HELL ON WHEELS

DEDICATION

For Gracie and Vincent – another big project I could never have done without you.

HELL ON WHEELS

A HISTORY OF BIKER MOVIES

STEPHEN CARVER

WHITE OWL
AN IMPRINT OF PEN & SWORD BOOKS LTD.
YORKSHIRE – PHILADELPHIA

First published in Great Britain in 2026 by
Pen and Sword WHITE OWL
An imprint of
Pen & Sword Books Ltd.
Yorkshire – Philadelphia

Print ISBN 978 1 03610 212 8
ePUB ISBN 978 1 03610 214 2
ePDF ISBN 978 1 03610 216 6

A CIP catalogue record for this book is available from the British Library.

Typeset in 11.5/14 pts Cormorant Infant
by SJmagic DESIGN SERVICES, India.

Printed and bound in India by Replika Press Pvt. Ltd.

The Publisher's authorised representative in the EU for product safety is Authorised Rep Compliance Ltd., Ground Floor, 71 Lower Baggot Street, Dublin D02 P593, Ireland. www.arccompliance.com

For a complete list of Pen & Sword titles please contact

PEN & SWORD BOOKS LIMITED
George House, Units 12 & 13, Beevor Street, Off Pontefract Road, Barnsley,
South Yorkshire, S71 1HN, England
E-mail: enquiries@pen-and-sword.co.uk
Website: www.pen-and-sword.co.uk

or

PEN AND SWORD BOOKS
1950 Lawrence Rd, Havertown, PA 19083, USA
E-mail: uspen-and-sword@casematepublishers.com
Website: www.penandswordbooks.com

FSC www.fsc.org MIX Paper | Supporting responsible forestry FSC™ C016779

CONTENTS

Acknowledgements 7

Introduction 8

Chapter 1 The Original Wild Ones 10

Chapter 2 Coffee Bar Cowboys 23

Chapter 3 We Are the Mods! 34

Chapter 4 All the Fallen Angels 43

Chapter 5 The Ballad of *Easy Rider* 75

Chapter 6 Silver Dream Racers 82

Chapter 7 Death Rides a Norton Commando 104

Chapter 8 Warriors of the Wasteland 122

Chapter 9 Heritage Classics 148

Chapter 10 Full Circle 174

Bibliography 179

Picture Credits 180

Index 184

How much hell on wheels can you take?
See mean brutes on wheels.
All action, all night!
All the Angels all in one mean programme ...
If it feels good, they do it bad.
Four super cycle shockers hitting town,
And they don't give a—!

Drive-in radio trailer, 1970

'The thing with the motorcycle movie, it's psychopathic in a sense that it's not interested in what anybody thinks about it ... It's almost like a motorcycle gang in real life. It's not looking for your approval. It's just a take it or leave it.'

Larry Bishop, *MovieWeb*, 2008

ACKNOWLEDGEMENTS

THIS BOOK WOULD not have come into existence without the faith of Jonathan Wright at Pen & Sword, or the eternal patience and support of his colleagues Olivia Camozzi-Jones and Janet Brookes. Then there was my friend Linne Matthews, who told me this publisher might be interested in a book on motorcycles. Special thanks must also go to the Design Team at SJmagic DESIGN SERVICES for putting it all together so beautifully. In spirit, this book belongs to Mick, Steve, Will, Womble, Rob, Martyn, Kev, and a whole bunch of other folks I rode with (you know who you are), and with whom I discovered many of these movies a lifetime ago – with an extra helping of thanks to Christopher and Daniel for locating the films I could not. Warmest regards, too, to Ollie and Kathy and everyone at Rooster's Bike Barn, especially Alan, Keith and Richard. Finally, love and thanks to my wife, Gracie, for her awesome cover design and without whom I would never achieve anything, and my son, Vincent, for all those mad movie nights.

INTRODUCTION

I WAS FIVE when I first felt the magic, when the local outlaw club cruised past our family car on a trip back from the beach in the summer of 1969. From that moment on, I knew I was going to be a biker. I got my first motorcycle when I was 15, a ratty Honda CB 125 with a furry seat that cost me 25 pounds which I tinkered with and largely rode around the backyard, hitting the road legally the day I turned 16. I'm 61 now and I've been riding ever since. I never bothered to get a car. That's about 75 per cent of my long and colourful life, and by far the most constant feature.

And I won't lie, another one of the inspirations for getting into this whole wonderful, crazy, and deeply rewarding lifestyle when I was a kid were the movies, back then caught on late-night TV and occasionally at the cinema, before home video made them more available in the Eighties. I appreciate that a lot of riders don't like biker movies, finding them at best stupid and unrealistic, at worst downright insulting and socially dangerous. For me, though, and maybe you, as you're presently reading this, biker movies have always been a guilty pleasure, regardless of quality. With a few exceptions, they are fundamentally exploitation movies and should be treated as such, like low budget horror movies. Cult classics, these are down and dirty drive-in movies of the old school. And like cheap and cheerful horror movies, if you manage your expectations they can be tremendous fun to watch, while a few, such as the seminal *Easy Rider*, will genuinely surprise you with their startling power and originality, whether or not you actually ride a bike. Sometimes, even the major studios release a bike picture. As we'll see, sometimes they get it, and sometimes they don't.

Biker movies remain a neglected, rebellious, and frequently misunderstood genre in film, with only a tiny handful of books ever written on the subject. What follows is an exploration of the history and the evolution of these stylishly weird movies and their cultural context: from early cinema to the juvenile delinquent films of the Fifties, the Sixties outlaw film cycle, kitchen sink rocker dramas, mod revival movies, racing films, horror hybrids, and the madness of Maxploitation. Key films are covered in detail, while the constraints of space mean that other entries are more brief and encyclopaedic. Collectively, I hope, these reviews and overviews offer a lively history of the genre, as well as introducing films that might be new to you that you feel are worth seeking out. I'm aware that I have not managed to list every single biker movie, but lord knows I tried.

We may argue about what defines a 'biker movie'. For my purposes, it is any movie in which at least one biker is present as a significant character or a major plot element. Movies that simply contain a motorcycle do not count. As a rider myself, I have also done my best to identify the motorcycles used whenever possible, given their importance to plot. Written for both bikers and fans of cult and extreme cinema, *Hell on Wheels* is intended to be at once a serious film history and an irreverent joyride that doesn't take itself or its subject too seriously. For me, this book is also a labour of love and a long-time life goal finally realised. May you enjoy reading it as much as I've enjoyed researching, writing, and living it.

So, how much Hell on Wheels can you take?

CHAPTER 1 THE ORIGINAL WILD ONES

IT ALL GOES back to *The Wild One.* Purists may argue that Charlie Chaplin rides a Thor Model M in *Mabel at the Wheel* (1914), and Buster Keaton is on a Harley Model F in *Sherlock Jr* (1924), but let's be honest, for the attitude, the swagger, and the look, Marlon Brando is the Elvis of biker movies. He may not have been the first, but he defined the genre. After *The Wild One* escaped at the end of 1953, nothing was ever going to be the same again.

The Wild One is the template for all the outlaw biker movies that would follow. It is also the first movie to engage seriously with juvenile delinquency (though Brando and co-star Lee Marvin were nearly 30), unless you count Crane Wilbur's clunky 1947 hot rod movie *The Devil on Wheels*. It predates *Blackboard Jungle*, *Rebel Without a Cause*, *Rock Around the Clock*, and *West Side Story*, and Elvis had yet to sign with Sun Records. Brando's Johnny was the unique and original rebel icon.

Watching the film now, the Black Rebel Motorcycle Club look as threatening as the cast of *Sergeant Bilko*, but in the winter of 1953 they were *terrifying*. The British Board of Film Classification repeatedly refused the film certification, but there were enough limited showings to turn a generation of teddy boys into ton-up boys. In America, Johnny's uniform was suddenly everywhere. In *Rebel Without a Cause*, James Dean wears a red Harrington jacket to stand out from all the Brando clones (including a very young Dennis Hopper).

But Johnny did not ride fully formed and original out of the imaginations of screenwriters John Paxton and the uncredited Ben Maddow. *The Wild One* is rather the moment when several evolving cultural narratives converge. As Hunter S. Thompson wrote in *Hell's Angels* (1966), *The Wild One* 'told a story that was only beginning to happen and which was inevitably influenced by the film'.

After the Second World War, thousands of battle-scarred young men were struggling to transition back to civilian life. Many purchased cheap army surplus motorcycles and went tearing off around California like the drifters who rode west after the Civil War. These initially informal gangs named themselves like air force squadrons, and motorcycle clubs like the Market Street Commandos, the POBOBS (Pissed Off Bastards of Bloomington), and the Boozefighters began to swarm, holding huge Gypsy Tours. One of these events was held at the sleepy Californian town of Hollister over the Fourth of July weekend in 1947. The POBOBS and the Boozefighters roared in, got a bit worse for wear and there were a few arrests. Eventually, the Highway Patrol had to be brought in to restore order. Then the press arrived, and the name of Hollister entered motorcycling mythology forever as bikers, according to C.J. Dourghty's report for *Life*, 'took over the town'. The piece was accompanied by an alarming photograph of a drunken rider astride a bobbed Harley parked in an ocean of empty beer bottles, a brew in each hand.

Buster Keaton points the way in *Sherlock Jr* (1924).

The identity of the biker in Barney Peterson's iconic photograph remains the subject of speculation to this day, and he may well not have owned that bike, or any bike. But the only thing that matters is the image. Peterson's portrait of the unknown rider created the image of the 'outlaw' biker virtually overnight. Then *The New York Times* and the *Los Angeles Times* picked up the story and turned a few misdemeanours and miscreants into a rampaging barbarian horde.

Middle America looked on in horror and the American Motorcycle Association went into damage control, hastily issuing a press release reassuring folk that '99 per cent of American Motorcyclists' were 'respectable, well-behaved citizens'. The so-called outlaws responded by proudly wearing patches bearing the sign '1%', a tradition that continues to this day. The Wild Ones had arrived.

The moral panic surrounding Hollister was the inspiration for Frank Rooney's short story 'Cyclists' Raid', published in *Harper's Magazine* in January 1951. With an added dash of *Romeo and Juliet*, this became the credited basis for the screenplay of *The Wild One*. The story leans heavily on the press reports, as the Angeleno Motorcycle Club rides into a sleepy Californian town, getting drunk and increasingly disorderly, leading to inevitable tragedy.

Rooney's bikers are a paramilitary unit, who all ride identical red bikes and sport identical khaki uniforms, aside from their leader, Gar Simpson, whose bike is white. They all wear green-tinted goggles which they never remove, leading a local to remark nervously that they look as if they come from

Marlon Brando as Johnny in *The Wild One* (1953) – the original rebel outlaw.

Mars, a familiar science fiction symbol for communism. The story is told by Joel Bleeker, a retired army officer. As a menacing evening progresses, the Angelenos split into smaller groups and methodically take over the town. Only one member sits this out, removing his googles and drinking Coke. Bleeker understands the boy's predicament: 'He didn't belong.' In a brutal climax, Bleeker's daughter Cathy is hit and killed by one of the marauding motorcyclists. No one can identify her murderer, and the Angelenos simply ride away. As the townsfolk pick up the pieces, the sober boy from the bar returns, having quit the club. Mad with grief, Bleeker attacks him, followed by other townspeople, until the old soldier is suddenly gripped with an urge to protect the boy.

Though sensational and politically conservative, Rooney's story has something serious to say about pack mentality and how quickly a civilised society can become brutalised. This moral appealed to *The Wild One*'s producer, Stanley Kramer, who made films with a social conscience, often dealing with subjects avoided by the mainstream studios. He had already explored the plight of disabled veterans in Marlon Brando's screen debut *The Men* (1950), and it was Brando's loyalty to Kramer that led him to play Johnny. This does not, however, appear to be the message that many of its audience took from the film. As Preetam Bobo of the Market Street Commandos and later the San Francisco Hells Angels told Hunter S. Thompson: 'We sat up there in the balcony and smoked cigars and drank wine and cheered like bastards. We could all see ourselves right there on the screen. We were all Marlon Brando.'

Early motorcycle clubs often named themselves like air force squadrons.

The Wild One has notional similarities to Rooney's short story, but Johnny is much more nuanced than Gar Simpson, blending Rooney's concept of an autocratic leader with the boy who didn't belong, as indicated in his opening monologue:

> It begins here for me on this road ... Mostly I remember the girl. I can't explain it – a sad chick like that, but somethin' changed in me. She got to me, but that's later anyway. This is where it begins for me, right on this road.

What follows is an extended flashback chronicling Johnny's epiphany, as rival clubs converge on a small town, the locals form an angry mob, and he inarticulately pursues Mary Murphy's Kathie.

The bikers themselves are also much more authentic, because of pre-production interviews with the real thing. As Kramer later explained:

> A lot of the dialogue is taken from our actual conversation with them ... And one of the most famous lines in the film came from my conversation with them, too. I asked one of the kids, 'What are you rebelling against?' and he answered, 'What have you got?'

Dozens of real bikers were also hired as extras. A Pacific War vet himself, Lee Marvin's interpretation of Chino was based on the notorious Boozefighter 'Wino Willie' Forkner.

As far as the nomad bikers go, however, Johnny's club is already a stylised cinematic depiction, albeit a very cool and immeasurably influential one. It is Chino's unnamed group that is the more realistic. Rather than the Levis and Schott Perfecto leather jackets (sales of which rocketed after the film's release), Chino's crew are mostly wearing army surplus and aviator gear. His gang are also on rusty Harleys and Indians, whereas the Black Rebels prefer pristine British sports bikes, Brando riding his own Triumph Thunderbird. The different looks delineate the two factions, with Johnny's group more of a Hollywood invention – what a motorcycle club *should* look like – creating a new sense

Kathie (Mary Murphy) and Johnny begin their courtship in *The Wild One*.

of subcultural style that became the physical reality. The image of the motorcycle, meanwhile, was also changed forever, from cheap blue-collar transport or middle-class toy to a symbol of working-class rebellion. As Thompson noted, you can actually see the subculture evolving within the movie. Something had happened, was happening, and was going to happen.

The Wild One made money, drawing in crowds of post-war teenagers hungry for a taste of rebellion and anyone who rode a motorcycle. Contemporary critics, however, reacted strongly against the film's apparent nihilism, seeing the movie as wallowing in violence and sensation, and showcasing jive-talking hoodlums who had no place on the silver screen. Religious groups and PTAs even campaigned (unsuccessfully) to stop screenings.

Johnson Motors, who imported and sold Triumphs, strongly objected to the presence of the brand in the film, and tried to get the production stopped. A journalist from *Motorcyclists* magazine was dispatched to the set, reporting that, 'I don't see where the motorcycle industry, including manufacturers, distributors, dealers and riders will benefit from *The Wild One*.' In fact, the movie cemented the popularity of the brand in the US, and Triumph still uses promotional images of Brando to this day. Similarly, *The Wild One* still features prominently on the Schott website, 'for the wild side in all of us'. *The Wild One* continues to resonate through time and popular culture. Elvis, James Dean, and Gene Vincent all bought their first motorcycle after seeing *The Wild One*.

Brando would go on to win his first Academy Award for *On the Waterfront* in 1954, and for him *The Wild One* was an enjoyable but minor role. He did, however, retain a soft spot for Johnny, later writing in his autobiography *Songs My Mother Taught Me* (1995) that, 'I related to Johnny ... There's a line in the picture where he snarls, "Nobody tells me what to do." That's exactly how I've felt all my life.'

Every generation of bikers has *their* movie, the one that inspired them, that both defined and created their era. In the Sixties it was *Easy Rider*, in the Seventies *Quadrophenia*, in the Eighties *The Road Warrior*. These were the genuine originals, and everything since owes something to these movies and their times. But it was *The Wild One* that started it all, that triggered the Fifties, that created the image of the modern biker, that turned the black leather jacket into a universal symbol of rebellion. Without *The Wild One*, motorcycling culture, its films and fashions, post-war youth culture, even rock 'n' roll itself, would all look very different, and likely diminished. It all begins here, on this road ...

Among other things, *The Wild One* had tapped into general post-war anxiety about juvenile delinquency, a term used first by the Victorians and resurrected in America by J. Edgar Hoover. The 1953 Senate Subcommittee to Investigate Juvenile Delinquency had concentrated public and political attention on the perceived causes: the breakdown in traditional family structures and values, the rise of consumerism and the attendant birth of a distinct teenage culture. What these teenagers consumed was deemed particularly pernicious, especially crime and horror comics and rock 'n' roll. Mainstream cinema responded in kind, with MGM releasing *Blackboard Jungle* in March 1955, and Warner Brothers following with *Rebel Without a Cause* in October. Independent film-makers were quick to capitalise, and when American International Pictures decided to add motorcycles to their JD output, it was the image created by Johnny rather than Chino that best suited their crazy teens. The Chinos of this world would have to wait another decade for AIP to catch up with them.

AIP was founded in 1954 by James H. Nicholson and Samuel Z. Arkoff, with a business model based on quickly made, low-budget films released as double features and intended to appeal

Lee Marvin's Chino was more authentic than Brando's Johnny in *The Wild One*.

to a predominantly teenage audience. Arkoff had a formula that was taught to writers and directors:

Action – Keep it exciting and pacey.
Revolution – Explore fresh or controversial subjects.
Killing – Keep the stakes high and the deaths lurid and creative.
Oratory – Make the dialogue memorable and quotable.
Fantasy – Consider what fantasies the audience might have and enact them.
Fornication – Don't be pornographic but maintain high levels of sensuality.

AIP quickly became known for science fiction, horror, and teens-in-torment double bills, with director Roger Corman emerging as a driving talent. Hot rodders featured regularly, often in genre crossovers. In *Invasion of the Saucer Men*, for example, the aliens are destroyed by the car headlights of the teen heroes.

Hot rod movies mined *Rebel Without a Cause* extensively for chickie runs, sympathetic cops, good kids with a past goaded into trouble by bad boys, and pretty girls who play both sides against the middle. AIP's *Hot Rod Girl* (1956), directed by Leslie H. Martinson, nailed this formula, which was recycled a year later as *Dragstrip Girl*, this time directed by Edward L. Cahn. Steve Terrell (from *Invasion of the Saucer Men*) was the earnest, working-class hero, while John Ashley took his first leading role as the bad boy, both courting the Dragstrip Girl Fay Spain. Then Cahn made it again, this time switching hot rods for motorcycles, with Terrell and Ashley essentially reprising their roles. Billed as 'Wild and wicked', *Motorcycle Gang* (1957) was the first of the *Wild One* copies. The biker movie was now officially a genre.

Twinned with Roger Corman's *Sorority Girl*, *Motorcycle Gang* was provisionally titled *Motorcycle Girl*, though this was likely ditched as too close to the source material. This is a shame, as Anne Neyland's Terry is really what gives this movie its edge – an independent and strong woman who knows what she wants in a genre that normally reduces her gender to victims, girls-next-door, tomboys, or tramps. Terry rides a big Triumph and 'Burning rubber is my one big vice,' she tells Steve Terrell's Randy, a poor kid on probation who dreams of college. To raise the money, he needs to stay out of trouble so he can win a police-sanctioned cross-country race. Randy was involved in a hit-and-run accident with his pal Nick (John Ashley), for which Nick pulled some time. These days, Randy's club has gone legit, with rules and dues and charters, overseen by benevolent bike-riding cop Russ Bender. But now Nick's out. Unimpressed by the new direction of the club, he sets out to humiliate Randy on the road, have him break his probation, and steal his new girl. Terry, meanwhile, is tempted, dallying with both.

Like all nice heroes, Steve Terrell doesn't have much to work with, but John Ashley plays Nick like an increasingly reckless sociopath, the textbook JD 'sickle cat' with his Schott leather, DA haircut and switchblade. Neyland, meanwhile, who also had a solid supporting role in *Jailhouse Rock* that year, is smart, sexy, and funny.

Distributed by AIP, Transworld Productions' *Dragstrip Riot* looks and feels older than *Motorcycle Gang*, though it was released in the spring of 1958. Inexpertly directed by David Bradley (who also made *They Saved Hitler's Brain*), *Dragstrip Riot* proves that 'cyclists and sportscar boys just don't mix'. Shot on location around Malibu, there's already trouble in paradise for the calypso-singing Corvette clubbers through the rivalry between alpha racers Rick Martin (Gary Clarke) and Bart Thorson (Bob Turnbull) for the same girl, Janet (*I Was a Teenage Werewolf's* Yvonne Lime). Bart tries to provoke a fight to which Rick won't rise,

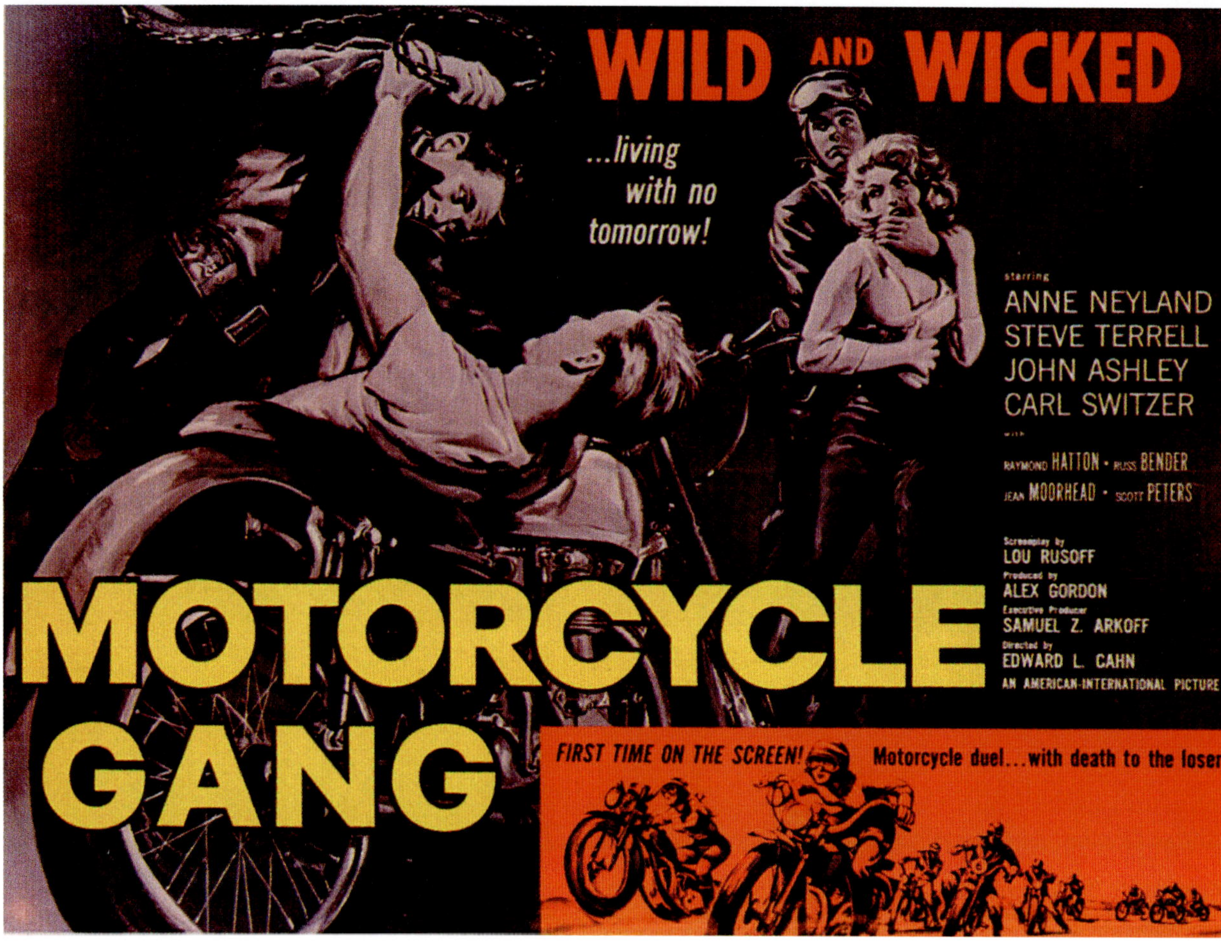

Motorcycle Gang (1957) was a remake of the hot rod movie *Dragstrip Girl.*

as he's vowed never to rumble again after spending time in reform school. Otherwise, the hot rodders are content to while away the summer racing, serenading girls on the beach (there are several incongruous musical numbers), and hanging out at Mom's Malt Shop. But as if Rick didn't have enough problems with Bart, their patch is invaded by a motorcycle gang led by John Garwood's Silva. Riding Triumphs and Harleys, these boys are straight out of *The Wild One*, though a deal snarlier and psychotic – switchblade-wielding, working-class antagonists to the more clean-cut, middle-class protagonists.

Bart contrives a confrontation between Rick and Silva, initiating a dangerous feud. The bikers attack Rick driving home on a mountain road with Silva riding alongside his car swinging a wrench while henchman Gordie (Barry Truex) closes in on the other side, providing the image for the movie's striking poster and the tagline 'MURDER at 120 miles per hour!' Rick slams on the brakes as Silva hurls the wrench, which hits Gordie instead, sending him off a cliff to his death. Silva, of course, blames Rick, vowing revenge.

Hero Gary Clarke would achieve modest fame in the NBC western *The Virginian*. Rick's mother, meanwhile, was played by King Kong's old girlfriend, Fay Wray. *Dragstrip Riot* was also a break-out role for Connie Stevens, popular American singer and *77 Sunset Strip* star who once dated Elvis. Silva was played by John Garwood in his first film role. He would go on to appear in the classic biker movies *Hells Angels on Wheels*, *The Savage Seven*, and *The Losers.*

As 1958 came to an end, so did the first wave of cheap Brando-inspired biker movies. Released in December, Joe Parker's *The Hot Angel* was a Paramount B-picture about uranium mining and claim-jumping in the Grand Canyon that mixed light aircraft with motorcycles in an awkward blend of JD drama and airplane thriller as 'Teenage gangs rip highways and skies with thrills and terror!'

Mandy (former Miss USA Jackie Loughery) runs a small airstrip and weather station. Having set up family friend Chuck Lawson (Ed Kemmer) with a flying job, she confesses she's really asked him down to help straighten out her little brother, Joe, played by baby-faced Mason Alan Dinehart – Bat Masterton from the TV show *The Life and Legend of Wyatt Earp*. Chuck feels obligated to the family as their older brother, Tom, died saving his life when they were pilots in Korea. Bereft of a male authority figure, teenaged Joe is running with a 'gang of delinquents on motorcycles' led by Mick (Boyd Santell). 'All he needs,' agrees Chuck, 'is a good steadying influence.'

Chuck and Mick battle for Joe's future, Mick supported by creepy, switchblade-swinging lieutenant Monk (Richard Stauffer). Joe had originally planned to follow his big brother into the air force but has now rebelled. Chuck is determined to reinitiate Joe's childhood love of flying. To humiliate Chuck, Joe challenges him to a game of off-road 'follow the leader' (as seen in *Motorcycle Gang*). If Chuck wins, Joe agrees to go up in a plane with him, confident that Chuck's a greenhorn rider. The gang all ride Ariel Square Fours, which miraculously turn into BSA scramblers for an impressive desert racing scene and hill climb. Chuck turns out to be a virtuoso rider and soon gets to work on Joe's moral compass, urging him to make his dead brother proud. Chuck offers to teach Joe to fly, and despite Mick's protests he walks away from the gang, who don't take it well. Joe trades his Ariel for a Cessna and starts flying with Chuck as observer as the claim-jumping plot takes over.

When everything's resolved and the sheriff leads Mick and Monk away, the first generation of movie wild ones was also leaving the silver screen, as fashion began to reset in preparation for the next decade. But paradigms do not shift without a clutch. As the Frustrating Fifties slowly gave way to the Swinging Sixties, Brando's original iconic image was to go in two very different yet parallel directions: parody and fetishism.

After Elvis joined the army, teenagers got a makeover in the media and, like rock 'n' roll, became a lot more vanilla. This can be seen in AIP's *Beach Party* (1963), a surprise hit that spawned a new genre of teen beach-oriented comedy musicals written by Lou Rusoff, who also penned *Dragstrip Girl* and *Motorcycle Gang*, starring pop singer Frankie Avalon and former Mouseketeer Annette Funicello. The principal comic foil is the biker gang the Ratz, goofy *Wild One* types on Triumphs lead by Harvey Lembeck's Eric Von Zipper. As

Hot rodders versus 'cyclists' in *Dragstrip Riot* (1958).

soon as they ride into shot for the first time and Von Zipper dismounts, his bike roars off by itself, leaving the leader and the pack staring out of the screen, emoting to a series of crashing sounds that end in a splash. 'You've done it again, boss,' says his right-hand man J.D.

Harvey Lembeck had been Corporal Rocco Barbella in *Sergeant Bilko*. Dressed in a Schott Perfecto and peaked cap and 40 years old, he sends up Brando something rotten as the 'carbon monoxide commando', with imperious, Napoleonic gestures, scratching and finger clicking punctuating statements of threat and rebellion delivered in his natural Brooklyn accent: 'Nobody tells Eric Von Zipper nuthin'!' When he pounds his chest for emphasis, he breaks the shades in his pocket. When he starts a fight with Bob Cummings' Professor Sutwell, he loses to a martial arts move in which a finger to the temple causes 'time suppression', freezing the victim for several hours. This becomes a running gag across several movies in which Von Zipper taps his head with his finger and turns statue – 'He gave himself the finger,' laments J.D. as the gang carry their rigid leader away like a two-by-four, J.D. always proclaiming 'Eric Von Zipper will return!' The climactic bar fight between surfers and bikers involves custard pies, and when Von Zipper gets on his bike as the credits roll, it won't start.

Von Zipper did not return in the follow-up film, *Muscle Beach Party* (1964), but audiences obviously noticed because he was back in *Bikini Beach* (1964), this time with a huge racing trophy on his headlight in mockery of Johnny's from *The Wild One*. Outraged at volleyballers 'getting footprints all over our beach' in *Pajama Party* (1964), Von Zipper hits the net when the gang rides in to chase them off and is catapulted into the ocean. 'Oh boy, he's gonna be mad,' says J.D., 'he hates fish!' Von Zipper ends up being chauffeured in a Harley sidecar that periodically detaches for laughs. He's last seen going over a cliff in it, as a new catchphrase is introduced: 'Why me? Why me all the time?'

In *Beach Blanket Bingo* (1965), Von Zipper falls for pop singer Sugar Cane (*Dynasty*'s Linda Evans) and tries to kidnap her, with predictable results, while in *How to Stuff a Wild Bikini* (1965), he attempts to go straight. Von Zipper had only a cameo in *Dr. Goldfoot and the Bikini Machine* (1965), and his swansong was *The Ghost in the Invisible Bikini* (1966), in which the Ratz blunder around a haunted house looking for treasure. Even Nancy Sinatra could not save this one, and despite a modest profit, the run was over. Eric Von Zipper would never return. Roger Corman was already working on *The Wild Angels.*

While Eric Von Zipper was first doing his thing, a much more reverential project was coming together on the LA underground film circuit. In a mere 28 minutes, *Scorpio Rising* (1963) by the gay avant-garde film-maker and occultist Kenneth Anger took biker movies to a place even the Angels feared to tread.

Scorpio Rising contains no dialogue, and scenes play out to contemporary pop songs Anger blew most of his budget licensing, including 'He's a Rebel' by The Crystals and 'Devil in Disguise' by Elvis. It has thus been hailed as a forerunner of the modern music video. Anger said that the theme was sex and death, which pretty much covers all his work. The film is divided into four symbol-laden parts. In 'Boys and Bolts', young men work on their bikes before putting on elaborately decorated jackets in preparation to ride, these scenes intercut with homoerotic shots of a 'beefcake' model in leather gear from photographer and male erotica pioneer Bob Mizer's Athletic Model Guild. 'Image Maker' introduces the character of Scorpio (Bruce Byron) getting ready to go out, snorting some speed, and arming himself. The wall is plastered with images of James Dean while *The Wild One* plays on the TV. In the days before home video, this was a live broadcast that Anger described as a 'magical coincidence'. The episode is intercut with real bikers riding around Coney

Island. Brando is replaced on the TV by Jesus and his disciples, cut in from *The Living Bible* Sunday school film, *Last Journey to Jerusalem*. 'Walpurgis Party' is a real Halloween party, in which the bikers horse around in costumes, moon each other, and initiate a new club member by stripping him and smearing mustard on his genitals to 'Torture' by Kris Jensen. Finally, in 'Rebel Rouser', Scorpio breaks into a condemned church next door and stages an impromptu political rally, declaiming from the pulpit surrounded by Nazi flags. His rant alternates with images of Christ, Brando, and Hitler, the scene transitioning into a climactic offroad race the next morning that ends in an accident. Like much of Anger's work, there is a sense of an invocation, of a spell being cast, of ritual magic, even sacrifice – the racer who crashed in the filmed accident really was killed. As Anger once said, 'making a movie is casting a spell'.

Often credited with introducing leather boys and full dresser Harleys to the New York gay scene, *Scorpio Rising* has a acquired a reputation for its undoubted homoeroticism, but it is also a fascinating historical document showcasing the lives of working-class Brooklyn bikers. In that sense, it is a forerunner of Hunter S. Thompson's *Hell's Angels* and *The Bikeriders* (1968) by Danny Lyon, a photo-book chronicling the Chicago Outlaws. 'This is the closest I've ever done to a documentary,' Anger later said. 'Basically, I was just photographing real things happening.' While living in Brooklyn, he had befriended a group of Italian American bikers that would meet under

Eric Von Zipper (Harvey Lembeck) tells it like it is in *Pajama Party* (1964).

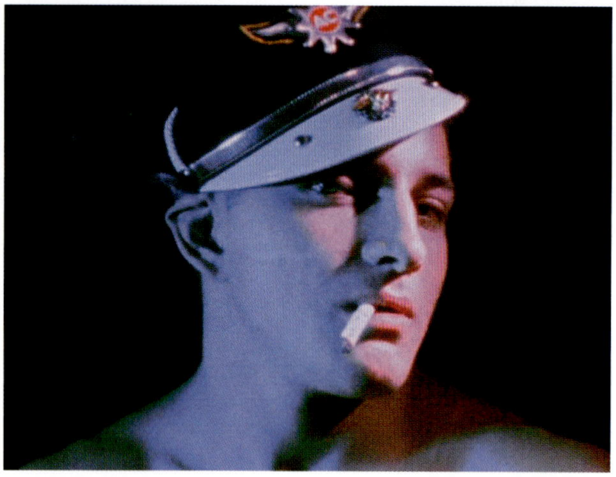

The homoerotic imagery of *Scorpio Rising* (1963).

the Cyclone rollercoaster at Coney Island. He photographed the bikes, which he saw as 'American Mechanical Folk Art'. To appear in his movie, all they asked was he supply the beer for the Halloween party.

Scorpio Rising has been cited as an influence by directors John Waters, Nicolas Winding Refn, Kathryn Bigelow, and Martin Scorsese, particularly for Anger's use of popular music to create atmosphere. It was a critical success on the arthouse circuit, although Anger was sued by the American Nazi Party for defamation, while the Lutherans went after him for copyright infringement. He won both cases. In 1964, LA cinema manager Michael Getz was prosecuted for obscenity for screening the film, but the case was overturned by the California Supreme Court, a landmark victory for artistic expression. The Hells Angels checked it out in Frisco, but the already-dated rocker imagery did not appeal.

In *Scorpio Rising*, as with the Ratz versus the surfers, there's a sense of the Fifties vying with the new style of the Sixties. The spell was cast, and the times, they were a-changing.

COFFEE BAR COWBOYS

CHAPTER 2

IN CONTRAST TO Henry Ford's American car culture, in Britain it was motorcycles that first emerged as powered everyday transport, replacing horses on roads that were little more than dirt tracks in the first years of the twentieth century. Like the early history of flight, two-wheeled technology leapt forward during the First World War, offering a traumatised generation the freedom and exhilaration of high-speed transport previously the preserve of those rich enough to afford private aircraft or sports cars. Riders were known as 'Promenade Percies' and as motorcycling evolved as a hobby, a sport, and cheap transport, the oil and dirt-encrusted bikers, geared up with storm coats and googles, began to acquire an image that was very different to that of car drivers. Their spiritual home was the Isle of Man Tourist Trophy (established in 1907), and British brands dominated the growing international racing scene. The Brough Superior SS100 was the first superbike, adored by T.E. Lawrence (Lawrence of Arabia), who was arguably the first ton-up boy.

During the Second World War, the British motorcycle industry – led by BSA – manufactured 400,000 bikes for the armed services. When the war was won, many of these were sold to civilians as War Department surplus, along with the gear worn by military dispatch riders. Enthusiasts' clubs were everywhere, a culture captured rather splendidly by the British mystery thriller *The Black Rider* in 1954.

Leslie Dwyer catches the motorcycling bug in *The Black Rider* (1954).

For centuries, the inhabitants of Brockham Village have believed the ruins of the old castle to be haunted by a monk on a black horse that breathes fire. Jerry Marsh (Jimmy Hanley), a new reporter on the Swanhaven *News & Mail*, believes it too, having interviewed an eyewitness, but his editor and prospective father-in-law, Mr Plack (Leslie Dwyer, later of *Hi-de-Hi!*) is sceptical. With his fiancée Mary (Rona Anderson), Jerry sets out to investigate the story anyway on his new Triumph Speed Twin.

Like George Formby's *No Limit* and the speedway dramas *Money for Speed* and *Once a Jolly Swagman*, *The Black Rider* is one of those rare British films that focuses on motorcycling before the era of mods, rockers, and Hells Angels. Jerry is supported by the wholesome, pipe-smoking Swanhaven Motorcycling Club, who help him track down the elusive Black Rider, solve the mystery, and catch the bad guys, but not before staging a charity gymkhana including a *concours d'elegance* and a two-wheeled egg-and-spoon race.

Director Wolf Rilla is most remembered for *Village of the Damned*, and art director John Stoll would go on to win an Academy Award for his work on *Lawrence of Arabia*. The script was by Arthur Richard Rawlinson OBE, a retired lieutenant colonel and former head of Military Intelligence who had notably worked on Hitchcock's *The Man Who Knew Too Much*. His military background explains *The Black Rider*'s apocalyptic plot, which plays out like the Famous Five busting a nuclear terrorist cell.

But plot aside, it is the authentic vision of post-war British motorcycling that makes *The Black Rider* such a charming film. The bikers are all lower middle-class enthusiasts, and their gymkhana feels like an old newsreel showcasing a new range of British bikes. For an idyllic snapshot of Britain after the war, when our motorcycle industry was on top of the world, *The Black Rider* really is joy to discover, another link in a short and uneven celluloid chain that is moving towards the working-class rocker angst of the early Sixties. Given that the motorcycle was such a ubiquitous form of cheap transport after the war, it is surprising, and a little sad, that the culture that grew up around them was so under-represented in British cinema.

Made a year after *The Wild One*, *The Black Rider* seems to have already belonged to a vanished world even when it was new. The riders are neither hip nor iconoclastic, there's no modern jazz, let alone rock 'n' roll, and there isn't a black leather jacket in sight. In post-war Britain, meanwhile, as rationing came to an end and the economy began to pick up, aspirational couples like Jerry and Mary wanted cars not motorbikes. As the decade progressed, however, a new demographic was emerging for which motorcycles would become a key accessory. Teenagers were consuming rock 'n' roll and American movies, and teddy boys were swapping their drapes for full leathers and motorbikes. They had jobs, disposable income, and higher purchase. Four quid a week for two years could get you a big British twin, then still the fastest and most stylish thing on two wheels. The ton-up boys had arrived as a very British working-class subculture, with their uniform of elaborately decorated leathers and bikes built for speed.

The teds had been the folk devils of the early Fifties. This outsider image consequently attached itself to the rockers, confusing parents, and outraging the conservative establishment. The first British film to address this new social threat was *Some People* (1962), directed by Clive Donner on the verge of his career breakthrough with *The Caretaker* the following year. In stark contrast to its sensational American counterparts, *Some People* is more closely related to bittersweet, neo-realist British films like *Saturday Night and Sunday Morning* and *A Taste of Honey*. Unusually shot in colour on location in Bristol, *Some People* is a vivid depiction of working-class life, the lure of rebellion and the validation of belonging to a subculture, a message snuck in under the radar of the Duke of Edinburgh Awards Scheme, who commissioned the project.

Ton-up boys Johnnie (Ray Brooks), Bert (David Hemmings, four years from international stardom in Antonioni's *Blow-Up*), and Beeza Bill (the Dickensian David Andrews) lose their licences after causing an accident. Robbed of their bikes, the aimless tearaways end up forming a band, supported by friendly choirmaster Mr Smith (Kenneth More), who lets them practise in his church hall, Johnnie

David Hemmings, Ray Brooks, Angela Douglas and David Andrews (on BSA) in *Some People* (1962).

soon falling for his daughter Anne (Anneke Wills – later Polly in *Doctor Who*). Only Bill is sceptical, fearing a 'catch', and withdrawing back into the world of rockers, dancehalls and pubs while Johnnie and Bert are recruited onto the Duke of Edinburgh scheme by Smith. Johnnie and Anne start going out, but of course it all ends in tears, as the different classes can never really connect.

In Bill's terms, there is a catch, and that's the clumsy promotion of current theories in British social engineering. The way for young working-class rebels to learn the rules – which include knowing your place – is through self-improvement schemes like the Duke of Edinburgh Awards and Outward Bound. There is thus a persuasive if subtle subtext to *Some People* that gives Bill's argument more credence than the film's producers would have liked had they realised. For Bill, the whole argument against the Duke of Edinburgh scheme is about class, of allowing those above them, like the kind but equally patronising Smith, to deprogramme their youthful rebellion and to slot them into an ordered place in society, always below their own.

Donner leaves us in no doubt that his heroes view their café racers and their identities as rockers as an antidote to the monotony of daily working-class life, Harry H. Corbett giving a poignant performance as Johnnie's father: an inarticulate and repressed blue collar drunk, old before his time, representing a fate that clearly appals his son. And whereas the American rebel movies of the Fifties always ended with the tortured protagonist returning to the fold of conformity and respectability,

Bill's continued rejection of the values of the Duke of Edinburgh scheme represents a necessary and continued rebellion against the soul-crushing job and council house that his social superiors have in store for him. 'What,' Bill seems to be asking, 'do I have to be grateful for?' Johnnie's journey perhaps ends more hopefully, but less honestly.

In another piece of early career genius, the next young Brit to play a motorcycle hooligan was Oliver Reed in *The Damned* from Hammer Films. Made in 1961 – before *Some People* – but not released until 1963 over censorship issues, *The Damned* trades realism for science fiction in a grim allegory of apocalypse. A government-sanctioned military research facility is experimenting with children to breed a race capable of surviving a nuclear war. An American tourist, a Bohemian artist, and a gang of rockers stumble upon the secret, and things do not end well. *The Damned* was adapted by Evan Jones from H.L. Lawrence's 1960 novel *The Children of Light*, and directed by American Joseph Losey. Though Lawrence's novel featured juvenile delinquents, it was Jones and Losey that turned them into Triumph-riding rockers who are not a million miles from Alex and his Droogs in Anthony Burgess' *A Clockwork Orange*. Burgess' novel was published in 1962, so the similarity between Oliver Reed's King and Alex is more a matter of convergent evolution and common cultural response than conscious imitation.

Losey had found sanctuary in Britain after being blacklisted in Hollywood for refusing to testify before the House of Un-American Activities Committee. In *The Damned*, he explores the relationship between institutional and street-level violence. Although completed in 1961, US co-producers

Oliver Reed (with signature weapon) in *The Damned* (1963).

Colombia Pictures stalled the release of *The Damned* until 1963 because of its politics. It was finally released quietly in London as the second feature in an X-rated Hammer double bill with Michael Carreras' *Maniac*. The film was released in the US as *These Are the Damned*, with 17 minutes of material removed, making the story practically incomprehensible.

On holiday in Dorset, middle-aged American tourist Simon Wells (Macdonald Carey from *Days of Our Lives*) gets picked up by pretty young waif Joanie (Shirley Anne Field) and led provocatively up a side street, where he's mugged by her brother King and his gang of rockers. 'I never expected a thing like this to happen to me in England,' says Simon, after being helped by some mysterious men wearing civilian clothes but referring to each other by rank. 'You thought England was a land of old ladies knitting socks,' replies Bernard (Alexander Knox), who is apparently in charge, 'The age of senseless violence has caught up with us too.'

King is a Byronic modern dandy in tweeds over motorcycle boots, affecting an upper-class accent. His signature weapon is an umbrella with a blade in the handle. His gang are more conventional rockers. King bizarrely looks more like a mod. He is obsessively possessive of Joanie, using a controlling 'You and me against the world' narrative suggesting they were evacuees or war orphans. Joanie challenges the gang to a drag, leading to an extended racing scene that culminates with King locking the brakes on his Bonnie in the town centre. She wins and finds herself by Simon's boat at the harbour. The two are attracted and Simon asks Joanie to make a choice, and she jumps on board. Outraged, King and the gang pursue along the quay on their bikes, beginning the long hunt that drives Simon, Joanie and King towards Bernard's terrible secret, where they must work together to survive.

The more intellectual rebel is represented by the doomed artist Freya (Viveca Lindfors), the conscience of the film. Her argument to everyone is that there might be a different way of seeing the world to their own. She rejects the nihilism of King, and Bernard's unwavering belief in impeding Armageddon.

As well as the Cold War politics and beatnik existentialism, Losey is obviously drawing on contemporary anxiety about juvenile delinquency, although the real villains of the film are government scientists and military police, making King's anti-establishment stance ultimately noble. It is the fluid and subversive nature of teenage subcultures that makes King so compelling, especially in that period in history. In *The Damned*, the sinister government scientist Bernard is the Frankensteinian villain, but it's King's rebellion against both English and American authority figures that resonates. King is chaos, the wild card, the rebel angel, who ultimately goes down fighting an evil eugenics project. Only it isn't being run by Nazis in South America, but by British civil servants just outside Weymouth.

Though the first act promises a British *Wild One*, *The Damned* soon morphs into something between *Dr. Strangelove* and *Village of the Damned*. King's rockers are therefore reduced to a subplot, but they are ultimately portrayed by Losey in a way no other director had done, at least in America, that is *sympathetically*. As a social problem, they are not even symptoms of the disease, just more of its victims. The disease, shows Losey, is the political system that has frivolously unleashed the threat of global annihilation with no idea how to contain it, and which lies to its citizens about the true nature of the threat by scapegoating harmless minorities, such as the rockers.

Completing this ton-up triumvirate was Sidney J. Furie's *The Leather Boys*. The film was released in 1964 at the height of the mods and rockers moral panic in the press. But Furie didn't care about subcultural combat. He was much more interested in social issues, and his source material was a novel published in 1961. Furie catches the tribalism of the rockers, shooting at the famous Ace Café in London and recruiting real riders as extras, but his focus is on the conflicts within the group, rather than external threats.

Rita Tushingham and Colin Campbell in the Ace Café in *The Leather Boys* (1964).

The Leather Boys initially follows all the narrative codes of kitchen sink drama, depicting working-class life in rented Victoria terraces, careworn parents old before their time, dead-end jobs, and never enough money. Like *Some People*, there's a sense of restricted destiny, pushed away by the roar of an engine and the brief freedom of the weekend. Shot in bleak black and white, it always seems to be raining or snowing, and you can feel the cold creeping out of the screen, reminding us why rockers preferred tea to beer, warming up those frozen hands.

The film opens with the familiar formula of the reckless working-class marriage between school-leaver Dot (Rita Tushingham) and Triumph 3TA-riding Reggie (Colin Campbell), who are already arguing on their honeymoon at Butlin's, and separate soon after. Reggie's world changes with the arrival of the free spirit Pete (Dudley Sutton), with his blond hair, leather jeans, and Norton Dominator. Reggie is drawn to Pete's spontaneous nature, and they're soon sharing a bedsit. When Reggie tries to chat up a couple of girls on a day trip to Brighton, though, it's obvious that Pete's not interested, while he and Dot loathe each other until she finally explodes, 'You look like a couple of queers!'

Like *Scorpio Rising*, *The Leather Boys* functions on two levels as an almost *cinema vérité* depiction of the ton-up boys, and as a pioneering landmark in queer cinema. Subtle though Pete's unrequited love for Reggie is, this was edgy stuff for 1964. Homosexuality between consenting adults over the age of 21 was not decriminalised in England until 1967. Because of the film's subject, Triumph refused to provide production company British Lion with new bikes, forcing them to use second-hand machines which added to the realism.

The screenplay was by Gillian Freeman, adapted from her novel of the same name. There are significant differences between the two versions, with the novel being much less coy about the relationship between the two friends, which is innocently sexual. Like the film, Freeman's novel has acquired a certain affectionate cult status among the LGBTQIA+ community. Working-class gay protagonists were virtually non-existent in the film and fiction of the time, and if the subject were addressed it was usually from the middle-class perspective.

The film showcases some excellent riding, with no camera trickery or back projection, as often real ton-up boys thunder around the North Circular and race to Scotland and back. They ride in rain, snow, and fog, and in one particularly haunting night scene, all that can be seen is a parade of Lucas headlights moving through the dark like ghostly orbs. Sutton and Tushingham are superb as the antagonistic rivals, and Furie shoots the film in the manner of the French *Nouvelle Vague*, a documentary style blended with emotional depth depicting a class and subculture rarely seen on film or television back then.

By the time *The Leather Boys* hit, rockers as a youth cult had already begun to go the way of the dinosaurs. As the Swinging Sixties kicked in, rockers were becoming unfashionably retro, a throwback to the Fifties. This cultural moment was later symbolised in *Quadrophenia* when mod Jimmy tries to drown out rocker Kevin in a public bath by singing the Kinks' 'You Really Got Me' over Gene Vincent's 'Be-Bop-A-Lula'. But British film had not quite done with them yet.

Kenneth Hume's 1965 *Mods and Rockers* is a 15-minute colour short from Anglo Amalgamated. Short films were all part of the cinema-going experience in the UK in the Sixties, content varying from entertainment to experimental, public information, and newsreels. *Mods and Rockers* was definitely experimental. A modern ballet performed by the Wester Theatre Ballet Company, the film's poster and the credits claimed 'With Music by The Beatles'. This wasn't strictly true. The music is an instrumental medley of early Beatles songs played by a garage band called The Cheynes. When *Mods and Rockers* was folded into a longer pop/variety film entitled *Go-Go Big Beat* the same year, Brian Epstein noticed and successfully sued.

The 'Mir Youth Club' is run by a groovy vicar in rocker gear and is presumably based on London's 59 Club. 'Mir' (Мир) is Russian for 'peace', Hume apparently conflating youth violence with the Cold War. The story, such as it is, is essentially *Romeo and Juliet* again as a mod girl and a rocker boy start dancing together, much to the chagrin of their different tribes. Eventually the couple slip away on the boy's Enfield Bullet while the dance degenerates into a massive fight. Though hardly *West Side Story*, *Mods and Rockers* is a colourful piece of period interpretative dance with some vivid costumes. The suits

'Leather Boys' Colin Campbell and Dudley Sutton.

are sharp, the dresses are tight, and the rockers' studded and painted leathers are glorious. There's a genuine attempt by Hume to capture the quickly evolving teen fashions of the decade, and to blend the high art of ballet with popular culture.

Also made in 1965, the short film *Roger Wonders Why* contains colour footage shot at the 59 Club in Paddington and a brief interview with 'Father Bill' Shergold. The 17-minute film was made by the Chelmsford St Andrews Young Communicants Fellowship, and explores the opening statement that, 'The modern Christian is serving the Lord on many frontiers,' in this case through the 59 Club and the Venture Scouts. The narrator, Roger Abbott, meets rocker Derek Jones at an after-service Sunday club and learns about the 59 Club. Derek takes him to the club in Paddington on his BSA. He meets Father Bill, who offers a nice history of the club, standing in full leathers and smoking a pipe. Roger asks him what advice he'd give to motorcyclists. 'Not to be selfish about our machines,' he says, 'but to use them in the sense of having a wonderful machine which we're entrusted with, and we've got to use, well, I would say, for the glory of God, and with a real sense of dedication and responsibility.' And that, of course, is what he did when he used his passion for motorcycles as a path to reach rockers and bring them into a youth club, keeping them out of trouble without any expectation that they attend church.

Late in the decade, Peter Collinson's *Up the Junction* (1968) starred Suzy Kendall as Polly, a rich Chelsea girl keen to experience the authenticity of working-class life, and Dennis Waterman as a Battersea mod desperate to get away from it. In addition to Waterman's Lambretta-riding Pete, *Up the Junction* also features a trio of long-haired lads on Triumphs led by the doomed Terry (the Bowie-like Michael Gothard).

Up the Junction was originally a collection of short stories by Baronet's daughter Nell Dunn published in 1963. In 1957, newlyweds Dunn and Oxford graduate Jeremy Sandford had given up their Chelsea lifestyle and moved across the river to Battersea. Her class tourism formed the basis of Dunn's short stories and her 1967 novel *Poor Cow*, while Sandford wrote the critically acclaimed BBC play *Cathy Come Home* (1966) directed by Ken Loach. Loosely framed around an unnamed female narrator, the stories show a side of British life still rarely represented at the time. Subjects include theft and imprisonment, racism, casual sex, domestic violence, sex work, and backstreet abortion.

Dunn adapted *Up the Junction* with Loach as a BBC *Wednesday Play* in 1965, the attendant controversy over its depiction of abortion leading the BBC Board of Governors to block its repeat and triggering a national debate that led to legalisation and regulation in 1967.

Loach also directed a film version of *Poor Cow* in 1967. Though not a critical success, it was a surprise box office hit, so a film version of *Up the Junction* was obviously appealing. Loach was not involved with the project, *Wednesday Play* script editor Roger Smith re-adapting Dunn's stories instead. Smith created a new throughline by making the narrator of the original stories into a Dunn-like protagonist who crosses Battersea Bridge in a chauffeur-driven Rolls and has a tragic fling with a local, anticipating Pulp's Britpop classic 'Common People'.

Waterman – best known on British TV for *The Sweeney* and *Minder* – plays Pete with a finely balanced combination of street smarts and vulnerability. His pursuit of the unobtainable girl and desire to escape the drudgery of working-class life is as deluded as the naïve Polly's belief that his world is 'natural' and 'free', but the fundamental difference is, of course, *choice*. Smith leaves us with the lingering possibility that Polly is, as Pete accuses her, playing with people's lives. And, by implication, so were Dunn and Sandford, whose writing could be interpreted as cultural appropriation.

Even with the addition of the Pete/Polly story, the film version of *Up the Junction* suffers in comparison with Loach's original play. Battersea looks less bleak in colour, the Manfred Mann soundtrack is catchy and cheerful, and the abortion scene, though harrowing, was the stuff of history by 1968. As film critic Leslie Halliwell put it, 'Socially obsolete sensationalism based on a television semi-documentary. An irritating heroine moves hygienically among motorbikes.'

Finally, Marianne Faithfull played an even more liberated middle-class woman in *Girl on a Motorcycle*, an Anglo-French co-production released in the UK in October 1968. Based on the erotic and surreal 1963 French novel *La Motocyclette* by André Pieyre de Mandiargues and directed by renowned British cinematographer Jack Cardiff, *Girl on a Motorcycle* is a long way from gritty social drama. It belongs more to the European arthouse tradition, although like *Up the Junction* it remains a quintessentially Sixties film in its exploration of identity and personal freedom, not to mention heavy-handed symbolism and psychedelic imagery.

After a feverish dream in which newlywed Rebecca (Faithfull) imagines her former lover Daniel (the mean, moody and magnificent Alain Delon) as a sadistic circus ringmaster removing her clothes with a whip as she rides around him on a horse, she wakes and resolves, 'I must go to him.' Donning a fur-lined black leather catsuit and a ridiculous egg-shaped crash helmet conceived by fashion designer and fetish photographer John Sutcliffe, she ditches her sleeping husband, jumps on her black Electra Glide and heads for Daniel in Heidelberg, doubled in unconvincing long shots by Grand Prix motorcycle champion Bill Ivy. Her ride from France to Germany becomes a framing narrative for a series of vivid memories of her relationships with the two men, while she muses on the restrictive nature of marriage against freedom and self-expression, and indulges in increasingly steamy sexual fantasies and flashbacks. The Harley is an obvious phallic symbol, on which she bounces and squirms around huskily proclaiming, 'My black devil makes love beautifully,' and 'Take me to him, my black pimp!'

Suzy Kendall slumming it in *Up the Junction* (1968).

Rebecca's ineffectual Swiss husband Raymond (Roger Mutton) is a classical musician and schoolteacher. Daniel, who she met before she married, is a bad boy intellectual who rides a Norton Atlas and says things like: 'Your body's like a violin in a velvet case,' and 'A motorbike becomes part of you. You are the sensations. They're there, between your thighs.' Daniel is a broken-hearted libertine who has no interest in marriage. Raymond is Rebecca's escape from Daniel's 'cruelty,' but Daniel gives her the

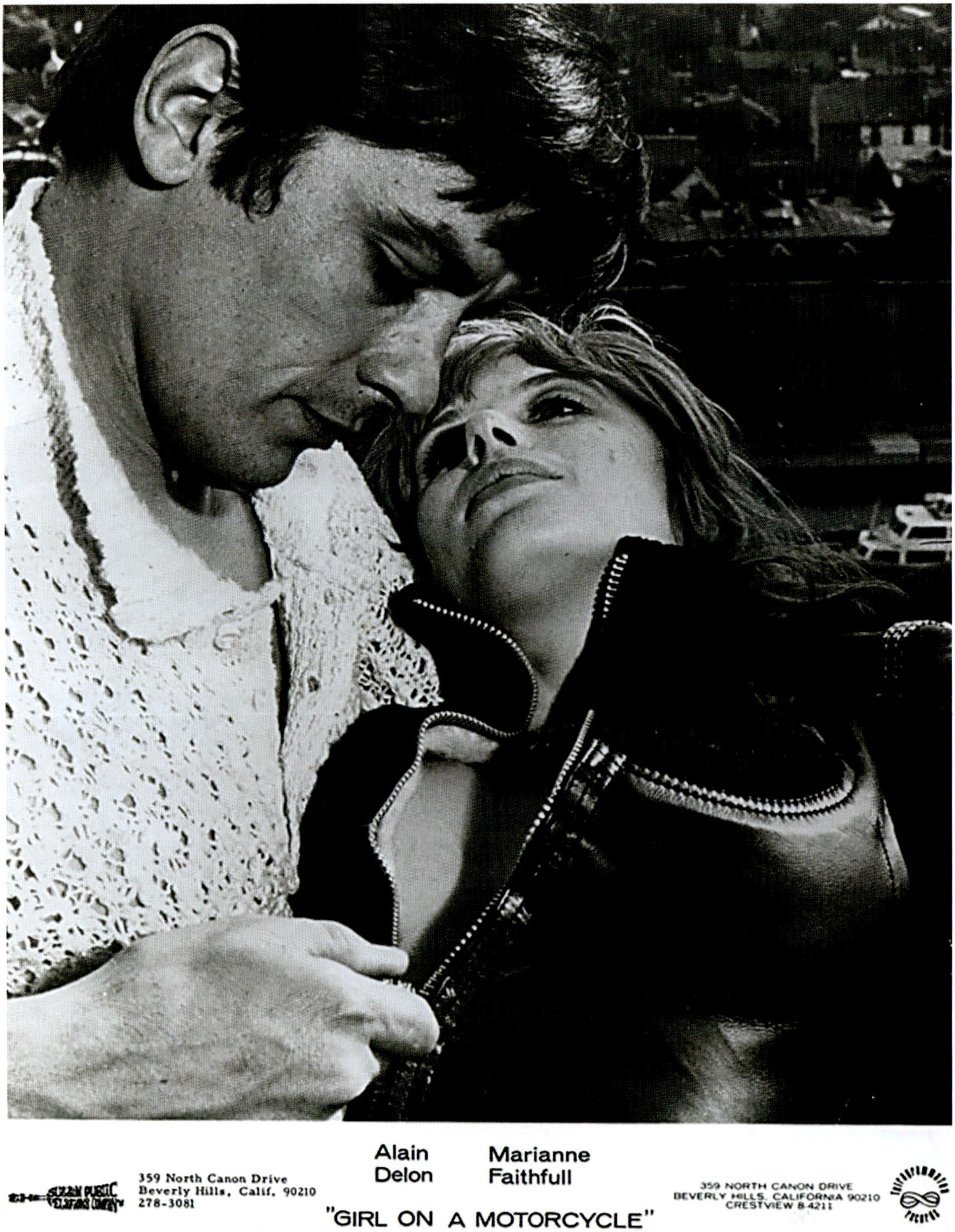

Alain Delon unwraps Marianne Faithfull in *Girl on a Motorcycle* (1968).

Harley as a wedding present and a way to return to him, and the affair soon fatally reignites. The film is therefore quite an honest exploration of destructive passion and sexual obsession in the manner of Pauline Réage's *Story of O* and Leopold von Sacher-Masoch's *Venus in Furs* – albeit with some florid dialogue and an overuse of solarisation that make the sex scenes look like something out of *Yellow Submarine.* The film was picked up by American distributors, given an X certificate and retitled *Naked Under Leather*, despite having about three minutes cut out of the European print.

And so ended Britain's small but significant contribution to the Sixties' biker movie, running in parallel yet totally different to the grindhouse outlaw pictures being mass-produced across the Atlantic. But perhaps the purest, most authentic Sixties British bike movie was yet to be made. A fusion of mod nostalgia, glam rock, and post-punk energy; *Quadrophenia* was set in the Sixties, but it took the Seventies to truly set it free.

CHAPTER 3 WE ARE THE MODS!

ALL THAT SIXTIES teenage angst and energy is most perfectly captured in Franc Roddam's *Quadrophenia*, a film released in 1979 that pays its dues to the kitchen sink dramas while at the same time transcending them with a realism that would have been impossible in the previous decade. Characters have sex on screen, masturbate, sell, steal and take drugs, and swear like wounded pirates in a depiction of working-class teenage life that reflects the immediate post-punk era that spawned it. Set in 1964, with a beautifully realised sense of time and place, the film's nostalgia somehow feels contemporary, because the sexual energy and confusion of being a teenager never changes. Phil Daniels' portrayal of the film's protagonist, mod Jimmy Cooper, therefore manages to combine the vulnerability and inner conflict of *Up the Junction*'s Pete with the snarling intensity of Johnny Rotten, who, apparently, screen-tested for the role. As Pete Townsend put it, '"Mod" is a shorter word for "young, beautiful and stupid" – we've all been there.' The film was also perfectly timed to trigger a full-blown mod revival, the seeds of which had already been sown by the English band The Jam and the Ska revival flowing out of 2 Tone Records in Coventry.

The source of *Quadrophenia* is the 1973 concept album of the same name by The Who, an elegant project that catches the essence of the band and their fans in the Sixties when 'My Generation' was as incendiary as 'Anarchy in the UK'. Like Pete Townsend's rock opera *Tommy*, *Quadrophenia* tells a story, the original double album including a written monologue by an unnamed mod and a booklet of black and white photos by Ethan Russell. The film's screenplay, by Roddam, Dave Humphries, and Martin Stellman, fundamentally follows Townsend's template of a young mod estranged from his parents, bombing 'blues' (the amphetamine Dexamyl), struggling to manage his emotions, hating his job, losing his girl, and returning to Brighton, a place he associates with a triumphant battle against rockers and being part of something greater than himself. Although some fans argue that the ending is ambiguous, the original text and photos suggest the kid accidentally drowns while out of his head, and that *Quadrophenia* is effectively his life flashing before his eyes. This is where the film parts company with the album, becoming more of a coming-of-age story.

Quadrophenia is episodic but with each scene structured around a core throughline: the build-up to a Bank Holiday confrontation with rockers in Brighton, followed by its repercussions. The first half of the film is therefore funny and exuberant, the second half more tragic as Jimmy's life, in his terms, starts to 'go backwards'.

Although sociologist Stanley Cohen famously debunked many of the mods and rocker stories circulating in the press in his seminal study *Folk Devils and Moral Panics* (1972) – like the Hollister

Original photoshoot for the *Quadrophenia* poster by Ethan Russell.

'riot', these confrontations were sensationally exaggerated by the media – 1964 certainly saw its share of tribal warfare. Rival gangs skirmished over the Easter weekend at Clacton and Hastings, followed by more trouble over the Whitsun weekend, most notably at Brighton. It's this second wave of violence that *Quadrophenia* covers, depicting epic running battles between mods, rockers, and police, during which Jimmy fights alongside the Ace Face (Sting) and finally pulls the girl of his dreams, Steph (Leslie Ash). Unfortunately, he's then arrested, after which his life spectacularly falls apart.

Quadrophenia was documentary maker Roddam's feature film debut, and as he later told the *Guardian*, producers Bill Curbishley (The Who's manager) and Roy Baird pretty much gave him free rein. He therefore decided against a known cast as they'd 'be too old' while accepting that, 'Any kids who are 18 will be unknown.' With that in mind, he figured, 'Let's just get the best of them,' and he did. *Quadrophenia* showcases a generation of emergent British talent, who unlike most stars of teen dramas really were teenagers. 'I think you just caught me at the right age,' Daniels tells Roddam on their charming commentary to the 2006 DVD release. Daniels was 19 at the time and his performance is nuanced and magnetic, taking Jimmy from the romantic dreamer who sees his subculture in mythic terms to streetfighter and, ultimately, suicidal despair followed by spiritual rebirth. Roddam, meanwhile, had been 18 in 1964, and he captures the mood of the period, the places, and working-class life perfectly, making excellent use of contemporary pop music around the operatic themes of The Who. Dialogue is fast, funny, and naturalistic, Roddam encouraging his actors to improvise. The bikes are great too, Jimmy on a Lambretta covered in extra lights and mirrors, the Ace Face on a chromed Vespa GS, and Jimmy's school friend Kevin (Ray Winstone) on a big BSA twin. The Brighton fight scenes are realistic and kinetic, and the magistrate's summing up on 'long-haired, mentally unstable, petty little hoodlums' is quoted artfully from a real contemporary court case.

Phil Daniels as Jimmy in *Quadrophenia* (1979).

The film also moves beyond its premise into something much more universal about the need to belong, to find some sort of cultural identity that transcends to banality of unskilled work and the kind of future the hero's parents represent. For Roddam, it was a memory of those years, while Daniels was still living them. Rarely, if ever, has the working-class British teenage experience been so honestly shown on film.

The stuff of double nostalgia – the original period, and the mod revival of the Eighties – *Quadrophenia* has been rediscovered by a new generation of British film-makers to the extent that there are now enough mod films to constitute a respectable subgenre of biker movies. Rowan Joffé's 2010 remake of Graham Greene' *Brighton Rock*, for example, updates the original 1938 novel and 1948 film adaptation to 1964, sticking psychopathic gangster Pinkie Brown (Sam Riley) on a Lambretta. Joffé uses the same Whitsun riots as *Quadrophenia* as his historical backdrop right down to the 'We are the mods!' seafront chant. Much was made of the mod angle by marketers, especially around the home media release, but the mods and rockers only appear in a couple of early scenes although Pinkie retains the sharp suit and the Lambretta. As a period piece, the story keeps dragging the setting back to the feel of the original, making *Brighton Rock* a lot more like *Peaky Blinders* than *Quadrophenia.*

More recently, 2021 saw Ray Burdis' *To Be Someone* and Chris Green's *The Pebble and the Boy*, post-Brexit films that are achingly nostalgic – albeit in very different ways – for the era of *Quadrophenia.* With a title taken from a Jam song and described by film critic Mark Kermode as 'a bunch of second stringers from *Quadrophenia* doing sub-Guy Ritchie schtick' (Phil Daniels isn't in it), *To Be Someone* started life as an unofficial sequel to *Quadrophenia* written by novice author Peter Meadows. Who manager Bill Curbishley was not impressed and Meadows was ordered to change character names and remove all references to the original film. Pete Townsend was more sympathetic, and suggested Meadows make his book a sequel to the album (the rights of which Townsend owned). Townsend endorsed the novel, and it was originally published through his Eel Pie Publishing house, the cover proclaiming, 'Jimmy's story continues'. Aside from using the same stream of consciousness device as the original sleeve notes, any connection to either version of *Quadrophenia* is peripheral at best, as now ex-con Jimmy ducks and dives through the world of early Seventies London gangsters and drug dealers. Townsend had changed his mind by 2016 when rumours of Burdis' film first hit the press, journalists quick to jump on the *Quadrophenia* connection despite Burdis' public denials he was making a sequel. The Who issued a statement disassociating themselves from the project, calling it 'totally ridiculous'.

Burdis and Meadows collaborated on the screenplay, which takes the rough storyline of Meadows' original but updates the backstory to the Eighties mod revival, the hero, Danny (Sam Gittins), being the son of the novel's now long-dead protagonist. Jack the lad, mod, and club owner Danny is drawn into an ancient dispute from his father's generation over a missing stash of blues by psychopathic gangster Mad Mike (Scott Peden) and bent copper Dickson (Burdis). Aided by a group of his dad's aging mod mates and their sex worker wives, Danny must figure a way out of a seemingly impossible situation comprising multiple factions in the manner of the hero of an early Guy Ritchie movie. Could the Isle of Wight August Bank Holiday International Scooter Rally be the key?

Director Ray Burdis brings an exaggerated Cockney swagger to *To Be Someone* that would have been dead cool in the era of *Lock, Stock and Two Smoking Barrels* but now seems incredibly dated. He also seems more comfortable depicting the criminal underworld than mod culture, which only gets a cursory look-in, while the humour is about as subtle as *Carry on Camping.*

Like the novel it's based on, the film trades on *Quadrophenia* while having nothing to do with it, the trailer promising 'Starring the original cast of *Quadrophenia*'. This is true; the film features

Steph (Leslie Ash) and Jimmy in *Quadrophenia*.

Sam Riley and Phil Davis in *Brighton Rock* (2010).

Mark Wingett, Trevor Laird, Gary Shail, Toyah Willcox, Leslie Ash, and Perry Benson in supporting roles, but playing completely different characters. There are some nice vintage scooters on show, though, alongside Danny's contemporary Royal Alloy, but as a *Quadrophenia* sequel, as Jimmy would say, it's diabolical.

The Pebble and the Boy, released a couple of months after *To Be Someone*, is a much more polished piece written and directed by Chris Green. Though the title sounds like something from Studio Ghibli, it's another Paul Weller song. *The Pebble and the Boy* is both road movie and coming-of-age drama. After the funeral of a father he barely knew (an Ace Face from the mod revival), directionless Manchester student John (Patrick McNamee) inherits his dad's Lambretta and resolves to ride it to Brighton to scatter his ashes. Though his mum and stepfather oppose the trip, John gives them the slip with the daughter of one of his dad's old friends, Nicki (*Coronation Street*'s Sacha Parkinson), who unlike John is a proper mod with her own scooter and a *This is England* poster on her bedroom wall (a nod to Green's obvious affinity with Shane Meadows). It's not that Nicki's particularly into John, but she's found a couple of tickets for a Paul Weller gig in Brighton in his dad's old parka. John is forever telling people 'I'm not a mod,' and doesn't even like Paul Weller. 'Once a mod, always a mod,' they invariably reply, this being the main theme of the movie. As John meets people from his father's past, he begins to build up a fuller picture of the man and the way of the mod.

With music by The Jam, Secret Affair, The Chords, and The Style Council, *The Pebble and the Boy* is a long love letter to the subculture itself across several generations. The trouble is, it's *very* long and would greatly benefit from being cut by about thirty minutes. It takes an hour to even get to Brighton,

Patrick McNamee as John in *The Pebble and the Boy* (2021).

and then another for John to learn the true story of his father, including the obligatory solo walk around the town at night and accompanying existential crisis. What ultimately saves the film is the barnstorming performance by Sacha Parkinson.

Also 'inspired by *Quadrophenia*', though with more of a *This is England* feel, *The Modern Way* (2022) is a historical piece set in the early Eighties during the tribal conflicts between second-generation mods, skinheads, and bikers. This isn't another Paul Weller title, but it's close, suggesting The Jam's 'The Modern World', both titles of course playing on 'mod'. Co-written by Jake Henderson (who also stars) and director Giuseppe Monticciolo, *The Modern Way* has some similarities with *The Hot Angel*, inasmuch as the friend of a dead older brother intervenes to help a kid that has fallen in with the wrong crowd. It also has the feel of a western, only with the hero driving a Ford Granada. Henderson plays Terry, a well-dressed, confident older mod returning to his old manor as a successful businessman to discover that the family of his best mate, Jack, has fallen apart following Jack's suicide, leaving his teenage sister Danni (Grace Long) confused and running wild with a local gang of skinheads. In a parallel intersecting plotline, little mod Frankie (Ashley Hodgson) has scored some drugs from a motorcycle gang he plans to shift in Brighton over the bank holiday but Danni's skinhead boyfriend Mason (Jack Parr) has nicked it, leaving him owing biker crime boss Harvey Grey (Nick Cornwall) five hundred quid. Terry – a friend of a friend – agrees to help, and all roads lead to Brighton.

Like *The Pebble and the Boy*, there's a real affection for mod culture, which is held up to Danni as a healthier alternative to the skins, Frankie and Terry even citing *Quadrophenia* in a potted history on the run down to Brighton. *The Modern Way* is also looking back to the gritty dramas of the era it's set

David Perkins as Steven in *The Fence* (2022).

in, like David Leland's *Made in Britain* (1982) and Mike Leigh's *Meantime* (1983), but without the talent that made Shane Meadows' *This is England* (2006) – which was attempting something similar – such an impressive period piece. There's no real sense of the social divide around Thatcherism, the racism, or the brutality and nihilism of the different youth cults. There isn't even much contemporary music to sell it. There's no real tension, no chemistry between actors, and the fake working-class accents are painful. Though *To Be Someone* is not much better, *The Modern Way* is certainly the weakest of these three films, and in each case, writers, directors, and marketers should be wary of citing *Quadrophenia*; all they do is remind us how good it was compared to the copies.

Finally, not a mod movie as such but also set in the Eighties, William Stone's coming-of-age movie *The Fence* (2022) is a breath of fresh air. There's an energy and authenticity about it that the previous films all lack, with strong working-class character design, superb acting, a tight script, and a story that is by turns tragic and extremely funny.

Apprentice Bristol butcher Steven Knight (David Perkins) hates his job but has finally saved up enough money to buy his first motorcycle, a second-hand Honda XL 125. This goal has kept him away from the temptations of petty crime, drugs, and glue sniffing that have claimed most of his mates on the council estate where he lives with his careworn mum and unemployed, alcoholic father. The problem is, someone's nicked it. With the help of local fence and old schoolfriend, Ritchie (Deshaye Gayle), and his older brother, Andy (*Game of Thrones'* Eugene Simon), a hard nut on a suspended sentence for assaulting a copper, Steve goes in search of his wheels, until the overdose of his best friend sets him on a new path: revenge.

The Fence is a feature-length development of a short film of the same name also written and directed by Stone in 2018. Stone establishes his setting well through music, with contemporary hits by The Selecter, Bad Manners, Madness, and Motörhead, as well as Andy's secret penchant for Nick Kershaw, Kim Wilde, Kajagoogoo, and Adam and the Ants.

While being the only recent period subcultural movie not to claim any links with *Quadrophenia*, it is *The Fence* that comes closest to recapturing its spirit. Stone had barely graduated from film school when he made the original *Fence*, and his cast was mostly young and unknown. *Quadrophenia* came out of a period of cultural revolution in the UK and had the same irrepressible energy as a punk rock record. Stone taps into a similar rawness, which Joffé, Burdis, Green, and Monticciolo all missed. But then, Stone had a strong story and a sense of humour while the others were trying to make movies out of nothing but nostalgia.

ALL THE FALLEN ANGELS

CHAPTER 4

RETURNING TO AMERICA, the spiritual home of the biker movie, the Sixties were to represent the high watermark of the genre. These were not mainstream movies. Instead, they came from the fringes of Hollywood, independent productions on low budgets made for the grindhouse and the drive-ins; cheap and cheerful exploitation movies churned out in record time to make money out of societal trends and anxieties using lurid and transgressive content.

Exploitation cinema, like wild rockabilly and punk rock, ran in parallel with the mainstream, pushing the boundaries of on-screen violence, sex and nudity in ways the big studios would not have dared. With cinemas reeling from the impact of television, these independents also did their bit in keeping the movie theatres from going under while mainstream Hollywood slowly modernised and realigned. And many of the young maverick actors, writers and directors that transformed Hollywood in the Sixties and Seventies came out of exploitation cinema. And then there were the mavericks and auteurs who stayed put and carried on turning out seat-of-the-pants shockers on micro-budgets as long as there were drive-ins to take 'em, before either retiring or moving into video in the Eighties. The story of the biker picture is their story, and it's notable how many names recur in these movies.

But before outlaw biker pictures spread like a virus across the drive-in screens of America, there were a couple of interesting antecedents. One of the most iconic motorcycle images on film isn't even from a biker movie, as Steve McQueen's Captain Virgil Hilts jumps a barbed wire fence pursued by German motorcycle troops on an artfully disguised Triumph Trophy in *The Great Escape* (1963). The studio included the climax chase scene to hook the gearhead actor. But although McQueen's riding ability made him more than capable of performing the stunt, the executives wouldn't risk it, so his friend and racing mentor Bud Ekins made the jump, launching McQueen into superstardom and Hollywood legend.

Paramount finally put the King on a motorcycle in 1964 in *Roustabout*, Elvis playing the same role he was usually stuck with: an itinerant working-class guy who's quick with his fists but has a beautiful singing voice. In this one, he's working on a travelling carnival for Barbara Stanwyck and romancing Joan Freeman. Though Elvis famously favoured Harleys, the studio was wary of the optics. Having made the King's image more family friendly after his stint in the army, they didn't want any of the negative associations of *The Wild One* and its impersonators, there being a thin line between a bit of marketable teenage rebellion and outlaw. Elvis therefore rides a Honda CB 77 Super Hawk, Honda having deliberately cultivated a non-threatening image in the US, running Robert Emmenegger's

Steve McQueen in *The Great Escape* (1963).

famous 'You meet the nicest people on a Honda' advertising campaign. 1964 was also the year The Beach Boys released 'Little Honda', again giving the brand a more wholesome feel than those noisy, oily British and American hogs ridden by the likes of Marlon Brando, and, indeed, Elvis, who did at least manage to sneak his black leather jacket into the movie.

The first sign of things to come was Russ Meyer's 1965 *Motorpsycho!*, part of what the king of sexploitation described as his 'Gothic' period, shot just before his better-known *Faster, Pussycat! Kill! Kill!* which essentially tells the same story but with sociopathic go-go-dancers in sports cars. *Motorpsycho!* anticipates Roger Corman's *The Wild Angels* in responding to developing media anxiety about a new generation of motorcycle gangs – most notably the Hells Angels – lobby cards promising 'The action beyond the headlines'.

The headlines in question had grown out of the Hells Angels' annual Labour Day run to Monterey in 1964, which had ended in heavily publicised allegations of the rape of two teenage girls although no charges were ever brought. California State Senator Fred Farr directed the state's new Attorney General, Thomas C. Lynch, to investigate outlaw motorcycle clubs. Described by Hunter S. Thompson as 'colourful, interesting, heavily biased and consistently alarming', the Lynch Report was presented at a press conference in March 1965, and although short on evidence of any real organised criminality, the melodramatic and hysterical prose was lapped up by the media, the *Saturday Evening Post* running a lurid cover story on 'The Strange Cult of Motorcycle Gangs', naming the Angels in particular. Similar articles appeared in *Newsweek*, *Esquire*, *Life*, and *Time*. The Hells Angels were suddenly notorious, and as with mods and rockers in the UK, politicians overreacted. Following the Lynch Report, local authorities in New Hampshire put the National Guard on high alert in anticipation of the Laconia Weir Beach motorcycle rally, an event that had been taking place peacefully for years. The charged atmosphere made conflict inevitable, leading to a pitched battle between bikers and police. New Hampshire is a long way from California and very few Angels bothered turning up. None were involved in the riot, which didn't stop the mayor of Laconia and the national press from blaming them, 'Hell's Angel' becoming a generic term for outlaw bikers, despite the club being no more prevalent than others such as the Outlaws and the Gypsy Jokers. Between the Miltonic connotations and the 1930 Howard Hughes film of the same name, 'Hell's Angels' was just more dramatic.

Motorpsycho! does not depict outlaw bikers the way Roger Corman would. There are no colours or choppers, just three hipsters on stripped down Honda C 100 Super Cubs looking for kicks, led by an increasingly psychotic Vietnam veteran, Brahmin, played by *Peyton Place*'s Stephen Oliver, making this an early vetsploitation movie as well. Oliver would also later appear in *Angels from Hell*, *Werewolves on Wheels*, and *Cycle Psycho*. *Motorpsycho!* is a relatively straightforward revenge tragedy in which veterinarian Cory Maddox (*The Godfather*'s Alex Rocco) and Cajun wildcat Ruby (Meyer regular and former exotic dancer Haji) team up in search of Brahmin and his gang, who have raped Cory's wife and murdered Ruby's husband. Fast paced and edgy, *Motorpsycho!* is a pretty wild ride though actually quite restrained for Meyer. At heart a western, *Motorpsycho!* is still well ahead of the curve when it comes to films about shellshocked Vietnam vets and psychedelic motorcycle gangs.

Elvis on a Honda Super Hawk in *Roustabout* (1964).

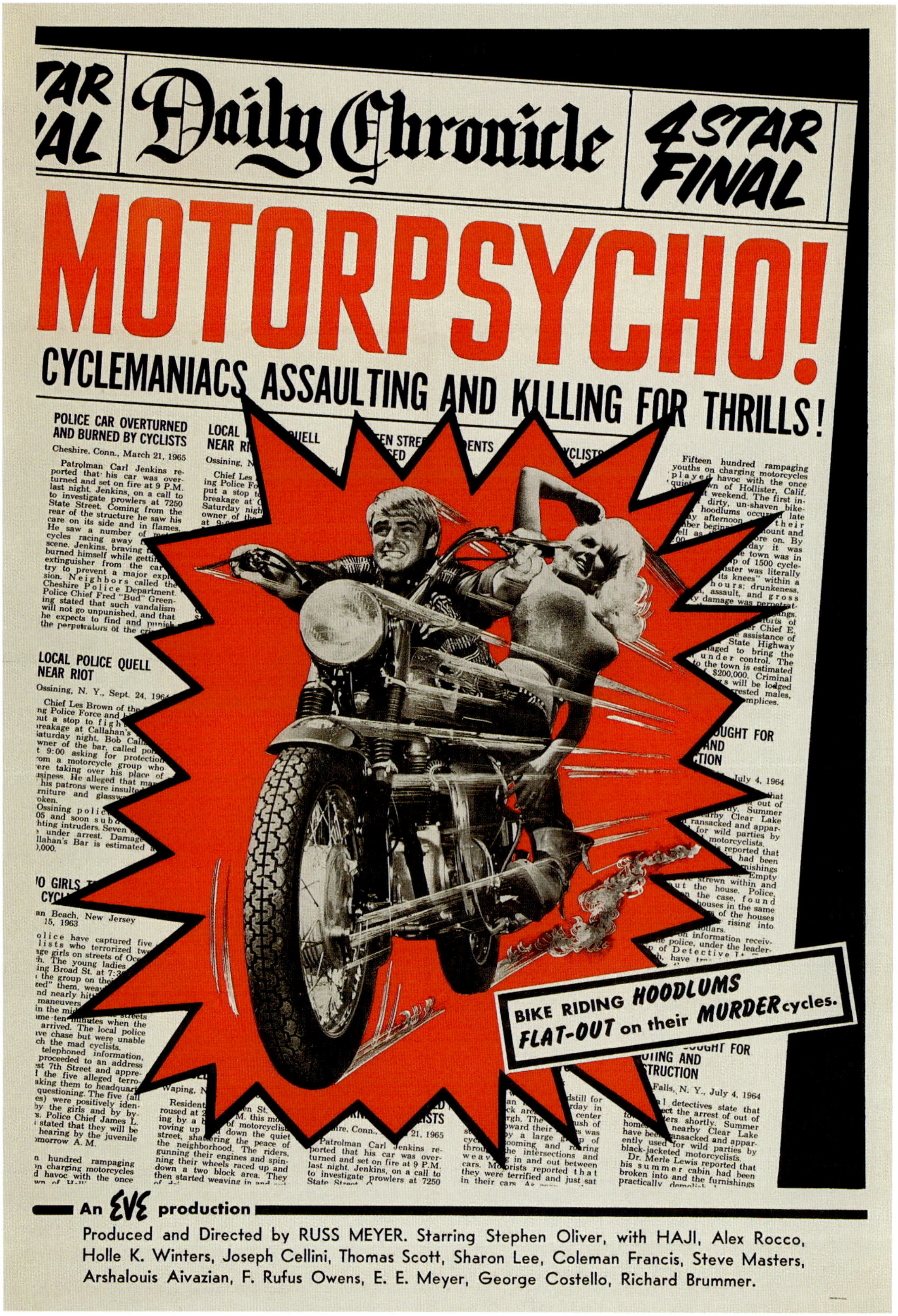

A cut 'n' paste poster for *Motorpsycho!* (1965) in which two characters who never meet awkwardly ride a bike not in the movie.

The canny piece of cultural response that spawned a genre, however, was Roger Corman's *The Wild Angels* (1966). As had happened with *The Wild One*, planets were aligning around this movie, which was both influenced by what was happening in American society and a prime influencer itself, as important as The Beatles, acid, and Vietnam in both reflecting and creating countercultural identity.

Like *Motorpsycho!*, *The Wild Angels* grew out of a news story. Corman later recalled in his autobiography *How I Made a Hundred Movies in Hollywood and Never Lost a Dime* (1998), 'It was a *Life* magazine photograph that gave me the idea for *The Wild Angels*. The photo, in a January 1966 issue, showed a group of Hells Angels on their choppers going to the funeral of one of their members.' This was the funeral of the much-loved James T. 'Mother' Miles, a legend in biker folklore killed in a collision with a truck. He was buried in his native Sacramento, his hearse followed by hundreds of motorcycles. Corman pitched a treatment to AIP provisionally entitled *All the Fallen Angels*, with a script to be written by Charles B. Griffith, the author of numerous AIP titles, including *The Little Shop of Horrors*. AIP had already dallied with biker pictures in the Fifties, though these had struggled to form a distinct identity outside the Juvenile Delinquent genre. Even *The Wild One* hadn't really escaped this orbit. This time, the cultural forces around the public fear and fascination with the Angels finally achieved critical mass, creating the first true biker movie and establishing most of the genre archetypes.

Roger Corman directs Peter Fonda in *The Wild Angels* (1966) while Peter Bogdanovich looks on.

Like Stanley Kramer during pre-production for *The Wild One*, Corman and Griffith researched the film by talking to real bikers, although the common claim that they were Hells Angels was always hotly disputed by Oakland Chapter President Sonny Barger, who sued Corman for implying that the Angels were involved. Griffith's original script played the outlaws off against a motorcycle cop, but Corman wasn't impressed and had Peter Bogdanovich rewrite it. This was before Bogdanovich's directorial career, when he was still a film critic hanging around with Corman and doing odd jobs on set and a bit of second unit work. Probably because Bogdanovich was only 27, he caught the subversive tone of the emerging counterculture much more authentically than Griffith, wisely moving the focus of the film exclusively to the outlaws. As AIP co-founder Samuel Z. Arkoff later explained: 'We started looking for our audience by removing the element of authority in our films. We saw the rebellion coming.'

This rebellion was perfectly captured by the film's star, Peter Fonda, as Heavenly Blues, the leader of the San Pedro 'Angels'. Though Fonda had started out as a conventional actor, by 1966 he had acquired a decidedly alternative rep, hanging around with The Byrds and The Beatles, dropping acid, and increasingly estranged from the mainstream Hollywood studios. Fonda was joined by Nancy Sinatra as Blues' girlfriend Mike (much to the chagrin of her father), with Bruce Dern and his then wife Diane Ladd as his old lady adding some dramatic clout. But though maybe not the best actor, Fonda was *cool*, his hair long, his shades dark, dressed in black on a chopped Harley panhead with chrome springers and a sissy bar that was taller than he was. From the moment the film starts, as Blues rides through Riverside County and the opening credits to a driving fuzz guitar theme by Davie Allan and the Arrows, he is completely captivating, the embodiment of the stylish nihilism Bogdanovich clearly saw in the rebel Angels. That Fonda was busted for possession soon after the film's release only added to his rebellious persona while also being great free marketing for AIP.

The film's throughline is built around Blue's best friend, Loser (Dern), who's lost his bike at the start of the story. Around episodic set pieces in which the bikers ride, party, and screw around, the club track Loser's bike to a Latino chop shop where a fight ensues, after which Loser is shot by a pursuing California Highway Patrolman. Blue decides to bust Loser out of the hospital, but without medical attention he soon dies. Picking up Corman's original premise, the club takes Loser on his last ride to his home town to be buried, the funeral service soon descending into anarchy.

Dark, decadent and nihilistic, the climax of the movie is intense, as Blues debates religion and personal freedom with preacher Frank Maxwell, his credo essentially do what thou wilt:

> We wanna be free to do what we wanna do ... And we wanna get loaded. And we wanna have a good time. And that's what we're gonna do. We're gonna have a good time. We're gonna have a party.

After all this soulless libertarianism, the film's bleak ending is a last turn of existential despair worthy of Albert Camus.

Shot in just over a fortnight with a budget of $360,000, *The Wild Angels* made $15.5 million at the box office, turning Fonda into a countercultural icon, and opening the floodgates on copycat biker movies.

While *The Wild Angels* was still running in theatres, AIP was already working on *Devil's Angels* (released in April 1967), written by Charles B. Griffith, directed by Daniel Haller, and starring maverick independent film-maker John Cassavetes, just working to fund his own projects, but bringing an emotional depth that Fonda did not possess in *The Wild Angels*. Cassavetes plays Cody, the leader of

Adam Roarke rides with Oakland Hells Angels President Sonny Barger in *Hells Angels on Wheels* (1967).

the Skulls MC, who dreams of finding Butch Cassidy's mythical hideout 'Hole-in-the-Wall' where there are no cops or straights. The quest goes off the rails when the club are falsely accused of raping a local girl in a small town and Cody is arrested. Despite Cody's orders, and aided by a larger club called the Stompers, the Skulls decide to take the town apart, the irony being that it's the world Cody wishes to lead them away from where they feel most comfortable.

Whereas, as far as they were concerned, Roger Corman had snubbed the Hells Angels while trading on their image, schlock producer Joe Solomon of Fanfare Films reached out to Sonny Barger to support his project *Hells Angels on Wheels*. Solomon gave the Oakland, Frisco, and Daly City Angels a credit, putting them in the opening scene of the movie, and paying Barger to be a technical adviser, a practice he continued on all his subsequent biker pictures. In return, Barger let him use the club's name and colours.

Written by seasoned AIP screenwriter Robert Wright Campbell and directed by future Academy Award nominee Richard Rush, *Hells Angels on Wheels* (released in June 1967) combines solid drama with tight action and very strong performances by Jack Nicholson, Adam Roarke, Jack Starrett as Sergeant Bingham, the cop trying to shut them down, and Sabrina Scharf as the girl that comes between them. Cinematographer Lászlό Kovács would go on to shoot *Easy Rider*.

Nicholson plays Poet, an intellectual rebel pumping gas who falls in with the Angels, led by Milton-quoting president Buddy (Roarke). He also meets Buddy's old lady, the middle-class Shill (Scharf), to whom he's instantly attracted. Though leading towards a predictably violent climax, the overall tone is as exuberant as *The Wild Angels* was bleak, with an upbeat, jazzy-psychedelic soundtrack by Stu Phillips that makes the rumbles feel like a fight out of the old *Batman* TV show. Instead of a funeral there's a wedding, and the film's structure shows that the outlaw tropes are already well established, with party scenes, road shots, a lot of drinking, dope smoking and making out, and mamas dancing in their underwear – all narrative gestures picked up and adapted from the *Beach Party* movies.

Adam Roarke had been a real street gang member when he was a teenager growing up in Brooklyn. He has a similar presence to Cassavetes' Cody only without the angst. He had obviously also learned from meeting Barger, and there's a swagger and a cockiness to Buddy that reflects the real pres in his heyday. He would go on to star in *The Savage Seven* (also directed by Richard Rush), *Hell's Belles*, and *The Losers*. Sabrina Scharf would go on to appear in *Easy Rider*. Like Roarke, Jack Starrett would become a central figure in outlaw biker movies. He also acted in *The Born Losers*, *Angels from Hell*, and *Hell's Bloody Devils*, as well as directing *Run, Angel, Run!*, *The Losers*, and *Race with the Devil*. Look out, too, for *Dragstrip Riot*'s John Garwood as Buddy's right-hand man, Jocko. The film, however, belongs to Nicholson, whose star was rising rapidly. Even Sonny Barger was impressed, writing in his autobiography *Hell's Angel* (2000): 'On the set, some of the crew thought Nicholson was a member from another charter, his style was so convincing. Even a few of our club members thought he was a Hell's Angel.'

The summer of 1967 also saw the release of Joseph G. Prieto's *Shanty Tramp* from K. Gordon Murray Productions, a mostly Mexploitation outfit that imported children's fantasy films and horror from south of the border, dubbed into English with a new title and poster and hawked round the drive-in circuit. Making his own movies was the logical next step, and former carney Murray threw *Shanty Tramp* together with first-time director Prieto and a bunch of amateur actors from Miami. In the movie, the succubus-like Emily (played by Eleanor Vaill as 'Lee Holland'), a wild but beautiful girl 'from the swamp infested backwoods of Georgia', wanders through a sultry night in her home town causing absolute chaos through her unbridled sexuality. She catches the eye of Savage (Lawrence Tobin), the leader of a nomadic motorcycle club called the Rats. By the end of the night, a lynch mob's been raised and three people are dead. No one is innocent, and no one is saved. The bikers are more *Wild One* than *Wild Angels*, provincial greasers on a mix of Triumphs and Harleys who know how to speak hip. There is a story that several of these guys were local policemen who lost their jobs over appearing in the movie.

Elizabeth James on a Yamaha YDS 3 in a promo shot for *The Born Losers* (1967).

With the style and production values of a stag film, the black and white *Shanty Tramp* does not look out of place next to Harold Daniels' notorious *Poor White Trash* (1957) – 'Too brutal and sadistic to be real' – and the films ran as a successful double drive-in feature for years. Prieto and Murray would repeat the same formula in colour the following year in *Savages from Hell*, in which a migrant farm worker called Teresa (Viola Lloyd) falls for the leader of the pack, much to the ire of his old lady, leaving it up to Teresa's brother (Diwaldo Myers) to save the day with his trusty 'swamp buggy'. Alas, there K. Gordon Murray Productions abruptly ceased when the IRS caught up with him.

William Grefe's *The Wild Rebels* from Crown International (1967) was another quick cash-in because 'It's now, it's what's happening', as down-at-heel stock car racer Rod Tillman (former teen idol Steve Alaimo) falls in with the Satan's Angels MC, who need a driver for a bank robbery as their bikes would draw too much attention. At the same time, he's recruited by the cops as an informer and when justice finally prevails, old lady Linda (Bobbie Byers) can only sob that it was 'all for kicks'.

The summer of 1967 also saw the release of AIP's third foray into biker movies, *The Born Losers*, the baby of the colourful independent film-maker Tom Laughlin, once described by Robert Altman as 'an unbelievable pain in the ass with a big Catholic hangup and a James Dean complex'. Laughlin co-produced, directed, and wrote the film under three different pseudonyms as well as starring in it, in his first of four outings as the mixed-race Native American ex-Green Beret Billy Jack. He ran out of money in post-production and managed to convince AIP to give him the funds to complete. It was one of the best returns on an investment AIP ever received, their highest-grossing release until *The Amityville Horror*. Much more dramatically sophisticated than the usual chop opera, *The Born Losers* was overtly political, written to explore discrimination against Native Americans, bystander apathy, and the establishment's failure to support and protect victims of rape.

The Born Losers is another movie to take its inspiration from the 1964 Monterey rape case. Three local girls are drawn into the mystique of the Born to Lose MC, unaware they are getting in way over their heads, raped then threatened into not pressing charges. College girl Vicky Barrington (Elizabeth James) also catches the eye of club president Daniel (Jeremy Slate) riding back from the beach in a white bikini on her white Yamaha YDS 3. Like the other girls, she is sexually assaulted, her pleas for help ignored by locals. Vicky's path crosses Billy Jack's when the bikers try to kidnap her to stop her speaking in court. The two form a relationship as Vicky agonises over whether to testify or just leave, as events propel them towards a violent and morally complex climax.

Though at times preachy to the point of sanctimony, and often poorly paced, *The Born Losers* is nonetheless a much more polished product than the majority of AIP biker movies. This is because it transcends its own genre, being more of a prototype for the modern lone hero action movie, while looking back to existential westerns like *Shane* and *High Noon*. Laughlin would go onto perfect his vision in *Billy Jack* (1971), in which the character defends a hippy Freedom School from prejudiced locals. *Billy Jack* was such a critical and commercial success it was followed by the direct sequel *The Trial of Billy Jack* (1974), and the less successful *Billy Jack Goes to Washington* (1977). AIP dropped out of *Billy Jack* over Laughlin's politics but made a mint reissuing *The Born Losers* on the back of it, as 'The film that introduced Billy Jack'.

AIP closed out the year with *The Glory Stompers*, released at the end of November, a relatively unremarkable and underwritten affair enlivened by the presence of Dennis Hopper as Chino, leader of the Black Souls MC. 'Black Souls vs. the Stompers in the deadliest cycle war ever waged!' promised the poster, which was a bit of an overstatement as both clubs together barely hit double figures and that's including the mamas. Originally written as a western by James Gordon Wright and John Lawrence, the Glory Stompers are a wholesome family of libertarians committed to partying and personal freedom led by Darryl 'Cowboy' Hudson (Jody McCrea). His girlfriend, Doreen (Astrid Warner), wants more

Before *Easy Rider*, Dennis Hopper starred in AIP's *The Glory Stompers* (1967).

security than this, though her romantic uncertainty becomes the least of her problems when she's kidnapped by the Black Souls. In the company of a former Glory Stomper called Smiley (played by Tarzan actor Jock Mahoney), Darryl sets off in pursuit of Chino and his girl.

With some trippy cinematography by Mario Tosi and art direction by custom car guru Ed 'Big Daddy' Roth, *The Glory Stompers* has a vivid visual style with some excellent riding by Hopper and his crew, including *The Born Losers'* Bob Tessier, and Casey Kasem, the future *American Top 40* DJ and voice of Shaggy in *Scooby-Doo*. Following his role in Roger Corman's *The Trip* (1967), Hopper continues to develop the edgy, intense, speedy persona that characterised Billy in *Easy Rider*.

A flurry of outlaw biker movies hit the drive-ins in May 1968, starting with *The Savage Seven* – the title supposedly a reference to Kurosawa's *The Seven Samurai* – bankrolled by rock 'n' roll impresario Dick Clark and distributed by AIP. The film was directed by Richard Rush, in a deal with AIP that allowed him to make his psychedelic film *Psych-Out* the same year. *The Savage Seven* reunites *Hells Angels on Wheels* alumni Adam Roarke, John Garwood, and Richard Anders as Bull (the same character he portrayed in the previous film). It also stars Robert Walker Jr. as the Native American Johnnie Little Hawk. The plot is looser than Rush's first biker picture. A Native American community led by Johnnie live in a shanty town built around a bar and general store owned by a seedy landowner who exploits their labour and robs them blind, backed up by hired muscle. An unnamed Californian motorcycle club led by Kisum (Roarke) breeze into town and shake everything up, naturally siding with the Indians against the greedy capitalists after a slightly shaky start. Kisum is attracted to Johnnie's sister, Maria (Joanna Frank), and despite his insistence that he's no Robin Hood, a softer side emerges in which he and the club help out Johnnie's people, although it all goes horribly wrong in the end.

The Savage Seven has a great soundtrack by influential surf 'n' drag producer Mike Curb of Sidewalk Records (who also scored *The Wild Angels*, *Devil's Angels*, and *The Born Losers*), elevated further by tracks from Iron Butterfly and Cream. This was Larry Bishop's second movie, and became the inspiration for his 2008 *Hell Ride*.

Meanwhile, could Godfather of Gore Herschell Gordon Lewis make a biker movie? Oh yes. Years ahead of the curve with splatter and sexploitation movies like his infamous *Blood Feast* and *Something Weird* (a film that blends LSD, witchcraft and kung fu), writer-director Lewis was looking for a new angle one day while driving in Miami when he clocked a tall woman on a Harley riding down the street like she owned it. This was Pat Poston, who he cast as Whitey in *She Devils on Wheels* (1968), along with a bunch of other local female bikers who had no acting experience whatsoever, bringing authenticity if not art, and creating the first genuine women's biker picture. In a unique take on female empowerment, the Maneaters all-girl motorcycle club race each other once a week for dibs on a 'stud line', a collection of grinning males who hang out at their clubhouse. The only rule is that you can't become attached, and when Maneater Karen (Christie Wagner) gets too close to Bill (David

The flamboyant Betty Connell in *She-Devils on Wheels* (1968).

Harris), she is forced to drag her unfortunate paramour behind her bike until there's not much left of him. Led by the raven-haired Queen (the larger-than-life Betty Connell), the girls have it all their own way until a gang of male hot rodders take over their turf. A battle of the sexes ensues, culminating in an on-screen decapitation. And if all this sounds mad, it is. Not a million miles conceptually from Russ Meyer's *Faster, Pussycat! Kill! Kill!*, *She Devils on Wheels* is a trash-o-rama classic and more camp than Christmas. As with his horror films, you can sense Lewis' tongue placed firmly in his cheek as he ladles on the sex and violence, interspersed with quickfire gags. There are also spinning scene breaks like something out of *The Man from UNCLE*, far out Sixties fashion, and very bad beat poetry. Then there's one of the first post-credit scenes in modern cinema, showing the Maneaters escaping the police and Queen and Whitey breaking the fourth wall with a final poem addressed to the audience:

> 'Can we ride a little faster?' said the leader to the pack.
> 'There's a fuzz right behind us
> And he's breathing down our backs ...'
> We don't owe nobody nothin',
> And we don't make no deals.
> We're swinging chicks on motors,
> And we're Maneaters on wheels.

Lewis and his son, Bob, also composed the film's theme song, which was memorably covered by The Cramps, the rock 'n' roll equivalent of movies like *She Devils on Wheels*. 'Get Off the Road' is the only Cramps song in which guitarist Poison Ivy Rorschach takes lead vocals, her husband Lux Interior reduced to an opening preface:

> 'Hey, who the hell do they think they are?'
> 'Ah, they're just a bunch of *girls* ...'

So close together it must have been synchronic, Crown International's *The Hellcats* (1968) dropped less than two weeks after *She Devils on Wheels*, the pressbook going as far as to claim: 'This is the first movie based on the exploits of a girl motorcycle gang, a way of life becoming part of today's scene.' Well, not quite. Based on another James Gordon White story and scripted by John Huston's son, Tony, and director Robert F. Slatzer, *The Hellcats* isn't as feminist as the marketing suggested. Unlike the Maneaters, the Hellcats MC have male and female members, though rather than being reduced to old ladies and mamas, the women ride their own bikes and are the equals of the men. The club is notionally led by a man, Snake (Elvis' former bodyguard, Del 'Sonny' West), though the shots are called by Sheila (Sharyn Kinzie), clearly the brains of the outfit.

This is a basic undercover story. After a cop is murdered surveilling the Hellcats and a gang of suspected heroin traffickers, his brother, returning soldier Monte (Ross Hagen), and his grieving fiancée, Linda (Dee Duffy), disguise themselves as bikers and infiltrate the club to solve the murder. This leads to several party scenes without dialogue in which bikers suddenly start dancing like extras in an Austin Powers movie, before a final battle between heroes, Hellcats and gangsters.

Lowering the bar even more was American General Pictures' *Hells Chosen Few* (1968), starring a bunch of people you've never heard of and directed by David L. Hewitt, whose previous work included *Monsters Crash the Pajama Party*. This is another undercover vet story with a Cain and Abel twist. Biker Willie Grady (Gary Kent) is framed for a murder he didn't commit. His estranged brother and

Vietnam veteran Joe (Jody Daniels) must join Willie's motorcycle club, the Hells Chosen Few, to get to the truth. The trailer claims that the film was made 'with members of the real Devil's Henchmen and allied motorcycle gangs of Southern California', which might explain why the acting is so egregious. Satan's Sadist and future biker movie regular William Bonner adds a little dignity, though legend has it that the film was a mash-up of two 16mm exploitation films directed by minor player Titus Moody, *Diary of a Teenage Bride* and *Outlaw Bikers.*

Ross Hagen was soon to return as the hero of the much more competent AIP film *The Mini-Skirt Mob* (1968), the Mini-Skirts being another girl gang, though the short skirts are hardly practical on their Hondas and Triumphs. Again written by the prolific James Gordon White, the film's title suggests something light-hearted, but *The Mini-Skirt Mob* is dark and bleak, as a vindictive woman stalks her ex-boyfriend and his new wife, gaslighting her crew into helping until it all gets out of hand and people start dying. Supported by an excellent score from the master of exotica Les Baxter, Maury Dexter's direction is slick and professional, though one-time Warner's starlet Diane McBain feels miscast as Shayne, the woman scorned, her bouffant hair and middle-class demeanour at odds with the character she's playing: the leader of a motorcycle club made up of rodeo performers including a young Harry

Diane McBain in *The Mini-Skirt Mob* (1968).

Dean Stanton and *The Born Losers'* Jeremy Slate. As a depiction of the escalating emotional violence of stalking, *The Mini-Skirt Mob* is disturbingly accurate, but as a biker picture it doesn't hold together.

Made by Joe Solomon's Fanfare Films, *Angels from Hell* (1968) has more going for it despite crude direction by former racing driver Bruce Kessler and a choppy script by Jerry Wish. This is another vetsploitation movie with former Marine Mike (Tom Stern) picking up with his old club, the Madcaps. Mike is another leader like Kisum in *The Savage Seven* whose moral compass swings wildly between healthy anarchy and sadism. His predecessor had a deal with local fuzz Captain Bingham (Jack Starrett, reprising his role from *Hells Angels on Wheels*) to keep the peace and stay out of the suburbs. Mike rejects this immediately, leading to escalating confrontations between the Madcaps and the police. In a particularly depressing scene, one of the Madcaps rapes and murders a hippy girl at a commune.

Despite its meandering, episodic narrative – and some hideous customised Triumphs – *Angels from Hell* has some interesting points to make about the alienation of returning veterans, civil rights, and the uneasy relationship between different branches of the underground culture. This would soon show itself brutally in the real world with the slaying of the black teenager Meredith Hunter by Hells Angels at Altamont. There's also a satire on biker movies built into the film, when the Madcaps visit a former member who's now a film star in Beverly Hills. His producer Sol Joseph (a cameo by Joe Solomon) is inspired to make a biker movie, sending his secretary to interview club members as Roger Corman had for *The Wild Angels*. Arlene Martel, Mr Spock's fickle Vulcan fiancée T'Pring, is aloof bar owner Ginger. The film also boasts another hip Stu Phillips soundtrack with songs by garage band The Peanut Butter Conspiracy.

Released on 5 June, *Angels from Hell* was oddly the last outlaw biker movie of 1968, but as the following year was to show, the genre had a fair few miles left in it.

Of course, 1969 was the year that saw the release of *Easy Rider*, premiered at Cannes in May and screened in New York in July. Though there are obvious links to the outlaw movies, this is a very different animal and is examined elsewhere in this book. The continuation of biker movies, which were already becoming formulaic and stale, owed a lot to the cultural impact of *Easy Rider*. Like the previous year, the trend was clearly slowing down in 1969, with only one outing from AIP and a desultory string of very low-budget and inexpert independents, only to pick up dramatically again in 1970.

Maury Dexter, James Gordon White, and Les Baxter followed *The Mini-Skirt Mob* with *Hell's Belles* for AIP, released on April 16, 1969. Loosely inspired by Anthony Mann's *Winchester '73* (1950), Jeremy Slate takes over from James Stewart, and instead of pursuing a valuable rifle the prize is a custom Norton P11 Ranger. Hero Dan (Slate) wins the bike in a race and plans to sell it to buy some land and settle down, only to have it stolen by a rival competitor who, in turn, loses it to an outlaw gang led by Tampa (Adam Roarke). Complete with cowboy hat and sheepskin jacket, Triumph-riding Dan follows in the footsteps of a legion of B-movie western heroes as he rides alone in pursuit of a black-hearted outlaw. Along the way, he acquires reluctant mama Cathy (played by UK model and actress Jocelyn Lane), whom Tampa 'gifts' to him in exchange for the bike and to resolve a conflict with his old lady Cherry (Angelique Pettyjohn). Stuck in the middle of the Arizona desert, Cathy has no choice but to jump on Dan's pillion and, unsurprisingly, their initial animosity transitions to romance over the next hour or so, although she remains torn between Dan and Tampa.

White's script is tight, Dexter's direction is fluid and assured, and Baxter's soundtrack is lush. Lane makes the most of her role; the poster shot of her looking cockily over her shoulder, hands on hips, in black leather boots, waistcoat and mini-skirt, became an iconic pop cultural image. As ever, Roarke steals the show, delivering every line with the same conviction and intensity one might expect of the stage or a much bigger Hollywood production.

Adam Roarke and Jocelyn Lane in a publicity shot for *Hell's Belles* (1969).

Somewhat less polished, *Scream Free!* (AKA *Free Grass*) reunited two of the stars of *West Side Story*, Russ Tamblyn and Richard Beymer, along with Natalie Wood's sister Lana. Actor and dancer Tamblyn had been a successful MGM contract player in the Fifties, his career zenith coming as Riff, the leader of the Jets in *West Side Story* (1961). In his own words, he 'dropped out' in the Sixties, losing interest in film and focusing on art. His film and TV work thus became much more eclectic, with some against-type exploitation roles. *Scream Free!* is the first of two biker movies Tamblyn made in 1969, the other being Al Adamson's *Satan's Sadists. Scream Free!* was written by James Gordon White and John Lawrence (who also co-wrote *The Glory Stompers*), and directed by former TV editor Bill Brame, who directed *The Cycle Savages* the same year.

Beymer (hero Tony in *West Side Story*) plays Dean, a hip bike rider with a custom Triumph who falls for Wood's hippy girl Karen. Karen is into the self-revelation of acid, but Dean is not so keen. Dean wants to split the scene and for that he needs bread. His speed freak friend Link (Tamblyn) offers him a grand to run some grass and cocaine across the Mexican border for some gangsters led by Phil (top-billed Casey Kasem). What could possibly go wrong?

Though mostly shot like a home movie, the film comes to life when Link spikes Dean with LSD and tries to burn him to death in an occult ritual, complete with psychedelic lighting and visual effects by Bob Beck and music by garage bands California Spectrum and The Boston Tea Party. There's a touch of Kenneth Anger about the acid scenes, doubly so because of Link's ritual magic. Though it even bombed at the drive-ins, *Scream Free!* is still a nice preface to Tamblyn's truly demented portrayal of Anchor, the leader of the Satan's MC in *Satan's Sadists*, released a couple of months later in June.

Described by Michael Weldon – a man who has seen it all – in *The Psychotronic Encyclopedia of Film* as 'probably the grossest biker movie of them all', Al Adamson's *Satan's Sadists* (1969) is a pure exploitation film, packed with sex, nudity, drugs and violence, starting with a rape and double murder before the opening credits even roll. Although the threat of sexual violence was always there in biker movies going back to *The Wild One*, Adamson goes further than even Corman had in *The Wild Angels* in making this threat explicit. This makes for uncomfortable viewing, but that's entirely the point. Like slasher movies, these films are directed towards a fundamentally prurient male audience, who come to be titillated and at the same time pass moral judgement on the social deviance portrayed on the screen. Bikers were a perfect folk devil, especially when conflated with the hippy underground culture that was currently terrifying the parents of Middle America. In *Satan's Sadists*, Russ Tamblyn develops the persona of the 'hippy-gone-bad' devil worshipper already seen in *Scream Free!* right down to wearing the same floppy hat from the previous movie.

The Satans' trail of mayhem leads them to a remote truck stop in the middle of the Colorado Desert in Southern California (a popular location for biker movies). Things kick off when a Satan makes a pass at a vacationing policeman's wife. The cop pulls a gun, which he promptly loses, Anchor using it to execute him, as well as his wife and the owner of the diner. Hitch-hiking Vietnam veteran Johnny Martin (Gary Kent) takes out a couple of Satans and manages to escape into the surrounding mountains with waitress Tracy (Jacqueline Cole), the remaining bikers in hot pursuit. Several of their custom Harley Sportsters and big British twins soon break down in the heat, the Satans hunting their prey on a dwindling supply of operational bikes while Anchor and Acid (Greydon Clark) take time out to terrorize a trio of female students who have the misfortune to be camping in the area, triggering his possessive old lady Gina (Adamson's wife Regina Carrol).

With its tagline 'Wild Beyond Belief', *Satan's Sadists* is tight, well acted and very well shot by Adamson, with some excellent riding scenes and a great soundtrack by Harley Hatcher, like Davie Allan another Mike Curb/Sidewalk Records artist. The film was so successful it generated the capital for Adamson to form Independent-International Pictures with his business partner Sam Sherman.

Not as deranged as *Satan's Sadists* but indicating a common move towards increased violence and depravity, 1969 also saw the ultra-low budget *Sinner's Blood* from Ray Dorn's Hollywood Star Pictures, which also made *Scream Free!* Like *Shanty Tramp* only in colour, the movie's rambling tagline pretty much covers it: 'The gut-ripping truth about a girl named Penny and a kill-for-kicks cycle-gang who in one single, shocking day, set the whole own ablaze with terror!' Director Neil Douglas never made another picture. Joe Solomon's Fanfare Films also contributed *Wild Wheels* (1969), in which a group of surfers and beach bunnies led by *Satan's Sadists*' Robert Dix use dune buggies to fend off an invading group of bikers led by Casey Kasem in a set-up not unlike AIP's *Bikini Beach*.

Russ Tamblyn goes bad in *Satan's Sadists* (1969).

Ross Hagen jumped into the producer's chair with *The Sidehackers* (AKA *Five the Hard Way*), released in May from Crown International. Sidehacking is sidecar motorcross, a fundamentally European sport that never really caught on in America. Filmed in Fantascope (which mostly seems to involve tiny split-screen letter boxing and dynamic freeze framing), there are some good racing scenes although *The Sidehackers* is not a racing movie. Instead, it quickly defaults into the more familiar menacing motorcycle gang plot written by Tony Huston. Hagen plays Rommel, a motorcycle mechanic who competes in sidehack races with his best friend Luke (Richard Merrifield from *The Hellcats*), and plans to marry his fiancée Rita (*The Mini-Skirt Mob*'s Diane McBain). The couple attract the attention of psychopathic exhibition rider J.C. (Michael Pataki) and his slutty girlfriend Paisley (Claire Polan). J.C. wants Rommel to join his crew while Paisley just wants Rommel. He politely rejects both, which triggers a predictably fatal cycle of violence and revenge.

Released in Europe in 1969 and the US in 1970, Bruce Clark's *Naked Angels* was bankrolled by Roger Corman and distributed theatrically through New World Pictures, the company Corman founded with his brother Gene after leaving AIP. Gritty and stylish, but formulaic, *Naked Angels* follows Mother (Michael Greene) as he tries to retake control of his former club and win back his old lady before going after the rival gang that hospitalised him in the first place. Craggy Michael Greene doesn't have much of an on-screen presence as the dictatorial Mother, though Richard Rust does well as his rival, Fingers, while there's a nice turn from Jennifer Gan, the future star of New World's *Women in Cages*. Supposedly, real bikers acted in the movie, although a lot of the cast were UCLA film students like Clark. The film is enlivened by some great night shots of the bikers riding around Vegas and a driving score by Jeff Simmons of The Mothers of Invention.

Released in August 1969, what was technically AIP's last biker movie of the year was in fact another Ray Dorn production, *The Cycle Savages*. (AIP just distributed it.) Despite the failure of *Scream Free!*, Dorn let Bill Brame loose on this one again as writer and director. *The Cycle Savages* looks a lot more polished than Brame's previous movie, with a decent rock instrumental soundtrack by Jerry Styner and The Cycle-Mates, again Sidewalk Records' artists. (Mike Curb was an executive producer, along with Casey Kasem.) It is also given a touch of class by an intense performance from Bruce Dern as sadistic biker Keeg, who wages a vendetta against street artist Romko (Chris Robinson) for sketching the gang. Keeg thinks this might be incriminating given his side hustle of kidnapping college girls, plying them with acid and then passing them on to his sex trafficking brother (Kasem). He resolves to destroy the pictures and stop Romko drawing any more. Romko, meanwhile, falls for club hanger-on Lea (Melody Patterson), whose loyalties are tested when Keeg sticks Romko's hand in a vice.

Finally, there was Harry Kerwin's *It's a Revolution Mother*, which slipped out, largely unnoticed, on 1 December 1969. Kerwin had previously made sexploitation movies and was looking to catch the countercultural wave as AIP had with their acid and biker movies. With no resources to fund a feature film, Kerwin went out and shot the real thing, hanging out with the Aliens Motorcycle Club in New York, filming an anti-Vietnam demonstration in Washington, and a rock festival in Florida (no bands, though, as licence fees are expensive). This so called 'Documentary of Love' has the same time capsule vibe as *Scorpio Rising* and Richard Chase's *Hells Angels Forever*, depicting real bikers on real bikes doing real biker stuff and, unlike Anger's earlier movie, we get to hear them speak too. This fascinating if random footage is tied together by a narration written by Thomas Casey (who also wrote *Flesh Feast*), delivered with the tone of a hipster on safari: 'When things get uptight, the open road stretches out like a tempting woman ...' Nice.

Always the dark side of the counterculture, the year ended with some real Hells Angel violence, an emphatic closer to the decade that should have changed the world for the better, already poisoned by Charles Manson and the Tate-LaBianca murders in August. On Saturday, 6 December, at a free Rolling Stones concert at Altamont Raceway Park in California, the black teenager Meredith Hunter was stabbed to death by Hells Angel Alan Passaro. In his autobiography, Sonny Barger, who was present at the concert, deflects the blame as he is wont to do, but in this case, he had a point. The venue was not well chosen, with the stage so low it could easily be accessed by members of the public. The Stones also needlessly delayed coming on stage, until the mood among the crowd got ugly. Though accounts differ, the Angels were vaguely engaged to act as nominal security, keeping people off the stage and away from the generators, their payment $500 worth of beer. Hunter was one of several concertgoers who invaded the stage and was roughly thrown off by the Angels and beaten. He then pulled out a .22 revolver (a moment captured in the Maysles Brothers' documentary *Gimme Shelter*) and was charged and killed by Passaro. He was acquitted of murder on the grounds of self-defence. Held less than four months after Woodstock, Altamont became its symbolic *other*, death and blood against peace and love, a complex metaphor for the end of a complex era.

Probably because of the press around Altamont and definitely because of the critical and commercial success of *Easy Rider*, the outlaw biker movie continued to roll into the Seventies, although really now past its sell-by date. To keep the format fresh, film-makers moved away from the social rebellion of the Sixties towards the more violent, salacious and action orientated – all components already present in the genre, only now more amplified, more extreme.

An attention-grabbing poster for *Run, Angel, Run!* (1969).

The Losers (1970), somewhere between *Rambo* and *The Road Warrior.*

The new decade literally kicked off with some blatant opportunism in the form of I-IP's *Hell's Bloody Devils*, released on 1 January. Directed by Al Adamson, the film had started out as *The Fakers*, a spy thriller about an FBI agent infiltrating a neo-Nazi crime syndicate in Las Vegas starring western actor Scott Brady. Adamson couldn't give *The Fakers* away, so he shot an extra 30 minutes of new footage adding a motorcycle gang led by Bob Dix. He released the film on a double bill with *Satan's Sadists*. Jack Starrett turns up as a gangster and there's a bizarre cameo by Colonel Sanders.

Speaking of opportunism, Martin B. Cohen's Paragon International Pictures' *The Rebel Rousers* starring B-movie legend Cameron Mitchell had been sitting in the can, unloved and unwanted, since 1967. As Jack Nicholson had a supporting role in it, after his Academy Award nominated turn in *Easy Rider*, Cohen released it as a Nicholson biker movie in 1970. Mitchell plays an architect visiting a small seaside town in search of his estranged and pregnant girlfriend (Diane Ladd, then carrying Laura Dern) at the same time as a bike gang led by Bruce Dern arrives. Harry Dean Stanton appears as comic relief, but even he, Nicholson, and Dern can't save this one.

Released in May 1970, *Run, Angel, Run!* is a much more ambitious film. Directed by Jack Starrett for Fanfare Films, it introduced actor and bodybuilder William Smith to the genre. Starrett creates some real existential depth while still delivering cool stunts (the hero jumping his chopper onto a moving train in one intense chase scene), babes, barroom brawls, and a powerful soundtrack by Stu Phillips, including a theme song by Tammy Wynette.

Angel (Smith) of the Devil's Advocates MC is splitting the scene. To bankroll this, he's sold an exposé of the outlaw lifestyle to a thinly disguised version of *Life*. With a vague plan to go to Europe, all Angel and his hipster girlfriend Laurie (played by Starrett's then wife Valerie) must do is ride from LA to San Franscisco to pick up the money, while the Devil's Advocates and every club in between try to waste them. The film could thus have played out like *The Warriors*. Instead, the script, co-written by Jerome Wish (who wrote *Angels from Hell*) and Valerie Starrett, explores the myth of freedom so often represented in these films, and the possibility of abandoning the road and putting down roots. A similar theme had been introduced in *The Glory Stompers* but never really developed. In an audacious change of pace after an action-packed first act, Angel and Laurie hide out in the country and Angel gets a job on a sheep farm, discovering for the first time the pleasures of honest work and domestic security. The serpent, of course, arrives in the garden as the Devil's Advocates finally track them down.

With an 80-minute running time, Starrett doesn't really have the space he needs to develop the characters, but like the superior *Easy Rider* he manages to push the dramatic and philosophic boundaries of the genre and move beyond them. The result is a serious movie that pays its dues to its influences. American cinema audiences took it seriously too, and the film was the seventeenth-highest grossing movie of the year.

Big Bill Smith was back on drive-in screens in July 1970 in *Angels Die Hard*, the first film out of Roger Corman's New World Pictures. This notionally typical small town invasion story is turned on its head when the threat comes not from the Angels MC that have descended on a small Californian mining town, but incompetent and corrupt law enforcement and local vigilantes. Writer-director Richard Compton's sympathies are with the Angels, one of whom is locked up on a trumped-up loitering charge and then murdered by a hit-and-run driver on release. The bikers hang around to bury their unlucky pal and go looking for payback, while bigoted local Mel Potter (played with suitable menace by Sam Peckinpah regular R.G. Armstrong) stirs the pot, and decent deputy Martin (Frank Leon) and the sheriff's daughter Nancy (Connie Nelson) try and fail to stop the inevitable battle between bikers, cops, and townsfolk.

AIP finally got the Hells Angels involved with a project in *Hell's Angels '69* (1970), the brainchild of bike movie actors Tom Stern and Jeremy Slate, who co-wrote, produced, and co-starred. Essentially a heist movie crossed with the standard Italian western premise of outlaws stealing a fortune and then losing it to other outlaws, *Hell's Angels '69* becomes historically significant through the casting of the Oakland Angels as themselves, all those characters folk had read about in Hunter Thompson's book: Skip, Tiny, Charlie Magoo, Terry the Tramp, and Sonny Barger, all taking prominent roles. This wasn't like the cameo in *Hells Angels on Wheels*; Sonny and the crew were central characters working alongside seasoned pros like Conny Van Dyke and G.D. Spradlin. The result is fascinating to watch.

Two bored rich brothers decide to rob Caesar's Palace for kicks. Disguised as out-of-town outlaws, they ingratiate themselves with the Oakland Angels and steer the club towards the idea of a run to Vegas (though the production never left California in reality), using them as a diversion while they change clothes and rob the casino. Unaware of the robbery, Sonny chases the brothers off for wasting club time and they split on dirt bikes heading for LA across open desert with Terry the Tramp's old lady Betsy (Conny Van Dyke), who has taken a shine to Wes (Jeremy Slate). When a detective (Spradlin) tells Sonny the truth, the club tear off after the robbers on big British scramblers. Barger notes in his autobiography that they wouldn't normally do this, but the script demanded it. Those boys would've done the Mojave on their Harleys.

As actors, the Angels turn the early scenes into what feels like documentary footage with everyone talking at once and horsing around, but after a while the film settles down and Sonny and Terry in particular emerge as perfectly credible actors within the limits of the genre. They achieve this by being themselves, and *Hell's Angels '69* is a nice way to see Sonny in his prime. Sadly, Terry the Tramp did not see the year out, dying of a drug overdose at age 30.

Well aware that the fad for traditional 'Beer, Broads, Bikes, and Boots' movies was running down after *Easy Rider*, Joe Solomon at Fanfare was always looking for a new angle to wring just that little bit more out of the genre and the drive-in cash registers. *The Losers* (AKA *Nam Angels*, 1970) was one impressive result, a film that combines as it anticipates the behind-enemy-lines carnage of *Rambo* and the neo-medieval motorcycles of *The Road Warrior* with a dash of *The Dirty Dozen* for good measure.

Possibly inspired by Sonny Barger's letter to President Johnson volunteering the Hells Angels as a 'gorilla' [*sic*] force fighting behind enemy lines in Vietnam, *The Losers* sends five Devil's Advocates across the border into Cambodia to rescue a CIA operative – Chet Davies (Jack Starrett) – from the Red Army. 'We can't go in there,' their military liaison tells leader Link (William Smith) 'but you can.' If they get caught, the US government has plausible deniability, and the army can't help them. 'This could really be a bummer,' Link replies sagely. And if all this sounds familiar, it's basically the premise of *Rambo: First Blood Part II* and *Missing in Action*, both made several years later. Link has history with Chet Davies, and two of his men are vets returning for a reason, Duke (Adam Roarke) for love, Dirty Denny (Houston Savage) for money. Speed (Gene Cornelius from *Run, Angel, Run!*) and Limpy (Paul Koslo, soon to be the panhead-riding plague survivor in *The Omega Man*) are less defined, though Limpy falls for a sex worker with a baby. The mad plan involves turning two-stroke Yamahas into 'weapons on wheels', and the guys add armour plate and machine guns to the handlebars, filling saddlebags with grenades and painting everything matt black. Limpy, meanwhile, builds a Harley/Volkswagen trike with 50 cal machine guns and a helicopter rocket launcher. Once the crash helmets are painted with flames and stars and stripes, they're good to go.

Having spent about an hour developing character, director Jack Starrett really goes for it in the last 35 minutes. The attack on the communist camp is action-packed, as the bikers pull wheelies to shoot and rocket guard towers and leap over command buildings dropping grenades. This isn't the climax of the movie either, which still has several twists and reversals of fortune in store for an audience now thoroughly invested in the fate of Link and his boys. The final confrontation between Davies (establishment) and Link (counterculture), two men who hate each other, is electric.

Written by British screenwriter Alan Caillou (Alan Samuel Lyle-Smythe) and shot on the Philippines sets from Robert Aldrich's *Too Late the Hero*, *The Losers* packs a heavy political punch, given that the war was still raging. Way ahead of the curve when it came to Hollywood action movies, *The Losers* was a big hit, grossing around $14 million against a budget of $210,000.

Using the conventions of a Range War western, director Lee Madden followed *Hell's Angels '69* with *Angel Unchained* for AIP, released in September 1970. There are also shades of *Run, Angel, Run!* as the protagonist – another 'Angel' (Don Stroud) – splits from his pack to find new meaning in a doomed pastoral environment. He takes off on his ugly Triumph chop, his paths crossing with hippie chick Merilee (Tyne Daly). Angel finds peace at the commune led by Tremaine (Luke Askew essentially reprising his role from *Easy Rider*), but a group of cowboys on dune buggies are trying to drive them off the land like cattle barons menacing homesteaders. Angel is convinced by pragmatist Tremaine to ask his former club, now led by Larry Bishop, for help, although they turn out to be almost as much trouble as the cowboys and no one really wins in the end.

Don Stroud and Tyne Daly in *Angel Unchained* (1970).

Looking like a young Brando, Stroud is an excellent lead, on the run from his past but not yet able to embrace or even understand the 'peace trip' Merilee is selling. He is similarly alienated from his 'ex-brothers', who view him as a 'dropout' and no longer respect or trust him while he ultimately realises they're 'animals'. Stroud was a good call for a biker movie, having previously duelled with Clint Eastwood on Triumphs in the climax to *Coogan's Bluff* (1968). Bud Ekins was stunt co-ordinator, which makes for an excellent climax with bikes and dune buggies flying everywhere. Marketed at the time as a kind of *Magnificent Seven* with bikes, *Angel Unchained* is much more nuanced than that. Bringing the hippie and biker countercultures together, Madden exposes their fundamental differences in a way that depressingly recalls Altamont.

Unique in the outlaw biker film cycle as a big budget movie from a mainstream studio, *77 Sunset Strip* star Roger Smith wrote and co-produced *C.C. and Company* (1970) for AVCO Embassy Pictures as a vehicle for his wife, Ann-Margret, and New York Jets' quarterback 'Broadway Joe' Namath. C.C. Ryder (Namath) is a slacker outlaw on a zebra-striped Harley shovelhead who saves fashionista Ann from being assaulted by other members of his club, the Heads. They later meet again at a motorcross event where she's running a fashion shoot. The Heads disrupt the first day, but C.C. pinches a Kawasaki G4TR and becomes an expert racer overnight, winning the competition and Ann's heart with his cornball one-liners. Club pres Moon (William Smith) is not impressed by all this, and eventually the Heads kidnap Ann and C.C. must race Moon to win her back.

C.C. and Company stands or falls on how you respond – like Ann – to Namath's goofy charm. He's either likeable or annoying as the lovable outlaw who can still ride hard, love hard, and fight his way out of trouble. In this respect, he's a prototype of the modern American action hero, who must be brave, handsome and funny. The tone of the movie is quite uneven, as it awkwardly mixes the normal codes of the biker movie, represented by Smith – the debauchery, sexism, casual violence, and sudden death – with screwball comedy. Even the soundtrack is all over the place, with driving rock, most notably a strident arrangement of Mitch Ryder & The Detroit Wheels' 'Jenny Take a Ride!' contrasted with silent movie hooks over the slapstick scenes. As Moon complains to C.C., 'We got the club here and you're over there, and it just never seems to blend.'

At the absolute other end of the budgetary scale, Laurence Merrick's *Black Angels* (AKA *Black Bikers from Hell*), released in October 1970, feels like a very early blaxploitation movie but doesn't quite commit politically. Made within six months of Ossie Davies' *Cotton Comes to Harlem*, which triggered the blaxploitation genre, and a year before *Sweet Sweetback's Baadasssss Song* and *Shaft*, *Black Angels* depicts a black motorcycle club – the Choppers – for the first time, barring the group that turns up briefly in the pre-credit scene to *Angels from Hell*. The Choppers and the white Satan's Serpents MC maintain an uneasy truce until an ambitious, newly initiated Chopper, Jimmy (James Young-El), decides to take down Serpents' pres Chainer (Des Roberts) and gets himself accidently killed. Long-suffering cop Lt Harper (Clancy Syrko) senses opportunity, and tells both clubs the other is gunning for them, with predictable results.

The film's opening scene suggests this is going to be a movie about racial conflict, with the doomed Jimmy denouncing 'Whitey' Chainer to his girlfriend and declaring, 'I'm a new shade of black. An all-new breed.' People who haven't seen the movie usually assume this is the premise, but being Californian, Chainer and his lieutenant Frenchy (John Donovan) are horrified by the racism of lone wolf Johnny Reb (John King III) when he complains about a black waitress in their favourite bar. Chainer tells him to 'take the white sheet off'. 'Black Angels', meanwhile, is a slang term both clubs use for the police. That said, there is an entirely unnecessary flashback scene of a Serpent mama being raped by two black men when she was a younger woman, so the movie is hardly free of negative stereotypes. Like Johnny Reb, however, her racism is held up to ridicule by the rest of the club. Ultimately, the film's message is a plea for reconciliation, hammered home by the closing song, 'Lord, Give us Peace' by Alan Bracket.

It's difficult to imagine getting from this to Reggie Rock Bythewood's *Biker Boyz* and the Black Knights MC. *Black Angels* is trying, but is let down by its amateurish direction, poor acting, incoherent script, and home movie production values. The film also feels dated, with bikers mugging to the camera trying to be outrageous but looking very last decade. It also fails as a blaxploitation movie, having none of the cultural or political Black Power motifs associated with the genre. Only the bikes are interesting, which may give some credence to the film's claim that the Choppers were a real club.

Ann-Margret and Joe Namath in a publicity shot for *C.C. and Company* (1970).

Dealing with race in a much more mature way, writer-director Burt Topper's *The Hard Ride* (released in April 1971) is a surprisingly sombre biker movie from AIP. Marine Phil (Robert Fuller) returns to the US escorting the body of his buddy Lenny (Alfonso Williams), killed in action in Vietnam. Lenny has left Phil 'Baby', his extravagant 1947 knucklehead chop, and charged him with assembling his biker 'family' for the funeral. Wearing Lenny's old gear, Phil sets off on Baby to find the club's elusive leader Big Red (Tony Russel), accompanied by Lenny's reluctant girlfriend Sheryl (Sherry Bain). The situation is complicated by a rival bike gang led by Grady (William Bonner), who wants to get his hands on Lenny's beautiful custom motorcycle. The couple's journey poignantly takes them through many of Lenny and Sheryl's old haunts and happy places, and we learn more about their relationship, complicated by race as Sheryl's white while Lenny was black.

The Hard Ride does not feel like an exploitation movie. Topper focuses on character while gently cascading social commentary. Less melodramatic than *The Born Losers*, the attitude to the war is balanced, respecting the sacrifice of the soldiers, but still suggesting a better way of living. Robert F. Sparks' cinematography is gorgeous, making much of the bikes in the desert landscape and Baby's ride along Interstate 5. There's also a resonant score by Harley Hatcher, including a moving rendition of 'Swing Low, Sweet Chariot' by Bill Medley of The Righteous Brothers. Fuller, familiar to US audiences as the star of *Laramie* and *Wagon Train*, plays Phil perfectly. His understated performance conveys a complex sense of grief, duty, and survivor's guilt. But most of all, *The Hard Ride* belongs to Sherry Bain as the waitress Sheryl, a dignified and authentic performance that is not too tough, sassy,

Charles Dierkop in *Angels Hard as They Come* (1971).

girl by mistake when trying to 'assassinate' him in a brawl. Long John figures it was one of General's ambitious lieutenants. The Dragons put the Angels on trial, and torture them until one escapes and brings the rest of the club back.

Although the outlaw biker film cycle was obviously coming to its natural end as the spirit of the Sixties passed into the history books as another failed social experiment, *Angels Hard as They Come* is one of the stronger entries, probably because of the talent involved, which also included a young Gary Busey in his first decent role as Henry, the leader of the commune, trying desperately to mediate between the two clubs, both of which despise his pacifism. Viola's assured direction gives the film a gritty, realistic feel while the ghost town of Lost Cause recalls a thousand Italian westerns. Characters drop the F-bomb (for the first time in a bike picture), and there's some interesting attempts to explore the relationship between the different countercultures and their collective opposition to the 'citizens'. Long John and Astrid trade subcultural stereotypes in a philosophical courtship, she raising Altamont, he the murder of Sharon Tate. As events unfold to a predictably violent conclusion, both sides come to understand more about the other's position, that sometimes talking is better (Henry), and that sometimes you have to fight (John). Glenn and Demme would work together again twenty years later on *The Silence of the Lambs*.

AIP, meanwhile, was still banging them out, albeit at a greatly reduced rate as their output moved more towards horror and blaxploitation. Director Lee Frost and producer Wes Bishop's evocatively entitled *Chrome and Hot Leather*, released at the end of September 1971, would be AIP's penultimate outlaw movie. It was also Big Bill Smith's final AIP outing, but he makes the most of it, delivering the film's killer line. Distracted by Larry Bishop's pinball playing in a sleazy late-night bar while sizing up hero-in-disguise Mitch (Tony Young), he turns to his subordinate with a pained look of almost paternal patience and explains, 'Can't you see we're menacing someone?' There's another memorable line on the film's poster: 'Don't muck around with a Green Beret's mama! He'll take his chopper and ram it down your throat!' The more honest pitch would be: 'Don't kill a Green Beret's fiancée because he'll come back from 'Nam on compassionate leave with his army buddies, pose as an outlaw biker to track you down, sleep with your old lady, capture you using military tactics and non-lethal ordnance, and then hand you over to the proper authorities.'

After *Angels Hard as They Come*, *Chrome and Hot Leather* feels dated, despite Frost's tight direction, great stunts courtesy of Bud Ekins, and strong performances from Smith and Bishop. *Gunslinger* star Tony Young is solid as the earnest soldier Mitch, backed up, oddly, by Motown legend Marvin Gaye in one of only two movies he ever made.

As philosopher Thomas Kuhn argued in *The Structure of Scientific Revolutions* (1962), periods of conceptual continuity and cumulative scientific progress – 'normal rationality' – are interrupted by periods of 'abnormal rationality', anomalies accumulating and precipitating revolutions leading to both dead ends and new paradigms. So it is with movies, with some of the most interesting and wacky stuff occurring when old and new genre paradigms are in flux. Thus did Crown International close out 1971 with *The Pink Angels*, an LGBTQIA+ road movie twenty-three years before *The Adventures of Priscilla, Queen of the Desert.*

It's not that *The Pink Angels* is a good movie (it really isn't) that makes it interesting, but that it exists at all. Written by Margaret McPherson – whose entire film career comprised a role in the 1965 stag movie *Wife Swappers* and crewing on Robert F. Slatzer's *Bigfoot* – and directed by Larry Brown (who didn't do much else), the film's heroes are six non-binary, cross-dressing bikers on three very cool and grungy wartime BMW sidecar outfits heading to a 'ladies' Cotillion' (a drag-queen contest) in Los Angeles. On the way, they run into some cops, a predatory waitress, some sex workers, a rival bike gang (including Dan Haggerty), and a deranged army general (G.J. Mitchell) who obsessively hates 'long-hairs'. The general's rants in front of an American flag punctuate the narrative while

Biker movie legend Big Bill Smith kicks back in *Chrome and Hot Leather* (1971).

being weirdly outside it, but watched through the lens of contemporary history, his ravings against the trans community and the fate of the heroes are particularly disturbing.

McPherson and Brown apparently viewed their film as a satire of biker movies. When it was re-released by Prism Entertainment on VHS in the Eighties, their pitch was '*La Cage Aux Folles* on Motorcycles!' But aside from comedic gay characters trying to get along in the straight world, these films don't have a lot in common. Film critics John Wooley and Michael H. Price more usefully suggest you imagine *Priscilla, Queen of the Desert* if Edward D. Wood directed it. This is a long way from Joe Orton, or even a *Carry On* movie, but for all the *double entendres* and inexpert production, there remains something quite satisfyingly subversive about *The Pink Angels*, though the great gay biker movie remains *The Leather Boys.*

Though the biker movie endures as an occasional subgeneric diversion to this day, there was never a period so prolific and popular as the Sixties again. In dating the cycle that begins with AIP's *The Wild Angels* in 1966, 1972 is definitely the year that it ends, with only three bike pictures released that year.

Dropping in April, the first of these, *The Loners* (1972) has the distinction of being the last film produced by prolific industry veteran Sam Katzman. Distributed by Fanfare, *The Loners* stars Dean Stockwell as Stein, a half-Navajo half-Irish scoot jockey – 'I never scalp on St Patrick's Day' – who is harassed by cops, the chase resulting in an accident in which one of them dies. Having no doubt he's facing a murder rap after the surviving policeman fires on him when he tries to help, Stein goes on the run on his ghastly Triumph chop with his neurodivergent best friend Alan (Todd Susman), playing a similar role to Michael J. Pollard's C.W. Moss in Arthur Penn's *Bonnie and Clyde* (1967). Along the way, they pick up Julio (Patricia Stich), a dope-smoking free spirit looking to escape her shrill and controlling mother, played by Oscar-winner Gloria Grahame. Pursued by the vengeful cop Hearn (ageing matinee idol Scott Brady) and a terrifying redneck sheriff (Alex Dreier), the trio manage to rack up more accidental fatalities until the film reaches its inevitable conclusion. What's interesting is that the narrative is entirely sympathetic to the fugitives, with establishment authority figures depicted as brutal, hypocritical and corrupt while the heroes are shown to have been disadvantaged since birth. Publicity material leaves no doubt what Katzman was going for: 'First there was "Bonnie and Clyde"' runs the original poster's tagline, 'Then there was "Easy Rider"...' Trailers made the same connection, further framing the film as 'The story of three young people who dared to be different' and, by implication, paid the price.

Al Adamson and Sam Sherman had a biker flick called *Screaming Angels* in the can at I-IP when the bike boom went bust in '72. What was, however, hot was New World's *The Big Doll's House* starring Pam Grier, Judy Brown, and Roberta Collins. Sherman and Adamson therefore adopted the same approach they had towards *Hell's Bloody Devils* only in reverse, shooting new scenes that de-emphasised the male biker content in favour of the old ladies. They renamed the film *Angels' Wild Women* to capitalize on the new fad for tough, independent and sexually aggressive female characters as seen in the emerging women's prison genre. Adamson, who also wrote the script, used the device of a men-only motorcycle run to get rid of the guys, and not only shot extra footage with the women but added entirely new female characters, most notably striking African American actress Maggie Bembry (a bit player in *Sweet Sweetback's Baadasssss Song*) to give the film a Pam Grier figure, and sexploitation actress Linda Vroom, who appears only in the first act and is then never seen again. Similarly, Linda Gordon becomes a prominent member of the group until the film's climax, when she disappears entirely. It's obvious from these inexplicable comings and goings that the original female bikers were limited to Vicki Volante, Jill Woelfel, and Regina

Carrol, whose collective plot function before the reshoot was just to be kidnapped by the bad guys.

This extra footage is then grafted onto the primary film narrative, about a bike club running into a Manson-inspired 'love cult' at the Spahn Movie Ranch in Los Angeles, the real hang-out of Charlie's Family. Biker leader Speed is played by a long-haired Ross Hagen, while William Bonner puts in a nice turn as the Manson figure King, a hippie guru selling peace and love while abusing his female followers and running a lucrative drug ring. The intertextual waters are further muddied by another film within a film, an unnamed Nazisploitation movie directed by Adamson himself on which Speed's girlfriend appears to work. Two long episodes with Hagen, meanwhile, now have little point in the new story so serve only as filler. All this editing renders *Angels' Wild Women* virtually incoherent. It was good enough for drive-in audiences, and the film went on to be a good earner for the studio, although Adamson and Sherman steered well clear of motorcycle pictures after that.

Director Al Adamson's wife Regina Carrol kicks ass in *Angels' Wild Women* (1971).

Finally, there was AIP's *The Dirt Gang*, released in November 1972, starring journeyman TV actors Paul Carr and Michael Forest and directed by Jerry Jameson, a former television editor. Jameson directs *The Dirt Gang* with some real flair, particularly in the opening scenes in which the large group of 'gypsy dirt bikers' tear through the desert on British, European, and Japanese scramblers. Jameson uses low angles, panoramas, aerial shots and rider points of view to create a sustained and high-energy explosion of sand, sound and movement, anticipating later post-apocalyptic road movies to the extent that several reviewers cite *The Dirt Gang* as the inspiration for *Mad Max*. There's certainly some *mise en scènic* commonality, even down to the riders themselves, who are no longer the long-haired, denim-wearing outlaw types of previous AIP biker movies, but instead sport beaten up crash helmets, goggles, and body armour, ten years before *The Road Warrior* cemented the look. The film also takes a similar line to *Angels' Wild Women*, making central female characters tougher and more assertive, such as Nancy Harris' Big Beth, a tomboyish biker girl who swings both ways and gets what she wants, and 'over the hill sex goddess' Dawn Christian (Jo Anne Meredith), an older actress who seduces leader Monk (Carr) because she finds him 'frightening but exciting'.

Screenwriters Michael DeForrest and Michael C. Healy didn't do much else, which is a pity as there are some great ideas in *The Dirt Gang*. There's a touch of *Moby Dick* about it in Monk's obsession with

The Dirt Gang (1972) was AIP's final outlaw biker movie.

finding the rider Zeno (Forest), who he blames for the loss of his eye during a previous race. Of course he does find him, working as a stuntman on a film set in the desert for a low-budget western, making *The Dirt Gang* meta as well as a revenge tragedy. In a classical allegory, Monk is warned several times by biker Stormy (Jessica Stuart) that the stars are not auspicious, but rejects her prophecy in favour of the religious ravings of Padre (a mad performance from Jon Shank), and his own belief that his lieutenant (and possibly bisexual lover) Biff (T.J. Escott) brings him luck. He's referred to several times metaphorically as a 'king', making his downfall feel almost Shakespearian.

And as the sun set on Monk's surprised-looking corpse, so it did on the outlaw biker film cycle that had dominated drive-ins and 42nd Street grindhouses since 1966, ending in every way appropriately with one last outing from AIP, the biker movie riding into film history not on a big Harley but a Triumph with knobbly tyres.

THE BALLAD OF *EASY RIDER*

5 CHAPTER

CONCEIVED AND THEN painfully born right in the middle of the outlaw biker film cycle, *Easy Rider* is the child of a lot of biker movie talent. And like all kids, it immediately rebels by being existential, reflective and deeply political, director Dennis Hopper drawing his influences from Indian and European arthouse cinema as much as the John Ford western to make what he described as the 'first American art film'. As Sonny Barger complained, '*Easy Rider*, supposedly the greatest bike movie ever made, wasn't really a bike movie at all.'

There are many different versions of the making of *Easy Rider*, the various perspectives, grievances, and counterclaims all adding to the legend. Peter Fonda came up with the basic premise – modern outlaws on bikes cross the country then get shot by rednecks – while signing *Wild Angels* photos in a hotel room. He called his friend Dennis Hopper, with whom he'd acted in the LSD-themed movie *The Trip*, written by Jack Nicholson and directed by Roger Corman. Hopper had been a promising leading man in the Fifties, but his confrontational behaviour on set, hard drinking, drug use, and womanising had made him a Hollywood pariah, forcing him to work outside the system. Like Fonda, he already had an AIP biker movie under his belt. He and his wife Brooke Hayward's house in the Hollywood Hills was one of the centres of LA hip counterculture, like the Psychedelic Temple in *The Trip*, regularly heaving with bohemian artists, writers, musicians, Black Panthers, Hells Angels, and hangers on. The plan was that Hopper would direct, Fonda would produce, and both would write and act in the picture. Fonda was looking to make some kind of provocative, anti-establishment statement, to 'shake the cage'. Hopper wanted to make a 'time capsule', something that actually captured the socio-political upheaval of the Sixties in America – psychedelic drugs, civil rights protests, Vietnam, and police brutality. Contemporary cinema offered young people only beach party or biker movies, neither of which had any bearing on reality, and in the latter case presented the counterculture as utterly depraved.

Co-writer Terry Southern was a major voice in the Sixties. A friend of Fonda, he had hung around with Camus, Sartre and Cocteau in Paris, been part of the Greenwich Village Beat generation, and a prime intellectual mover in Swinging London. Tom Wolfe credited him as the father of New Journalism, and his work as a script doctor on Kubrick's *Dr. Strangelove* turned him into a significant and bankable screenwriter. When Fonda told him about the project, Southern waived his usual fee in order to get involved, also suggesting the title 'Easy Rider' – a song by bluesman Lead Belly and slang for a man who lives off a prostitute but is not her pimp.

Fonda initially took the project to AIP, but Nicholson and Arkoff weren't keen on first-time director Hopper. Instead, *Easy Rider* was funded by Bob Rafelson and Bert Schneider's Raybert Productions, the company behind *The Monkees* TV show and its surreal and disastrous follow-up movie *Head*, directed by Rafelson and co-written by Jack Nicholson. Fonda pitched a budget of $360,000 as that had been the cost of *The Wild Angels* and he had no idea what figure to ask. Several bike movie alumni turn up in the cast and crew, for example Sabrina Scharf and Jack Nicholson, Robert Walker Jr., Michael Pataki, Luke Askew, Dan Haggerty, stuntmen Tex Hall and Gary Littlejohn, and Hungarian cinematographer László Kovács. Nicholson replaced Southern's friend Rip Torn as alcoholic civil rights lawyer George Hanson after Hopper pulled a knife on Torn in a pre-production meeting, allegedly basing his laconic southern drawl on Jack Starrett. Nicholson would go on to be nominated for an Academy Award and this role marks the beginning of his superstardom. The film's iconic motorcycles were designed and built by African American custom pioneers Cliff Vaughs and Ben Hardy, who inexplicably received no credit.

On the surface, *Easy Rider* is a simple road movie. Two long-hairs with Wild West names we don't know anything about, Billy (Hopper) and Wyatt (Fonda), buy cocaine cheap in Mexico and sell big in LA. They buy two Hydra-Glide panhead chops and set off for Mardi Gras in New Orleans, 'Looking for America.' As characters, Wyatt is contemplative, curious and calm, whereas Billy is permanently antsy, distrustful of others and always wanting to move on. In essence, they play themselves. Billy is upbeat about being rich and dreams of retiring to Florida. In reply, all Wyatt offers is, 'We blew it.'

The genius of *Easy Rider* is in the social commentary and symbolism, as well as Kovács' stunning cinematography. There are sublime shots of tiny bikes riding across Monument Valley and landscapes that look like photographs by Ansel Adams. Kovács intuits the movements of the bikes, reframing in real time so that the ride feels like a dance. Hopper and Kovács show us everything the riders see, frequently juxtaposing the natural with the urban, rivers (God's design, says Fonda) and man-made

Peter Fonda and Dennis Hopper in *Easy Rider* (1969).

Hopper as Billy in *Easy Rider.*

roads, the eye of the camera taking in rich southern suburbs, black shanty towns, and industrial decay. The road south takes them further towards a heart of darkness where anyone different is despised, the atmosphere becoming ever more menacing.

Dialogue was frequently improvised, conveying naturalism and *verité*, which managed to sit quite comfortably alongside Southern's scripted scenes and Hopper's use of symbolism. On-screen soft drug use was authentic, Hopper later remarking wryly that this was 'The first time marijuana had been smoked in a movie and they didn't go out and kill a bunch of nuns or something.'

The spirit of the age is further established by a score of contemporary rock music, including The Byrds and Jimi Hendrix, while The Byrds' Roger McGuinn sings Bob Dylan's 'It's Alright, Ma' and the 'Ballad of Easy Rider', which Dylan wrote specifically for the film. Steppenwolf's 'Born to be Wild' has become a biker anthem, and the songs together form a literary commentary to the story in a similar way to *Scorpio Rising*. The 16mm Mardis Gras/LSD episode feels like Kenneth Anger too, some sort of magical invocation that accidently summons something dark and malign.

The film's most obvious symbolism is Fonda himself, styled 'Captain America', a huge American flag on the back of his leather jacket, stars and stripes on both crash helmet and petrol tank. The innocent, optimistic, thoughtful, questing Wyatt *is* an embodiment of the American Dream, destroyed by prejudice and corruption. When Billy argues, 'You go for the big money then you're free,' Wyatt understands this means the exact opposite.

Easy Rider wrapped in the summer of 1968 but it took Hopper the better part of a year to edit, creating rough cuts as long as five hours. Various cast and crew members have since claimed to have had a hand

Fonda's Wyatt 'Looking for America' in *Easy Rider.*

in editing the film, including associate producer Bill Hayward, Southern, and Fonda himself. What is certain is that Rafelson and Schneider got Hopper out of the way and then got someone else in to cut the movie, possibly Jack Nicholson and the actor Henry Jaglom, who was part of the hip LA film circle. Whoever it was got the movie down to 96 minutes, which Hopper begrudgingly accepted.

Easy Rider was shown for the first time at the 22nd Cannes Film Festival, where Hopper won the Best First Work award while also being nominated for the *Palme d'Or*. Hopper also won a Special Award at the 1969 National Society of Film Critics' Awards, Nicholson picking up Best Supporting Actor, which he also won at the 1969 New York Film Critics' Circle Awards, losing out at the Oscars. Fonda, Hopper and Southern were also nominated for the Academy Award for Best Original Screenplay. Distributed by Columbia Pictures, one of the first independent movies to be put out by a major studio, the film grossed $60 million at the box office. It was one of the heralds of the New Hollywood era, in which major studios began to invest in low-budget projects and *avant-garde* directors, paving the way for a new generation of film-makers and actors such as Nicholson, De Niro, Coppola and Scorsese.

And as for those iconic choppers, of which two of each were built, one was blown up for the film's climax, while the other three were stolen. There is a legend that the Hells Angels were responsible and that Barger had the original Captain America bike, but this seems unlikely given his disdain for the film and 'that pretty boy Fonda'. Tex Hall, who had been looking after the bikes, believed they'd gone to a chop shop. Fonda let Dan Haggerty have the remaining burned-up wreck, which he rebuilt around the original frame. The trouble is that Haggerty – who had done time for dealing cocaine and tax evasion – seems to have sold the 'original' Captain America chopper three or four times.

Easy Rider remains not only a great bike picture but a great American movie. Its success undoubtedly kept the outlaw biker film cycle going longer than it perhaps would have done otherwise, though its influence remains hard to detect in what follows in the genre. *Easy Rider* had a huge influence on the direction of American film, but not, oddly, on the biker movie, which still seemed to prefer fantasy outlaws to confused loners in search of spiritual enlightenment.

American TV viewers, however, were more receptive to the concept, having already been introduced to Michael Parks' James Bronson, another vagabond seeker on a Harley in NBC's *Then Came Bronson.* Created by former war correspondent Denne Bart Petitclerc, the show is so in tune with the values of *Easy Rider* that it is often assumed to be a copy, although the pilot was broadcast in March 1969, two months ahead of the movie. Admittedly, the show itself didn't air until September, so it's likely the success of *Easy Rider* led to the green light. Parks plays a newspaperman disillusioned with the rat race after the suicide of his best friend (Martin Sheen). He quits his job and takes to the road on a red Sportster with the Eye of Providence on the tank in search of some kind of meaning and authenticity. Each week his wanderings take him somewhere he needs to be, acting as an agent of change for a stranger at a turning point or moment of crisis. More wholesome and drug free than *Easy Rider*, the show went a long way to restoring the image of Harley riders in the US after years of relentlessly negative portrayals.

In a film that feels like an unofficial companion to *Easy Rider*, James William Guercio's *Electra Glide in Blue* from United Artists (1973) explores the prejudice against hippies and bikers from a law enforcement perspective. Robert Blake plays John Wintergreen, an Arizona motorcycle cop who yearns to be a homicide detective. He gets his chance when he correctly argues that the apparent suicide of an eccentric recluse was murder, and is seconded to Homicide to assist seasoned detective Harvey Poole (Mitchell Ryan, who also appeared in the Dirty Harry movie *Magnum Force* that year, another film featuring motorcycle patrolmen). Poole is convinced the killer is a member of a local hippie commune, a group Wintergreen has already seen harassed and framed by his partner Zipper (Billy Green Bush). Wintergreen is uncomfortable with Poole's interrogation of the hippies, leading to a downbeat ending that mirrors that of *Easy Rider.*

Guercio came out of the music business and *Electra Glide in Blue* is his only film. It's ambitious, idiosyncratic and experimental, while also a realistic police procedural. Guercio waived his directorial salary so he could afford to hire cinematographer Conrad Hall, who'd won an Academy Award for *Butch Cassidy and the Sundance Kid.* Shot in and around Monument Valley, the film conveys the spirit of John Ford with the dynamic juxtaposition of human subjects and the natural landscape. Blake got the role for which he is most remembered – *Baretta* – through this movie.

Almost twenty years later, *Sid and Nancy* co-writer Abbe Wool's *Roadside Prophets* (1991) quietly contributed an *Easy Rider* for Generation X. John Doe of the LA punk band X plays Joe, a divorcee with a dead-end job and a '57 panhead who meets a biker called Dave (David Anthony Marshall) who tells him about a wondrous place in Nevada called El Dorado with a casino full of beautiful girls and good luck he can't exactly remember the name of. When

Jack Nicholson as ill-fated lawyer George Hanson in *Easy Rider.*

Dave is killed in a freak accident, Joe resolves to scatter his ashes at the place he loved, if only he can find it. He's joined on the road by the puppy-like Sam (The Beastie Boy's Adam Horovitz) on a ratty Triumph Bonneville, setting up a loose series of encounters with eccentrics along the way until the quest is fulfilled, Joe finds himself, and Sam comes to terms with his troubled childhood. The Roadside Prophets are a mix of Sixties survivors, including Arlo Guthrie, Timothy Leary, and a hookah-smoking David Carradine, X-ers like Joe with names like Prudence Kierkegaard (Jennifer Balgobin), and the rising generation of new, clueless revolutionaries represented by Sam and John Cusack as a radical 'dine and dasher', all offering homespun philosophy from 'Be on the lookout for transcendent reality' (Leary) to 'Stick with the one who can see the truth of your soul and don't take any wooden nickels' (Balgobin). Harry Caesar as aging and lonely hotel manager Jesse delivers the point of the movie when he laments a life spent following the rules, and wishes he'd 'lived a little more reckless'.

In a strange and depressing coda, there was also *Easy Rider: The Ride Back*, a sequel released direct-to-video in 2012 produced, co-written and starring Phil Pitzer, a Cincinnati attorney with no industry experience but very deep pockets. Pitzer had successfully sued Rafelson and Schneider to uphold his company's purchase of the sequel rights after the previous holder went into receivership.

Directed and co-written by Dustin Rikert – an efficient low-budget, direct-to-video director/producer – *The Ride Back* is an unremarkable family saga set during the Iraq War in which Pitzer cosplays Peter Fonda as Wyatt's younger brother Morgan, right down to the shades, flag jacket and Captain America chopper, all supposedly reclaimed after Wyatt's death. (There's another brother called Virgil. As there wasn't a famous Earp sister, Wyatt's is called Shane.) Morgan has been estranged from his father since he burnt his draft card, but Shane tracks him down in Mexico and begs him to return to Ohio to see their dying dad on his birthday. The film is framed by Morgan's ride back with Jeff Fahey as the Dennis Hopper figure, while the post-war history of the family is told in voiceovers and flashbacks moving between Morgan and his father Wild Bill (Newell Alexander). Wyatt only turns up in a couple of scenes as a kid before he runs away to California, which judging by the state of his family was absolutely the right move. The family are all proud military stock. Wild Bill fought in the Second World War, and Virgil did two tours in 'Nam. Shane's son is serving in Iraq, and the film's tone is relentlessly nationalistic and pro-military. You know what you're in for when Morgan's opening

Robert Blake in a promo shot for *Electra Glide in Blue* (1973).

monologue, describing the day Wyatt died, begins 'The sky was crystal blue, just like 9/11 ...'

Pitzer had never acted before (or since), and simply can't carry the movie. Throughout a stiff performance, he looks like what he is: a rich, sixty-something lawyer with very obviously dyed hair starring in his own vanity project. Expository dialogue and passive narration suck the life out of the drama, and the big family reunion is perfunctory and mawkish. With a budget of $10 million, the film was a critical and commercial bomb and Pitzer's plans for a further sequel and a TV show have, thankfully, not come to pass, so hopefully Hopper and Fonda have now stopped spinning in their graves.

John Doe and Adam Horovitz in *Roadside Prophets* (1991).

Viewed as an undemanding family drama with a couple of nice bikes in it, *The Ride Back* is not the worst straight-to-video movie you'll ever see. The problem is in linking it to *Easy Rider*. On that level, it's a travesty. The tragedy is that the sequel Fonda and Hopper wanted to make in the Eighties never happened because of a long legal dispute between Columbia and Raybert over the rights to the original movie. *Easy Rider A.D.* would have seen Wyatt and Billy brought back from the dead in the far future, riding across a post-apocalyptic America. Now *that* would've been something.

CHAPTER 6 SILVER DREAM RACERS

AS SOON AS motorcycles first appeared, riders started racing. The *Fédération Internationale des Clubs Motocyclistes* was founded in Paris in 1904 as a governing body for motorcycle racing, creating a five nations International Cup between France, Germany, Britain, Austria and Denmark, the first race taking place the following year. The British Auto-Cycle Union was a founding member, staging the first International Tourist Trophy on the Isle of Man in 1907. The Federation of American Motorcyclists was formed in New York City in 1903, evolving into the American Motorcyclist Association in 1924 (although African American riders were not admitted until 1954). In the US, early races took place on horseracing ovals and bicycle velodromes, before wooden tracks known as motordromes began to appear around 1910. Motorcycle Grand Prix racing began in the US soon after the end of the Great War, European countries quickly following their example.

With its long and distinguished history, you would think that motorcycle racing would be a rich source for film-makers. And you would be wrong. Whereas motor racing has intense dramas like Lee H. Katzin's *Le Mans*, Ron Howard's *Rush*, and James Mangold's *Ford v Ferrari*, there are as yet no equivalents exploring any of the epic rivalries in MotoGP, such as Mike Hailwood vying with his up-and-coming teammate at MV Augusta, Giacomo Agostini; the bitter feud between Yamaha teammates Phil Read and Bill Ivy; Barry Sheene and Kenny Roberts duelling on the track like Great War flying aces; Kevin Schwantz versus Wayne Rainey, or Valentino Rossi versus everyone. And while riders like Hailwood, Sheene, and Rossi cry out for biopics, motorcycle racing pictures are more like *Rocky*: unrealistic Cinderella stories of semi-skilled independents and underdogs succeeding against impossible odds, a formula in Hollywood sports pictures that was already decades old when Stallone exploited it. As with the outlaw film cycle, it is often difficult to detect any real understanding of motorcycles or the men and women that ride them, let alone race them, on the part of film-makers, who rely instead to some half-understood romantic image of bike riding that can usually be traced back to westerns.

The first motorcycle racing picture is the British *Money for Speed* (1933) directed by Bernard Vorhaus, an American director blacklisted in his own country for his communist sympathies. Set in the world of speedway racing, then at its popular zenith in the UK, *Money for Speed* is a dark, cynical tale of rivalry and revenge between champion rider Mitch (John Loder) and cocky Australian newcomer Big Bill Summers (Cyril McLaglen). Mitch conspires with his streetwise girlfriend Jane (a very young Ida Lupino) to affect an innocent country girl persona and dupe Bill into a relationship, getting as much money out of him as possible. The plan is to humiliate Bill by revealing the truth before a big race, throwing him off his game.

The track scenes are authentic and intense, featuring star riders of the day Ginger Lees and Australian Lionel Van Praag of the Wembley Lions, and the 'Red Devil' Frank Varey of the Belle Vue Aces. Promoter and father of modern speedway Jack Stark Hoskins also appears as himself. With a running time of 73 minutes, Vorhaus had to shoehorn a big plot into a short movie, leaving little space for character development, although Ida Lupino shines through as the 'tart with a heart', and spotted by a Paramount talent scout, *Money for Speed* got her to Hollywood. John Loder made it to Hollywood too, though here he's really just a melodramatic villain with a motorcycle. Cyril McLaglen's Bill has more emotional depth, progressing from cock of the walk to feather duster. The film was considered lost for decades until two European copies turned up in the Eighties.

Much easier to see, *No Limit* (1935) is a British musical comedy starring the Lancashire Chaplin, George Formby, much of it shot on location at the Isle of Man TT the year Stanley Woods won the Senior for Moto Guzzi, after an epic battle with Jimmy Guthrie on his Norton. It was directed by the Italian comedian and actor Monty Banks – who also directed Laurel and Hardy – and produced by Basil Dean for his company Associated Talking Pictures (Ealing Studios), Warner's having rejected Formby as 'too stupid to play the bad guy and too ugly to play the hero'. *No Limit* established the rags to riches formula for most of Formby's subsequent films, in which the lovable but accident-prone northern working-class everyman pursues a dream, winning the heart of a nice southern middle-class girl in the process.

George Shuttleworth is a chimney sweep from Wigan whose hobbies are motorcycling and playing the ukulele. He is desperate to get on the Rainbow racing team (a fictional British bike brand) and has adapted one of their models into the Shuttleworth Snap (a heavily disguised AJS H5). George heads for the TT in the hope of winning the £1,000 prize and making a name for himself. He is supported by the Rainbow director's secretary Florrie Dibney (comedian Florence Desmond), who is falling for the dopey, big-hearted dreamer, despite being courted by the arrogant and urbane Bert Tyldesley (Jack Hobbs), Rainbow's posh star rider.

George Formby in *No Limit* (1935).

No Limit is all about social class, urban poverty, the north-south divide and the outsider versus the elite. This is hardly surprising, given that the original story was written by Walter Greenwood, the working-class Salford author of the bestselling novel *Love on the Dole* (1933). It is also a film about the bravery and skill of the road racers and the risks they take, and it doesn't hold back in depicting the violent reality. In the race segments, real Manx footage is used, while stunt riders smash through gates, brick walls and, in one case, the doors of a pub; others fall into rivers, hit each other, and routinely slide down the road. (Two years later, Jimmy Guthrie was killed in the German Grand Prix.) Stunts were done by local racers, the brothers Bertie and Harold Rowell, and members of the Peveril Motorcycle and Light Car Club. Formby also did some of his own stunts, including a nice run on the Cronk-y-Voddy Straight. And for all the daftness and unlikely story events, you do get a sense of the bravado and energy of the TT before the war, with a lot of great footage of the riders, the spectators, and the bikes. Formby's character is now a TT icon, memorialised as a statue by the Manx artist Amanda Barton in Douglas.

There's also a sense of something coming to an end. George V's Silver Jubilee was in 1935. It was a beautiful summer, with national celebrations, and the general population, having survived the Great War and Depression, must have thought the worst was over. But this was also the year Hitler broke with the Treaty of Versailles, re-forming the Luftwaffe and rearming, the Nazis flaunting Germany's growing military machine at the Leipzig Fair. One of the visitors was James Leek, a senior executive at BSA. When he returned to England, he recommended the company's plant be immediately repurposed for war.

Also made in Britain, Jack Lee's *Once a Jolly Swagman* (1949) remains one of the best motorcycle racing films, chronicling the rise, fall and redemption of a speedway champion played by 27-year-old Dirk Bogarde in his first starring role. Set either side of the Second World War, the film is based on the 1946 novel of the same name by the left-wing intellectual Montagu Slater. The title is taken from the opening line of 'Waltzing Matilda', the Australian bush ballad and unofficial national anthem. This is an elegant title, referring to speedway's origins in Australia. It is also used as the theme for the burnt-out Australian track star, Lagg Gibbon (Bill Owen), who takes Bogarde's Bill Fox under his wing.

Bill is a bored, skint unskilled factory worker from a large Cockney family who rides a BSA R34-4 and dreams of better things. He blags his way into a try-out for the Cobras speedway team, managed by cigar-chewing Rowton (Sid James). Lagg sees potential and convinces Rowton to take Bill on. Bill is so happy he fails to realise he's just jumped into an insatiable meatgrinder that makes and breaks track heroes in a very fast turnover, as Lagg's shakes, dodgy leg and obvious drink problem demonstrates.

With a reckless disregard for his own personal safety, Bill quickly becomes the Cobra's rising star, just as Lagg's pales. The American title of this movie was *Maniacs on Wheels*, which doesn't really do justice to the complex drama but is a pretty fair assessment of those early speedway racers, screaming sideways around a shale track on bikes with one gear and no brakes or left foot peg, keeping themselves upright with a steel boot originally fashioned from old coal shovels, churning up great rooster tails of gravel. Lagg's younger sister Pat, played by the Shakespearean actress Renée Asherson, falls for the handsome and ambitious Bill. The fraught trajectory of their romance forms the main plotline of the movie, alongside Bill's attempt to unionise the riders, all the while driven forward by edge-of-seat racing scenes shot at night at New Cross Stadium.

Though Hollywood was lagging behind, something was clearly in the air as RKO's flat track racing B-picture *The Pace That Thrills* (1952) was only a year ahead of *The Wild One*, although the two films could not have been more different. In comparison to the outlaw ethos of *The Wild One*, *The Pace That Thrills* is effectively an AMA movie, depicting bike riders as cheerful, law-abiding enthusiasts, and introducing the audience to the culture alongside romantic lead Eve Drake (Carla Balenda), a

Dirk Bogarde on an Excelsior-J.A.P. 500 in *Once a Jolly Swagman* (1949).

Lobby card for the beautiful documentary *On Any Sunday* (1971).

the different personalities of the businesslike and professional Lawwill, the happy-go-lucky virtuoso Malcolm Smith, and talented amateur racer Steve McQueen, who co-produced the film. McQueen's presence certainly adds a bit of stardust, but he's here as a racer not an actor and is down to earth and dedicated.

There have been four sequels, starting with *On Any Sunday II* (1981), directed by Ed Forsyth and Don Shoemaker, and three made between 2000 and 2014 by Brown's son, Dana, none of which manage to capture the energy and exuberance of the original. Almost sixty years on, *On Any Sunday* still offers the most eloquent answer to the question Brown poses: 'Why do they do it?'

Earl Bellamy knew his way around a racetrack, having directed *Munster, Go Home!* in 1966. Bellamy directed two motorcycle racing movies; the first, *Sidecar Racers* (1975), in Australia. Released the year after Sandy Harbutt's *Stone*, *Sidecar Racers* is not, unfortunately, another precursor to *Mad Max* or part of the New Australian Film Renaissance, although its female lead, Wendy Hughes, was. Instead, the film goes back to the privateer archetype, with John Clayton's broke but determined Dave Ferguson trying to win sidecarcross, dirt track, and road races to secure sponsorship and fulfil his dream of competing in Europe. After Dave's passenger is killed in an accident, his on again/off again girlfriend Lynn (Hughes) introduces him to American surfer and former Olympic swimmer Jeff Rayburn

(*Alias Smith and Jones*' Ben Murphy), believing he has the balance and control to help Dave win the championship. Though the single-minded, working-class Jeff is touchy and abrasive, Jeff sticks around because he's attracted to Lynn, a rich girl slumming it, and perhaps to have another crack at sporting glory. Predictably, it all comes down to the final race of the season. The race scenes are well shot and intense, and despite the American lead the film retains its national character, with 'barbies', 'bikies', and everyone calling each other 'Sport'. It was written by Australian novelist Jon Cleary, who didn't know anything about motorcycles or sidecar racing.

Bellamy also tackled motocross in the much more elegantly crafted *Sidewinder 1* (1977), a little gem starring *Then Came Bronson*'s Michael Parks as J.W. Wyatt, an aging indie motocross rider who's gone through a lot of factory teams because of his maverick attitude. Approached by industrialist Packard Gentry (Alex Cord), Wyatt becomes the partner, chief designer, and lead rider on the Sidewinder 1 team, promoting Gentry's new production bike. The Sidewinder (a Maico with Rokon wheels), is twitchy but fast, and Gentry manages to kill himself riding one offroad without a helmet. Wyatt has to persuade his new partner, Gentry's sister and heir Chris (*Dallas*' Susan Howard), to back the team through the racing season. Chris, an urbane executive, is less than enthusiastic and wants to sell out to a Japanese corporation. 'We're just not her kind of people,' explains Wyatt's colourful teammate

Lobby card for the Australian movie *Sidecar Racers* (1975).

Digger (the equally colourful Marjoe Gortner). The mismatched trio travel from race to race, winning a few, and dealing with mechanical and emotional breakdowns until they inevitably bond, duelling for the championship title with unscrupulous rival Bill Vint. Again, it all comes down to the final race of the season.

David Wickes' *Silver Dream Racer* (1980) covers similar ground as single-minded hero Nick Freeman (David Essex) tries to fund, ride and prove the worth of a prototype racing bike designed by his late brother. Essex was a real biker, and the 500cc Silver Dream Racer was a real bike designed by Barry Hart of Barton Motors and ridden by Essex himself, doubled by racer Roger Marshall. Pop star Essex also scored the film. Wickes wrote the script from an original story by *UFO* actor Michael Billington. That this was Billington's only attempt to write a film is telling, because *Silver Dream Racer* is full of sentimental sports drama clichés. Nick is a privateer who's struggling for money; his dream overrides all other aspects of his life, his job, his relationships, and he's reckless and self-destructive. With the help of his loyal mechanic and best friend Cider (Clarke Peters), and the widow of another racer, Julie Prince (Cristina Raines), Nick must overcome numerous setbacks to ride his brother's space-age bike at Silverstone, and beat smarmy American professional racer Bruce McBride (Beau Bridges).

As ever in British film, this is all about class. Factory worker Nick is bitter about his circumstances. He has skill and drive, and now a blurringly fast experimental sports bike has fallen into his hands that he can't afford to race. McBride thinks Nick has a chip on his shoulder and he's right. 'I just want to show them, just once,' Nick tells Julie, *them* by implication being everyone that has put him down and made him feel like dirt since childhood: teachers, bosses, bank managers, the middle classes in general and, especially, cocky professional racers. There's a lot more drama than track scenes, but the three big races are very well shot, with a sense of multi-camera live TV coverage, and excellent location work at Brands Hatch and Silverstone.

Although the underdog story's been done to death, *Silver Dream Racer* does look more closely than its US counterparts at the essentially Thanatotic nature of racing. When Nick invokes 'The Great God Speed' you just know there's going to be a sacrifice. The film was shot with two different endings, and if you were scarred for life by *Silver Dream Racer* then you saw the one favoured by Essex and the writers over the one the Rank Organisation imposed.

Promo shot of David Essex for *Silver Dream Racer* (1980).

Showing how little things had changed, the HBO movie *Race for Glory* (1989), written and directed by Rocky Lang, covered the same ground as gifted amateur Cody Gifford (Alex McArthur) builds a 500cc superbike with 'the speed of a rice-burner and the heart of a Harley' with his best friend and his girlfriend in his garage. After implausibly getting onto the European Grand Prix circuit, Cody deserts his friends to ride for made-up Japanese racing team 'Samurai', blocking for their star rider Klaus Kroeter (Oliver Stritzel), an arrogant, unscrupulous, and dangerous blowhard. After a lot of melodrama and some good racing

James Caan in the original *Rollerball* (1975).

scenes shot in France, Belgium, and Yugoslavia during the 1988 season, Cody returns to his friends and fulfils his now dead father's wishes by beating Kroeter to win the French Grand Prix and the Championship. The film's alternative title was *American Built*, and with German and Japanese villains, buffoonish Italians, and stars and stripes all over the bike, the film is unashamedly jingoistic and formulaic.

Although Norman Jewison's *Rollerball* (1975) is not a real sport, it deserves a mention for the sheer realism of the gameplay. This looks like a cross between roller derby, hockey, American football, and speedway, as two teams in football armour and leathers wearing roller-skates chase a 21lb steel ball around a banked track supported by bikers on armoured Honda CB 125s, all beating the hell out of each other trying to get the ball into a tiny magnetic goal. Based on a short story by William Harrison (who also wrote the script), *Rollerball* is a dystopian science fiction film set in a near-future corporate technocracy. Rollerball is a hugely popular sport and its undoubted superstar is Jonathan E (James Caan), who plays for Houston. The players are modern gladiators in a violent and dangerous sport, and are depicted as mostly macho, childish, and narcissistic celebrities. Jonathan is being put under pressure to retire by management and is resisting. As he investigates the reasons behind this and the history of his own society, he uncovers a dark secret.

Like all good science fiction, *Rollerball* is philosophic and political, and a sharp satire of corporate government and mass media. The film contains only three games but these are incredibly realistic spectacles (each including a TV commentary). Jewison opens with a game, establishing character and premise; there's another mid-point in the film as things are starting to go wrong, and an intense final, by which point the game's organisers have removed all the rules to make it impossible to not only win but to survive. You can see the influence of *Rollerball* in later dystopian and apocalyptic movies in look, style, and action. The film was remade in 2002, director John McTiernan deliberately ignoring the social commentary of the original film and focusing more on the game, resulting in a critical and commercial disaster.

Roger Corman's New World Pictures also knocked off *Rollerball* in 1978 with the gladiatorial *Deathsport*. After an overlong first act building a pretty standard post-apocalyptic dystopia – oppressive city states separated by an atomic wasteland – Richard Lynch chases David Carradine and former Playmate Claudia Jennings around the Hollywood Hills on 'Death Machines', Yamaha SR 500s with so much aluminium shielding and weaponry that stunt co-ordinator Gene Hartline is to be commended for keeping them upright. Pitched as a sequel to the vastly superior *Death Race 2000* (1975), *Deathsport* has none of the wit or political satire, and the budget doesn't match the ambitious world-building. Carradine and Jennings were on some serious drugs when they made the movie, and original director and co-writer Nicholas Niciphor was a Vietnam vet with PTSD who couldn't handle the on-set pyrotechnics. Joe Dante's frequent collaborator Allan Arkush finished the film, later telling web series *Trailers from Hell*, 'Mostly we just blew up motorcycles.'

While the great motorcycle racer biopic remains yet to be made, it feels like there's an entire sub-genre based around the flamboyant daredevil Evel Knievel (1938–2007). The best of these is the first. Fanfare Films' *Evel Knievel* (1971) is tremendous fun to watch, largely because of John Milius' jaunty script and the charm and complexity George Hamilton brings to the title role.

The film is framed by Knievel preparing for a nineteen-car jump at the Ontario Motor Speedway in California, with an opening monologue delivered to camera in a pre-credit scene. The opening fanfare and shot of the track looking down from the bleachers conveys a sense of the Colosseum, and the metaphor is carried through the film until Knievel's closing monologue, when he declares: 'I am the last gladiator in the New Rome.' This was an image the original Evel Knievel subsequently adopted, merging his on-screen persona with real life. This also links to another recurring theme, that the audience actually wants to see the performer get killed. This classical image is combined with American libertarianism in a country and western theme song called 'I Do What I Please'. The story then flashes back to Knievel's early life in Butte, Montana, his first stunts for a rodeo show, and courting his future wife Linda (Sue Lyon), all breezily narrated by Hamilton. Non-linear insertions include a newsreel montage of the original's hair-raising stunts, and the ill-fated 1967 Caesar's Palace jump. The Ontario framing narrative also moves forward in scenes between Knievel and his wife, his crew, and his doctor, depicting the battle-scarred rider as nervous and prima donna-ish, but ultimately heroic. The past narrative closes with Knievel and Linda deciding to get married, the present with the Ontario jump, successfully completed by the real Knievel. The closing monologue hints at the much-vaunted Grand Canyon jump (which never happened), ending with a flourish: 'The only thing really left to us is a choice about our death. And mine will be glorious!'

Despite being made by Warner Brothers on a $5 million budget with an ensemble cast including Gene Kelly, Lauren Hutton, Leslie Nielsen, and Marjoe Gortner, *Viva Knievel!* (1977) is not so much fun to watch. Knievel plays himself in a story that starts with him distributing action figures of himself to orphans, one of whom throws aside his crutches and announces, 'You're the reason I'm walkin', Evel,' inspired by his hero's recuperative and, presumably, messianic powers. It ends with him thwarting

LL Cool J in John McTiernan's 2002 *Rollerball* remake.

drug lord Leslie Nielsen. Though a natural showman, Knievel is out of his depth as an actor, and nowhere near as good as George Hamilton at playing himself.

TNT's *Evel Knievel* (2004) is a partial rerun of the 1971 movie; another rags to riches flashback biopic, in this case framed by the Caesar's Palace jump, that also spends a lot of time on Knievel's pursuit of Linda before ending up at the Snake River Canyon debacle. Like its predecessor, there's also a montage of Knievel's real jumps and crashes, this time appended to the end of the movie. Based on Steve Mandich's candid biography *Evel Incarnate: The Life and Legend of Evel Knievel* (2000) and directed by John Badham, this isn't a bad historical drama but it looks like what it is, an episodic TV movie that lacks any real character development or depth. There's also some glaring historical errors and anachronisms that can't be put down to the needs of the drama. *CSI*'s George Eads plays Knievel like an ambitious working-class rebel turned ego monster, but unlike Hamilton he doesn't really convey how much of an American folk hero the larger-than-life Knievel was in the Sixties and Seventies. He's also out-acted by Jaime Pressly as Linda, while Lance Henriksen and Beau Bridges steal every scene they're in.

Finally, American documentary film-maker Daniel Junge did the complicated, flawed and brilliant Prince of Daredevilry some justice with *Being Evel* (2015), an honest yet also reverential documentary that finally gets to the contradictions, showmanship and crazy genius of the man who could make a 324lb Harley XR-750 fly, the truth being much stranger than the fiction.

British stunt rider Eddie Kidd also made a movie. *Riding High* (1981) directed by Ross Cramer came out a year after *Silver Dream Racer* and although the two films share a similarly Dickensian sensibility common to British drama of that era, Kidd's outing is much more upbeat and light-hearted. Kidd, who was then

George Hamilton in *Evel Knievel* (1971).

21, lean and cocky, plays Cockney motorcycle courier Dave 'The Kid' Munday, who lives by the sea with his eccentric Gran (the legendary Irene Handl). Dave is a motorcycling virtuoso on his Yamaha YZ 400 who dreams of becoming a professional stunt rider. Opportunity presents itself in the form of an open competition to take on over-the-top American stunt rider Judas S. Chariot (Bill Mitchell doing Evel Knievel) by jumping the Devil's Leap, a partially collapsed railway viaduct across the Blackwater River in Essex. The winner gets a gold-plated Yamaha XS 1100. Of course, this is just a publicity stunt by Chariot. He doesn't actually expect anyone to take him up on this, because that would be suicide, right?

Kidd did all his own stunts, including the 80ft viaduct jump. His natural working-class charm came over well on camera, but despite Kidd being a regular face on the TV at the time, and a great contemporary pop soundtrack, *Riding High* was not a commercial or critical success. His film career continued as a stunt man instead, until his luck ran out and he was paralysed in an accident at the Bulldog Bash in 1996.

A million miles from all that glitzy showmanship, Roger Donaldson's splendid biographical drama *The World's Fastest Indian* (2005) tells the story of eccentric New Zealander Burt Munro (1899–1978), who set the under-1,000cc world speed record (184.087mph) at Bonneville in 1967 on a 1920 Indian Scout he modified himself. He was 68 years old, and at time of writing, the record remains unbroken.

The real Monro cast his own barrels and pistons in his shed, making specialist tools and parts himself because of his modest income, spending forty-odd years modifying a bike he'd bought new that's original top end was 55mph. Retired and divorced, he visited the Bonneville salt flats fourteen times, setting world records in 1962, 1966, and 1967.

Donaldson, who wrote and directed, dramatically compresses Monro's visits to Utah, strongly implying the 1967 run was his first, while also simplifying his family connections. Thus stripped down to its essence, the story is about a solitary and elderly man pursuing a dream. Donaldson had previously made a TV documentary about Munro called *Burt Munro: Offerings to the God of Speed* in 1971.

Anthony Hopkins is stunning as Burt, bringing a naïve nobility to the character, and making his homespun philosophy profound, even though he doesn't even bother to try a Kiwi accent. Donaldson and Hopkins explore Burt's obsession together, its long deferment making it burn all the brighter. The film is also a meditation on aging, on dealing with infirmity and loss, and also on making the most of every second you have left. *The World's Fastest Indian* is a quirky and unapologetic feelgood movie, and the best thing of all is that Burt Monro's dream really did come true.

Regrettably, biopics of notable women riders remain significant by their absence. There is no movie, for example, about Clara Wagner who, at 18, won a 365-mile enduro from Chicago to Indianapolis in 1910 on a bike designed by her father, but was denied her trophy by the AMA because of her gender. There was also mother and daughter team Avis and Effie Hotchkiss, who completed a 5000-mile transcontinental run from New York to San Francisco in 1915 on a Harley sidecar outfit, and the Van Buren sisters, Augusta and Adeline, who did the same on solo Indians the year after. A little more recently, film-makers might care to celebrate Elspeth Beard, who went around the world on a 1975 BMW R 60/6 between 1982 and 1984, or Steph Jeavons, the first motorcyclist to circumnavigate the globe, covering 74,000 miles on all seven continents on a Honda CRF 250L between 2014 and 2018. Brazilian film-maker Walter Salles has demonstrated how dramatically effective this type of travel narrative can be in *The Motorcycle Diaries* (2004), adapting Che Guevara's posthumously published memoir of his journey through South America with friend Alberto Granado in 1952, on a clapped-out Norton Model 18 they called the 'Mighty One'.

Half arthouse, half grindhouse, Paul Verhoeven's Dutch film *Spetters* (1980) starts out as a coming-of-age drama about three working-class mates from Rotterdam trying to make it in motocross then mutates into something much deeper, darker and weirder. Rien (Hans van Tongeren) has genuine talent, Hans (Maarten Spanjer) is a klutz, and Eef (Toon Agterberg) is their mechanic. They all dream of beating their provincial destiny, and aspire to be like champion Gerrit Witkamp (Rutger Hauer), in reality a shallow and spiteful diva. All three are drawn to concession stand beauty Fientje (Renée Soutendijk), an ambitious and frustrated young woman who sees the young riders as a possible escape from low-paid, blue-collar drudgery. The title is a Dutch slang word for a good-looking guy or girl, but it also means 'splatter' – the splatter of mud from the track, the hot cooking oil from Fientje's *kroket* stand, semen, and blood.

Anthony Hopkins as Burt Munro in *The World's Fastest Indian* (2005).

The guys measuring their manhoods with Eef's vernier gauge to decide who can chat up Fientje first is an early indication of cinematic provocateur Verhoeven's direction of travel, as social taboos are transgressed, performative masculinity deconstructed, and early dreams suffer tragic, Kafkaesque reversals. And as in all Verhoeven's work, violence, sexuality, and religion cannot be separated. *Spetters* is also brutally naturalistic, and does not shy away from either the dangers of motorcycling (and unrealistic expectations), or the small town mindset, which led to a critical backlash in the Netherlands. Brilliant, bleak and cynical, *Spetters* often makes for uncomfortable viewing. As Amy Simmons wrote of it for the BFI: 'We feel uneasy watching *Spetters* as we're unsure how to respond to anything.'

Chalking another one up for Roger Corman, *Fast Charlie ... The Moonbeam Rider* (1979) is a historical race movie set in 1919 featuring flat-tank veteran motorcycles. This is a real curio from a mainstream studio (Universal), co-produced by Corman and directed by my more successful namesake Steve Carver. In a role initially conceived for Steve McQueen, David Carradine excels as a likeable rogue and Great War dispatch rider (and possibly deserter) competing in the First Intercontinental Motorcycle Race from St Louis to San Francisco on his barn-built bike the 'Moonbeam Special'. Charlie is a liar and a grifter who abandoned his unit during a battle, although he manages to convince three of the survivors to be his pit crew, played by character actors R.G. Armstrong, Terry Kiser, and L.Q. Jones, who bring a lot of class to the movie, as does Brenda Vaccaro as Grace, the romantic interest who, like Charlie, is not what she seems. About half the film is set-up and character development, after which the pre-road network rural race scenes are

Renée Soutendijk in *Spetters* (1980).

downright scary, with riders kicking each other off their antique bikes and some spectacular crashes. In a witty and smart screenplay by TV writer Michael Gleason, the climax of the race replicates Charlie's war experiences as dodgy motorcycle manufacturer Pop Bauer (Noble Willingham) sends thugs to stop him winning with guns and high explosives. Will Charlie crumble under fire and desert his friends again, or beat smarmy factory racer Calvin Hawk (Jesse Vint), redeem himself and get the girl? You can probably figure it out, which doesn't make the movie any less enjoyable.

David Carradine in *Fast Charlie... The Moonbeam Rider* (1979).

Decades later, one of the best motorcycle racing dramas returned to this era with the Discovery Channel TV miniseries *Harley and the Davidsons* (2016), directed by Ciarán Donnelly and Stephen Kay, and co-written by Nick Schenk, Evan Wright and Seth Fisher. This beautifully rendered three-part period drama covers the foundation of Harley-Davidson in 1903, beginning with brothers Arthur and Walter Davidson (Bug Hall and Michiel Huisman) building their first motor-bicycle in a shed in Milwaukee based on designs by their childhood friend and engineering student William Harley (Robert Aramayo). The series follows the company's early attempts to make an impression in a crowded and rapidly developing market at that time dominated by Indian, showcasing its models in the evolving racing scene, from enduros to the lethal motordromes and the growth of flat-track events. Early racing champions like Ray Weishaar, Albert 'Shrimp' Burns, Gene Walker and Eddie Hasha are central characters and the recreations of those early races and the bikes are stunning in their energy and realism.

There's a certain legendary quality about the whole thing that suits the brand; *Harley and the Davidsons* is thus a proud salute to the spirit of American entrepreneurship and patriotism, which does get a little economical with the truth sometimes, especially when it comes to the rivalry with Indian, in which George Hendee (Philip Brodie) and the entirely fictional CEO Randell James (Dougray Scott) are portrayed like moustache-twirling Victorian villains. Characters also sometimes talk as if the hand of history is on their shoulders, but let's face it, it was.

While not a racing picture, like *Rollerball*, George Romero's *Knightriders* (1981) still boasts some realistic motorcycle competition. After the success of *Dawn of the Dead* (1978), Romero could write his own ticket and did so with a passion project about a travelling community attempting to live by chivalric codes of honour. Inspired by the Renaissance Fayre circuit and an argument with Samuel Arkoff, Romero's original idea about a realistic portrayal of Camelot evolved into a story about modern knights who joust on motorcycles.

Led by King Billy (Ed Harris in his first starring role), the troupe move from small town to small town supporting themselves by putting on jousting displays. They ride scramblers with shields on the bars and wear leather armour and crash helmets based on medieval designs, using melee

Michiel Huisman as Walter Davidson in *Harley and the Davidsons* (2016).

weapons. Though the crowd treat this as a circus act, the troupe take it incredibly seriously, and if Billy or his champion is defeated he will lose his crown. His chief rival is Morgan (played by effects wizard and frequent Romero collaborator Tom Savini), who is more into the bikes than the code, and wants Billy to use the show's growing notoriety to earn some serious money. As the idealistic Billy becomes more spiritual and mystical, the troupe begins to factionalise and fall apart. The symbol he uses is 'fighting the dragon', rejecting what he sees as the morally corrupt business ethics of modern America. Again like *Rollerball*, this is a long reflective movie structured around three tournaments: the first establishes King Billy and the troupe, the second shows things falling apart as Morgan's riders abandon the code and local bikers invade the field, and the third represents the film's climax as Morgan's champions and Billy's fight with honour for the crown, leading to a beautiful and incredibly moving denouement.

Romero bought sixty bikes (mostly Honda XR 250s) for the picture, many of which are gleefully destroyed on camera. Some had their frames partly sawn through so they would break in half on impact. Stunt co-ordinator Gary Davis had also worked on *Viva Knievel!*, *C.C. and Company*, and *Race with the Devil*, and would go on to be stunt co-ordinator on *Terminator 2*. *Knightriders* garnered a lot of positive critical attention but fell stillborn from the box office. This was partly the curse of the maverick independent film-maker that dogged Romero throughout his career, and also because it was buried by John Boorman's *Excalibur*. It is likely, too, that Romero's fanbase did not get the film, wanting more zombies, while the poster – by noted fantasy artist Boris Vallejo – depicting King Billy in full armour on his 6-cylinder Honda CBX 1050, a mace hanging from his hand, suggests a movie like *Rollerball*, *Death Race 2000*, or *Mad Max* a lot more than a rebirth story about a glorified and, by 1981, outdated hippie commune.

Fast forward a couple of decades, and after illegal street racing was glamourised and popularised by *The Fast and the Furious* and its interminable sequels, there were a couple of biker movies made around the millennium hoping to catch a similar wave.

Reggie Rock Bythewood's Oedipal coming-of-age story *Biker Boyz* (2003) from DreamWorks is a pretty good depiction of the underground LA racing scene, with a focus on the black motorcycle clubs, loosely based on Manuel 'Pokey' Galloway, the president of the Pasadena Valiant Riders. The ensemble cast of iconic black actors includes Laurence Fishburne, Djimon Hounsou, Orlando Jones, Lisa Bonet and Vanessa Bell Calloway, while then relative newcomers Derek Luke, Meagan Good, Rick Gonzalez, and Canadian Brendan Fehr represent the rising generation. As a film about working-class black American culture, it's refreshingly free of reductive clichés and stereotypes. Many of the cast were keen motorcyclists, which brought authenticity to their roles, although their characters' on-screen stunt riding and lavish entrance choreography goes well over the top at times, even for the US, with a lot of unironic performative masculinity.

Unfortunately, the story itself is clichéd and melodramatic. Fishburne plays Smoke, president of the Black Knights MC, an aging philanderer and undisputed 'King of Cali', unbeatable on his Suzuki Hayabusa. Jalil AKA 'Kid' (Luke) – on a Suzuki GSX-R 750 – dreams of racing Smoke, and yearns for recognition. Kid and his friends Stuntman (Fehr) and Primo (Gonzalez), start their own club, the Biker Boyz, and race and hustle their way into the big leagues, with various romantic and family dramas along the way, until Smoke finally agrees to race Jalil. Though a lot deeper than anything in the *Fast & Furious* franchise, *Biker Boyz* was a critical and commercial flop, and did not make back its $24 million budget.

Two Renaissance Fayre knights battle it out in *Knightriders* (1981).

With all that death and black leather, it's hardly surprising that film-makers have often incorporated bikes and bikers into horror, like the nomadic raiders of George Romero's *Dawn of the Dead*, the Hells Angel-like henchmen in Hammer's *The Satanic Rites of Dracula*, and Adrienne Barbeau's Harley-riding demon hunter in *The Convent*. And let's not forget Daryl Dixon (Norman Reedus) in *The Walking Dead*, or Triumph-riding bad boy Kevin Dillon taking over Steve McQueen's role in Chuck Russell's 1988 remake of *The Blob*. But none of these movies focus on the motorcycles; they're just stylish props in a wider narrative. There is, however, a modest yet significant subgenre of horror films that do.

The true motorcycle horror film emerged from the death throes of the outlaw biker film cycle, when production companies were looking for fresh angles and creating bizarre genre hybrids. The first of these was notorious B-movie producer Anthony Cardoza's *Bigfoot* (1970). *Bigfoot* was inspired by the famous footage shot in California in 1967 by amateur cryptozoologists Roger Patterson and Robert Gimlin. Cardoza had done quite well out of *The Hellcats* and *Outlaw Riders*, so why not mash up a newsworthy cryptid with a motorcycle gang? – a classic example of Price and Wooley's 'Just Add Monsters' formula.

The tagline 'Bigfoot breeds with anything' gives a good idea of the premise. Directed and co-written by Bob Slatzer (who also directed *The Hellcats*), *Bigfoot* isn't the worst drive-in movie you'll ever see, though the comparisons with *King Kong* are pushing it. John Carradine even paraphrases the famous line 'T'was beauty killed the beast' at the end. The bikers all wear bright-coloured windbreakers and ride small Yamaha two-strokes, and are thus more like the 30-year-old teenagers in beach party movies. As with Cardoza's other biker movies, Sonny West puts in an appearance.

Daryl Dixon (Norman Reedus) in *The Walking Dead* (2010–2022), on a Honda 750 Nighthawk with a Yamaha YZF-R6 front end.

Never believe the ads! A rather misleading poster for *Bigfoot* (1971).

Original poster for *Werewolves on Wheels* (1971).

When lovers Rick (Robert Mitchum's son Christopher) and Chris (Judy Jordan) slip away from the group on an offroad run in the Tehachapi Mountains, they discover a Bigfoot burial ground and are attacked by a live one, which knocks out Rick and kidnaps Chris. Back in town, the sheriff doesn't believe Rick's story but it catches the attention of sideshow barker Jasper B. Hawks (Carradine), who sees a financial opportunity in capturing the beast. Jasper, his partner Elmer (John Mitchum, Robert's little brother), and Rick explore the woods, eventually discovering Chris and pilot Joi Landis (pin-up model Joi Lansing), who was grabbed in the opening scene. They are being held captive by a Bigfoot tribe who offer up human women to the alpha male, and there are hybrid human-Sasquatch children running around. Though the rescuers end up tied to trees as well, the rest of the bikers go in search of Rick with some townspeople and save the day.

There are some good ideas in *Bigfoot*, but the pacing is glacial. The film did, however, trigger a whole genre of Bigfoot movies, several of which borrowed the interbreeding premise, such as the notorious video nasty *Night of the Demon*, and Bob Goldthwait's excellent found footage movie *Willow Creek*.

Making *Bigfoot* look polished, meanwhile, Brad F. Grinter's super low budget *Blood Freak* (1972) concerns a Sportster-riding Vietnam veteran played by Steve Hawkes who gets addicted to pot after one smoke and hallucinates most of the remainder of the film, in which he apparently grows the head of a giant turkey and craves the blood of other dope fiends. He is eventually saved by the power of prayer. With rambling interruptions from director Grinter, the film is unique in being an R rated splatter movie intended to convey a strong Christian and antidrug message, which makes you wonder what audience Grinter was trying to attract.

The evocatively titled *Werewolves on Wheels* (1971) from Joe Solomon's Fanfare Corporation is a much slicker combination of outlaw biker and gothic codes, because of the assured direction of Michel Levesque and a sharp script by Levesque and David M. Kaufman. Steve Oliver of *Motorpsycho!* and *Angels from Hell* returns to the saddle as Adam, leader of the Devil's Advocates MC, and the film poses the metaphysical question: *What would happen if Hells Angels came face to face with the Devil?* – the answer being in this case punch him out and then get cursed. It is also an early reflection of the Seventies fad for the occult that grew out of the more optimistic esotericism of the Sixties, spawning a generation of middle-class suburban devil worshippers because that crowd will take any excuse to have an orgy.

Werewolves on Wheels starts like a conventional biker movie before things start to go sideways. The story is triggered by Deuce Barry's Tarot giving Adam's old lady Helen (Donna Anderson) an ill-omened reading, anticipating the club later blundering into the grounds of a deconsecrated church full of satanic monks led by comedian and character actor Severn Darden. The club get into the Satan trip and accept bread and wine, knocking them out while the monks make Helen the 'Bride of Satan'. Adam grabs her back after some exotic dancing with a skull and a snake. The club splits, but as they continue their run into the desert members start to die violently and mysteriously. Tarot knows this is a 'bad spiritual scene' but Adam keeps rationalising and denying, denouncing Tarot for laying a bad trip on everyone and bumming them out. Eventually, the werewolves reveal themselves, leading to a chase that finally validates the title and a weird and unsettling occult ending. Folk singer Barry McGuire plays one of the bikers. The film was released the same year he was born again, but I'm going to guess that happened after he made the Devil worship movie.

Psychomania (1973) is one of the smoothest blends of the biker movie and the Gothic, this time with a very dark and British sense of humour. You know you're in for a treat when the opening credits are accompanied by bikers riding around a misty stone circle in slow motion at twilight to spooky, psychedelic music by John Cameron, with skulls painted on their crash helmet visors.

When not leading the Living Dead MC on rampages through town, charming middle-class psychopath Tom Latham (Nicky Henson) likes to hang out in graveyards and at the Seven Witches stone circle. He's obsessed with the 'other side', and wonders why his mother (Beryl Reid) and her butler Shadwell (George Sanders in his final role) never seem to get any older. Discovering his mother made a satanic pact, Tom tricks her out of the secret of the 'Living Dead', which is to willingly go to your death with absolute faith you will come back. The next day, Tom rides off a motorway bridge then comes back to life. As you can only die once, he is now indestructible. He returns to the gang and shares his secret, leading to a darkly comic series of suicides. Now really the Living Dead, the gang embark on a murder spree. Can bemused copper Chief Inspector Hesseltine (Robert Hardy) stop them before they commence their plan to slaughter the entire Establishment?

Psychomania was directed by Australian Don Sharp, who'd made several films for Hammer. He catches the tone perfectly, blending genuine horror with black comedy. Surprisingly, given its Englishness, *Psychomania* was written by Americans Arnaud d'Usseau and Julian Zimet, who also wrote *Horror Express.* Nicky Henson had gothic form too, having appeared alongside Vincent Price in *Witchfinder General*. An avid motorcyclist, Henson was occasionally doubled by stuntman Cliff Diggins, who had to ride a Bonnie through a brick wall, out of a grave, and off a bridge on the M3. Though *Psychomania* is viewed with great affection in the UK, contemporary reviews were harsh, *The Times* floridly suggesting the film was only fit to be screened 'at an SS reunion party'. That was probably because one of the gang run over a pram. Some people have no sense of humour.

Warren Oates and Peter Fonda fight off satanists in *Race with the Devil* (1975).

Written by exploitation veterans Wes Bishop and Lee Frost, 20th Century Fox's *Race with the Devil* (1975) shares its basic premise with new wave American horror films like *The Texas Chainsaw Massacre* and *The Hills Have Eyes*, in which middle-class city folk venture into the middle of rural nowhere and get hunted and slaughtered by atavistic psychos and mutants.

San Antonio motorcycle dealers Roger Marsh (Peter Fonda) and Frank Stewart (Warren Oates) and their wives Kelly (Lara Parker – Angelique from *Dark Shadows*) and Alice (*M*A*S*H*'s Loretta Swit) are travelling to Aspen in Frank's RV, dirt bikes on the back. On their first night under the stars, Roger and Frank spot what they initially assume is a bunch of hippies until they witness a hooded figure ritualistically murder a naked girl. The local sheriff, played

Japanese poster for *Psychomania* (1973).

What Have They Done To Your Daughters? (1974).

with charming menace by R.G. Armstrong, doesn't believe them, while Alice and Kelly find a paper covered in weird symbols stuck on the RV. Someone has cast the runes. Back on the road, events escalate eerily until a climactic chase in which redneck satanists in pick-up trucks pursue the RV at high speed while Frank tries to fight them off with a shotgun. Pre-dating *The Road Warrior* by seven years, director Jack Starrett uses the same device that George Miller would later refine in having the climax function like a mobile siege. Starrett claimed that he'd hired real satanists as extras, which seems unlikely but is a wonderful promotional hook.

Giallo is an Italian genre pioneered by Mario Bava and Dario Argento that blended mystery and horror with eroticism and exploitation. (*Giallo* means 'yellow', referencing the distinctive yellow covers of Italian pulp crime novels.) Anticipating the slasher movie, *giallo* plots usually involve a mysterious killer whose identity is not revealed until the end of the movie. One way of doing this is to stick them in a full-face crash helmet, which is exactly what director Massimo Dallamano did in *What Have They Done to Your Daughters?* in 1974.

This is an angry and polemical movie about the abuse of schoolgirls by rich and powerful men in Rome. While investigating the apparent suicide of a teenage girl, Deputy DA Vittoria Stori (Giovanna Ralli) realises it was murder. As she digs deeper, she gradually uncovers a paedophile ring that one of the dead girl's lovers was blackmailing. At the same time, more potential witnesses are being horribly murdered by an apparent serial killer wielding a meat cleaver. He appears throughout in full black leathers, boots and gauntlets, and a black crash helmet obscuring his features, riding a Ducati 450 Scrambler. Rather than risk exposure, the great and the good at the heart of the conspiracy are cleaning house, employing a psychopathic assassin to make the killings look random. The film is tight and intense, and frequently downright disturbing, especially the exploitation of children, which is artfully limited to audio tape recordings retrieved from the dead blackmailer.

This was not the first time a biker had appeared in a *giallo*. Sergio Martino's *Your Vice is a Locked Room and Only I Have the Key* (1972) starring Edwige Fenech featured a motorcycle racer and the hero of Jorge Grau's Spanish/Italian zombie movie *The Living Dead at the Manchester Morgue* (1974) rides a Norton. The following year, Andrea Bianchi replicated the look of Dallamano's psycho in *Strip Nude for Your Killer*, also starring Fenech (only this time there was no bike), while Ken Hughes did the same in the 1981 American slasher *Night School*, the murderer on a Honda XR 125 disguised by a tinted visor.

Moving from *giallo* to full-on horror, Umberto Lenzi's *Nightmare Beach* (1989) is another slasher movie with a mystery killer in full leathers and a black full-face. This one rides around on a Honda Goldwing with a pillion converted into an electric chair. When not on the bike, he improvises with power cables.

The film opens with the execution of Diablo (Tony Bolano), the leader of the Florida Demons MC, for murder. Diablo goes to the chair proclaiming his innocence and vowing to return to exact his revenge. A year later, during Spring Break in Miami, after a bunch of teen comedy scenes, dead bodies start turning up, inexplicably electrocuted. Could Diablo have returned from the dead? That's certainly what his former gang thinks, while teen heroes Skip (Nicolas de Toth) and Gail (Sara Buxton) embark on a *Scooby-Doo*-like investigation. Meanwhile, police chief Strycher (horror stalwart John Saxon), and medical examiner Doc Willet (Michael Parks) cover up the murders to avoid a panic and disruption to the local economy, like the mayor keeping the beaches open in *Jaws*. Retaining the common *giallo* device, the killer never takes off his tinted crash helmet until the big reveal, and he would've got away with it too, if it weren't for those meddlin' kids.

Back in the US, 1989 was also a good year for feminist-biker-comedy-horror in the tradition of *She Devils on Wheels* and *Angels' Wild Women*. Released within a month of each other, David O'Malley's *Easy Wheels* offered a unique take on the werewolf, while Troma's *Chopper Chicks in Zombie Town* does exactly what it says on the tin.

Easy Wheels had a lot of *Evil Dead* talent on board. Sam Raimi, Bruce Campbell, and Rob Tapert were all producers, while Raimi co-wrote the script with his older brother, Ivan, and director O'Malley. *Evil Dead II* actors Dan Hicks and Ted Raimi also appear. *Easy Wheels* is a satire of the biker movie that at the same time is actually quite a good one, with a wry sense of humour and a dark underlying premise.

The Born Losers are a group of acolytes following Bruce (*American Graffiti*'s Paul Le Mat), a 'Nam vet with shrapnel in his brain that causes him to have visions. Sensing a great evil in Iowa, Bruce and

Don't get on the back of that bike! Jennifer Hingel and Lance LeGault in *Nightmare Beach* (1989).

the gang embark on a mission to 'Find the evil, destroy the evil, and find a really great lite beer,' joined by an unnamed reporter (Barry Livingston) researching baby kidnappings and essentially playing Nick Carraway to Bruce's Gatsby. The baby nappers are the Women of the Wolf, an all-woman bike club led by the sultry She-Wolf (soap star Eileen Davidson), who was raised by wolves and believes her destiny is to, 'Raise a new nation of women – fearless, wild and free.' Girl babies are left for the wolves; the boys are sold, their family homes burned, and their parents left for dead. The women all ride big Japanese cruisers and dress like *Vogue* models. Bruce falls for the beautiful She-Wolf, but in a vision he sees her true self, an insane human-wolf hybrid. Will he follow his heart or the hunk of metal in his head? And will he ever find a really great lite beer?

Though hardly *Sean of the Dead* and a lot rougher around the edges, Dan Hoskins' *Chopper Chicks in Zombie Town* has a better balance of humour and horror than *Easy Wheels* and a similar sense of female empowerment. The Harley-riding Cycle Sluts led by lesbian Rox (Catherine Carlen) roll into the small town of Zariah in search of new recruits, a drink, and some casual sex. When one of their number disappears, they uncover a fiendish plan by local mortician Ralph Willum (*The Return of the Living Dead*'s Don Calfa) to raise the dead as slaves to mine uranium – basically the same premise as Hammer's *Plague of the Zombies*. Despite having been run out of town, the Sluts return to help fight off the zombies when they break out of the mine, using chainsaws, baseball bats, welding torches, dynamite, and a staple gun, while saving a busload of blind orphans. Years away from his Academy Award, Billy Bob Thornton was still a struggling actor when he took a small part in *Chopper Chicks*.

Kiefer Sutherland in *The Lost Boys* (1987).

It's worth tracking down the 'Tromilleninium' DVD release, because the way Lloyd Kaufman exploits this is hilarious.

Shot in twelve days with rooms in the director's house serving as interiors, Michael Roush's *Hot Wax Zombies on Wheels* (1999) feels like it belongs in this group. Women bikers again feature prominently, and there's that same surreal sense of humour overlaying a classic horror plot, in this case *Invasion of the Body Snatchers.* In the sleepy town of Daneport, a new beauty parlour specialising in hair removal has been opened by the mysterious and exotic Yvonne Wayne (Gwen Somers), a Harley-riding dominatrix commanding a gang of unnaturally shiny biker bodybuilders. Lingerie seller Sharon (Jill Miller) and her adventure biking buddy Sven (Tre Lovell) decide to investigate as the townspeople become increasingly odd after visiting *Chez Yvonne. Hot Wax Zombies on Wheels* never really achieved cult status, and has thus become quite difficult to track down, which is probably for the best.

Biker Zombies from Detroit (2001) is another film with a great title that doesn't quite live up to it, although at least this time there are actuals zombies, in make-up, which is more than can be said for the *Hot Wax* variety. There are more motorcycles, too. Bear in mind, however, that this is a pretty low bar. A demon transforms a bunch of street people and petty criminals into a legion of zombie bikers to reclaim the world, starting in the Detroit suburbs, while two teenage riders fight for the heart of the same girl, one of them literally.

Some great low-budget indie horror has come out of the Detroit suburbs, most notably Sam Raimi's *The Evil Dead.* Unfortunately, novice director Todd Brunswick is not in the same league, and *Biker Zombies* represents a lot of learning by doing. As clumsy as *Bigfoot* and *Blood Freak*, this one's only for the true gorehound. Otherwise, treat the tagline as a warning: 'Evil never looked so bad.'

The Lost Boys (1987) is also regarded as a 'comedy horror' film, which I'd dispute. A scary movie with some funny dialogue isn't a comedy, although like Lenzi's *Nightmare Beach*, director Joel Schumacher does throw some teensploitation into the mix as two brothers try to find their way in a new town. Older brother Michael (Jason Patric) rides a Honda XL 500 and soon attracts the attention of the local dirt bike-riding juvenile delinquents led by David (Kiefer Sutherland, fresh from *Stand by Me*) on his chopped Yamaha XT 500. Moving away from the outlaw stereotype, these kids are punky and goth and presumably graduated from skateboard culture, like a much more stylish version of the 'Cretins' from Troma's *Class of Nuke 'Em High* (1986). They're also vampires, and like the Lost Boys from J.M. Barrie's *Peter Pan*, they will never grow old. The premise is similar to Kathryn Bigelow's *Near Dark*, released the same year, as a young man is unwillingly drawn into a vampire cult by a girl to whom he's attracted. David challenges Michael to 'keep up', resulting in a high-speed night-time ride during which David's crew take insane risks. This is because, unbeknown to Michael and the audience at this point, they're invulnerable, as long as they can avoid wooden stakes, garlic, and holy water, none of which are common motorcycling hazards, though in real life, Sutherland broke his wrist on set pulling a wheelie.

Speaking of vampires, Dirk Campbell's British horror comedy *I Bought a Vampire Motorcycle* (1990) channels *Psychomania* and Alex R. Stuart's 1973 pulp novels *The Devil Rider* and *The Bike from Hell* (which involved a cursed Norton Dominator), with a demonically possessed, blood-drinking Norton Commando.

Outlaws the Road Toads take out a rival club trying to summon a demon on their turf in Birmingham. Denied a living human host, the demon Ahriman jumps into a dead satanist's Commando, which is subsequently picked up cheap by motorcycle courier Noddy (Neil Morrissey before *Men Behaving Badly* made him a household name). The trouble is the bike seems to have a mind of its own. It only runs at night, and when Noddy's girlfriend Kim (Amanda Noar) orders garlic prawns from a Chinese

Around the same time, there were independent film-makers doing much more imaginative stuff in the spirit of directors like Roger Corman and Al Adamson, and paying homage to the high-watermark American Nightmare period of horror between the Seventies and Eighties.

The 'Butcher Brothers' (Mitchell Altieri and Phil Flores) had already made a name for themselves with the *Chainsaw*-inspired *The Hamiltons* and the remake of *April Fool's Day* when they turned their attention to biker horror with *The Violent Kind* in 2010: a cabin in the woods movie set in the remote clubhouse of The Crew MC. After a party that sets up the main characters, the bulk of the club split leaving a few stragglers stranded after all their vehicles mysteriously die. Then party girl Michelle (Tiffany Shepis) staggers back up the road covered in blood and talking weird, triggering a demonic possession story. Things are further complicated by the arrival of a group of rockabillies who've been missing in the area since the Fifties and are 'looking for a good time – the violent kind'. They seem to be drawn by whatever's inside Michelle. After torturing and killing about half the cast and re-enacting a scene from *Rebel Without a Cause*, they let biker Cody (Cory Knauf) and Michelle's sister Megan (Christina Prousalis) go just in time to witness what could be either an alien invasion or a biblical apocalypse. Like their previous films, the directors are throwing in a lot of influences. Whether there's any genuine inspiration here or just a bunch of intertextual referencing is open to debate, but with some decent effects and spirited

Nicolas Cage with VMAX, *Ghost Rider: Spirit of Vengeance* (2011).

Final Girl Chrissie (Jordana Brewster) runs into Holden (Lee Tergesen) in *The Texas Chainsaw Massacre: The Beginning* (2006).

acting, and a plot that is insanely unpredictable, *The Violent Kind* is much better than the reviews would have you believe.

Closing the circle, James Bickert's retro homage to Seventies exploitation movies *Dear God No!* (2011) returns us to bikes, babes, beer, and Bigfoot. 'Your mind will be violated!' promises the trailer, which is a pretty accurate description of the viewing experience. This includes exotic dancers in Richard Nixon masks firing machine guns, the improper use of feminine hygiene products, a man strangled by his own intestines, a lot of dead nuns, multiple decapitations, and an improvised Caesarean section that I don't ever want to think about again. The bikes are pretty cool too, with a couple of the Impalers MC out of Georgia riding real knuckleheads.

Since Robert Rodriguez and Quentin Tarantino's *Grindhouse* in 2007, a whole genre of independent films has grown up trying to recreate that period low-budget drive-in aesthetic, but very few have genuinely succeeded. (Even *Grindhouse* itself doesn't really manage it.) But Bickert has absolutely nailed it. Shot in two weeks on 16mm, *Dear God No!* is about as close in spirit to films like *Satan's Sadists* and *Werewolves on Wheels* as it's possible to get: a micro-budgeted orgy of saturated colour, perversion, nudity, and gore. The film has a deranged, carnivalesque intensity similar to Rob Zombie's *House of a 1000 Corpses* and the original *Texas Chainsaw Massacre*. When Bickert and his co-producers ran out of money, they managed to crowd fund post-production through Kickstarter.

BIG WORLD PICTURES PRESENTS
DEAR GOD NO!

IN HELL
L-R: MADELINE BRUMBY, OLIVIA LACROIX, PAUL MCCOMISKEY
CREDIT: BRYAN G. MALONE

Dr Marco (Paul McComiskey) already anticipating *Frankenstein Created Bikers* in *Dear God No!* (2011).

The Impalers are on a murder spree and they never leave any witnesses. Having wasted two cops at a gas station, they set off in pursuit of a married couple that could identify them, tracking them to a cabin in the woods where they're visiting their old university supervisor. A standard and escalating Al Adamson-style home invasion ensues, only Dr Marco (Paul McComiskey) is a mad Nazi scientist who's found Bigfoot and discovered a prehistoric virus he's introduced into the local eco-system. He's also infected his wife, who's now a sex-crazed fiend locked in the basement. As the gang torture and murder their way through the household, Bigfoot begins to do the same to them. Finally, only Marco's daughter Edna (Madeline Brumby) and leader of the Impalers Jett (Jett Bryant) remain, and it's not looking good for either of them.

Almost as good and just as mad, *All Hell Breaks Loose* (2014) was shot in three weeks in and around Oregon on a budget of $20,000. Written by indie horror author Jacy Morris and directed by special effects artist Jeremy Garner, *All Hell Breaks Loose* sees nerdy newlywed Nick (Nick Forrest) out to save his wife Bobby Sue (Sarah Kobel Marquette) from the Satan's Sinners MC, who are literally bikers from Hell. Killed by the bikers on his wedding day, Nick is resurrected by a mysterious cowboy dressed in white who may or may not be God. Nick is pretty clear on his mission, 'Get the girl. Save the day,' but he's a complete wimp, so the bikers keep killing him and the cowboy keeps bringing him back, until, like a dedicated video game player, he has acquired the skills he needs to kick some satanic ass.

Finally, Jett, Edna and the Impalers return in *Frankenstein Created Bikers* in 2016, again written and directed by Bickert, despite all being dead at the end of the previous movie. The Impalers are now zombie bikers working for Dr Marco as 'Bigfoot wranglers', that being the source of the serum that keeps them reanimated and the key to fully resurrecting Edna, who's now just a conscious head like Virginia Leith in *The Brain That Wouldn't Die*. But Nazis are not the most trustworthy employers, and the Impalers are also being pursued by the brother of one of the cops they killed in the first film, rival bike club the Satan's Own, and a group of psychotic bounty hunters led by eyepatch-wearing badass Val (Tristan Risk) that include the Reverend Chainsaw from the Church of the Screaming Epileptic Jesus (Nick Hood). You get the general idea.

At the more authentic side of the grindhouse that has so inspired a new generation of guerrilla film-makers, honourable mentions should also go to a couple of Eighties straight-to-video slashers. Wes Craven's *The Hills Have Eyes Part 2* (1985) was a rushed and underwritten sequel to his groundbreaking 1977 survival horror, in which a motorcycle racing team run by survivors of the original movie get lost taking a shortcut across the desert and discover that the hills still have eyes. It's worth it for an extended desert motorcycle chase featuring Michael Berryman's Pluto, returning from the first film because it wouldn't be a *Hills Have Eyes* movie without him. Meanwhile, in Bruce Hickey's *Necropolis* (1986), LeeAnne Baker plays a seventeenth century witch reincarnated as a punky biker chick out for revenge against the descendants of her executioners, riding a US-spec Yamaha XS1100. At the other end of the scale, there was also New Line's $16 million prequel *The Texas Chainsaw Massacre: The Beginning* (2006), directed by Jonathan Liebesman, which featured outlaw bikers Holden (Lee Tergesen) and Alex (Cyia Batten) as secondary characters who run into the deranged Hewitt family in 1969. They recreate the feel of Sixties biker films beautifully, and it's a shame they weren't the leads. That would have made for a more interesting movie. We need to see Leatherface on a Harley!

The iconography of the death's head is everywhere in motorcycle culture for a reason. Like ghost stories, biker horror is a way to face your own fragile mortality, the thing Hunter S. Thompson called the 'Edge' – that liminal space between life and death; your head, the road. Bikes can kill you. Part of the thrill of the burn is survival, not life-affirming so much as death-affirming. Like the Ghost Rider, every mile we ride takes us a little bit closer to Hell.

But isn't it fun?

CHAPTER

8 WARRIORS OF THE WASTELAND

WELCOME TO THE new Dark Age. Civilisation has collapsed. There is no government, police force, or functioning military. Health care, electricity, and running water are distant memories, and all the shopping malls are closed. Most of the global population is dead, and life for the few remaining survivors is harsh and brutally Darwinian. You now live in a primitive, neo-medieval world of warlords, warriors, and slaves. On the plus side, there seems to be a plentiful supply of exotic vehicles and leather clothing.

In the evolution of the biker movie, the post-apocalyptic dystopian action film represents the final stage of truly original development. Everything after this is a legacy picture – either a sequel or a remake.

Though George Miller's *The Road Warrior* (AKA *Mad Max 2*, 1981) wasn't the first post-apocalyptic movie – it wasn't even the first Mad Max movie – its international success, its energy, and its inspired post-punk design aesthetic popularised the genre in the same way George Romero's *Dawn of the Dead* had zombie films. Like *The Wild One*, Its influence is vast.

There were, however, antecedents.

To this day, when Australian bikies talk about a film that means something to them, that reflects their lifestyle, it's not *Mad Max* they'll cite but Sandy Harbutt's cult outlaw biker movie *Stone* (1974). Described by Luke Buckmaster of the *Guardian* as 'akin to watching celluloid soaked in LSD and set on fire', Harbutt's directorial debut is a true countercultural testament in the way that all those American outlaw films failed to be because the director/writer/co-star actually understood his subject and believed in its credo. Harbutt was a bikie himself, and continued to ride until old age and ill health got the better of him. When he conceived the movie, he was a law school dropout turned actor taking a lot of drugs and drifting round the fringes of the outlaw scene in Sydney on his Triumph. This was a good time to be a film-maker in Australia, whose domestic film industry had virtually collapsed in the Sixties. The government intervened, and the newly created Australian Film Development Corporation (now Screen Australia), put up $154,000 AUD of the film's $192,000 AUD budget. Somehow, Harbutt found the rest, among other things convincing the Sydney Hells Angels to appear in the film as rival club the Black Hawks for beer and weed.

Ostensibly, *Stone* is about an undercover cop, Stone (Ken Shorter), joining the Sydney bike club the Gravediggers led by the Undertaker (Harbutt), to investigate why several members have been murdered. He earns their respect when he almost beats their best rider in a street race, although a Commando keeping up with a Z1 is probably the most unrealistic thing in the movie. As he gets to know the Gravediggers, learning they're all Vietnam and Korean War veterans, Stone comes to admire their sense of honour and camaraderie, and uncompromising social rebellion.

But the crime story's not the point, or the reason Australian bikies love this film so much. The true power of *Stone* is that Harbutt told the story from their perspective, with an honest and authentic depiction of the outlaw lifestyle. In contemporary interviews, he was quick to state his admiration for the outlaws, their code, and their refusal to conform.

'They call him... Stone.' German lobby card for *Stone* (1974).

Though critical reviews were mixed, *Stone* made a lot of money. With its depiction of bikies on colourful Kwaka 9s with full-face lids instead of chopped Harleys and the conventional US outlaw look, it introduced American audiences to the performance bike culture growing in Europe and around the Pacific Rim. This style – including the Z1s and bubble fairings – was picked up by George Miller in *Mad Max*, which shared several actors with *Stone*, notably Hugh Keays-Byrne and Roger Ward. As the Australian Film Renaissance grew, with arthouse director Peter Weir quickly gaining international recognition, Screen Australia was clearly wary of promoting *Stone*, which they viewed more as Ozploitation. Harbutt therefore found his film excluded from prestigious Australian film festivals, which made it very difficult to find distributors or backers for future projects. His idealistic and iconoclastic nature was also a serious impediment, and tragically he never made another movie.

Enthusiasm for *Stone* among Australian bikies shows no sign of diminishing, however. Some 34,000 of them descended on Sydney to celebrate the film's twenty-fifth anniversary, recreating its opening funeral run along the Gosport Expressway, and in 2023 they did it again for the fiftieth anniversary, with a rally the following year in Queensland. Two clubs have also grown out of the movie: the Vietnam Veterans MC and the Stone Social Club. After the success of *Mad Max*, reissues of *Stone* were quick to capitalise, adding the tagline: 'Before *Mad Max* there was *Stone*'. I still prefer the original though: 'Take the trip'.

Also funded by the Australian Film Development Corporation, Peter Weir's second film, *The Cars That Ate Paris* (1974), is also worth a mention as another step on the path leading to *Mad Max*. A difficult film to categorise – is it horror, arthouse, social satire, or all three? – *The Cars That Ate Paris* is about a small rural community of modern-day wreckers who cause unwary travellers to crash their cars and then harvest the spares, the contents, and even the occupants. The tiny hamlet of Paris in New South Wales is divided between a small-town conservative establishment and a group of younger 'Hoons' (including *The Road Warrior*'s Bruce Spence) – an Australasian term for reckless and showy drivers – who build grungy custom cars out of salvaged parts and eventually destroy the town. The film's iconic image is a VW Beetle bristling with metal spikes, a reproduction of which turns up in *Mad Max: Fury Road*.

'A few years from now ...' begins George Miller's *Mad Max* (1979), a canny bit of ambiguous futurism that was about to change the world. Society is on the edge, but it hasn't gone over yet, with

Mel Gibson and Tim Burns in *Mad Max* (1979).

under-resourced cops and medics still trying to desperately hold it all together. A bikie calling himself the Nightrider (*Stone*'s Vince Gil) has killed a rookie cop and escaped in a Main Force Pursuit vehicle, precipitating a trail of carnage until MFP's top driver Max Rockatansky (Mel Gibson in his second film) takes him out.

Gil's Nightrider is pumped, paraphrasing AC/DC as he monologues to the cops and his brothers on the radio: 'I am the chosen one, the mighty hand of vengeance sent down to strike the unroadworthy!' His high-speed driving is perfect and he knows it, until Max enters the race and his confidence collapses. Later, when Max's wife asks who he was, he replies, 'Just another glory-roader, I guess.' And this seems to be the point. This is carmageddon. Everyone in this culture – including the cops – is obsessed with speed, a kind of reckless last turn as the oil runs out. The film fetishises fast cars and bikes with an almost religious intensity that is matched by the elegant and eulogistic dialogue. Everyone talks like the Nightrider. It's almost prose poetry at times, as if Shakespeare had written a road movie.

The story is a basic revenge tragedy, *High Noon* meets *Death Wish*. The Nightrider's friends, a nomadic gang of scoot jockeys led by the eloquent but deranged Toecutter (Hugh Keays-Byrne), are out to get Max. Max, meanwhile, is attempting to live a normal life with his wife and his baby, and is trying to quit the Force for the sake of his sanity. Tension mounts as the narrative moves between scenes of Max with his family and his best friend, Jim Goose (Steve Bisley), and the bikies getting closer ...

Mad Max was the directorial debut of future Academy Award winner George Miller, who was still working as an emergency room doctor in Sydney during pre-production. With friend and producer

Byron Kennedy, Miller managed to raise a budget of around $350,000 AUD without going to the Australian Film Development Corporation, because they seemed to favour arthouse projects. He co-wrote the script with journalist James McCausland, who contributed the baroque dialogue. Though McCausland never wrote another script, his influence remains in the literary dialogue of the subsequent Mad Max series. Recent National Institute of Dramatic Art graduates Gibson and Bisley had previously appeared together in the 1977 thriller *Summer City*. As Gibson was an unknown, the film's trailer focused on action over character, while it's actually Bisley on the original poster.

Like Harbutt, Miller hired real bikies as extras, the Vigilantes and Barbarian MCs, and the Victorian Four Owners Club, mostly paying them in beer. The Toecutter's gang form a conceptual bridge between Harbutt's Gravediggers and the post-apocalyptic raiders of *The Road Warrior*. On dusty KZ 1000s dressed somewhere between street racers and Visigoths, they look like they live on the road.

What makes this film so special is Miller's ability to choreograph speed and movement, putting cameras on the front of cars and convincing cinematographer David Eggby to sit on the back of a Z 1000 going well over the ton with a camera. Even today, the film conveys a realistic sensation of riding and driving very fast indeed that's both exhilarating and disconcerting. There's also excellent character development. Toecutter is grooming prospect Johnny the Boy (fellow Shakespearian actor Tim Burns) to replace the Nightrider, but his lieutenant Bubba Zanetti (a wonderfully wry performance by Geoff Parry) doesn't think he has the style. Joanne Samuel, as Max's wife Jessie, grounds his character and we feel genuine concern whenever the family is threatened. Max's journey, meanwhile, takes him from good cop, husband and father to burnt-out, revenge-fuelled vigilante. The film also looks great, as Miller shot it with a widescreen anamorphic lens picked up cheap having been abandoned by Sam Peckinpah after shooting *The Getaway* in Australia. Finally, the orchestral score by Brian May is dramatic and gothic.

Mad Max made over $5 million AUD at the Australian box office and over $100 million US worldwide, holding the Guinness World Record for the most profitable film ever made based on box-office-to-budget ratio until the release of *The Blair Witch Project*. It was picked up and distributed in the US by AIP. Fearing American audiences would not understand Australian accents and idioms, AIP redubbed the entire picture, making it sound like a spaghetti western, which perversely enhances the grindhouse viewing experience. DVD releases usually include the original audio, which allows you to discover the movie all over again. Even the engine noises are different.

Contemporary reviews were, unsurprisingly, harsh. In an article for *The Bulletin* in 1979 entitled 'The dangerous pornography of death', the Australian broadcaster Phillip Adams wrote that the film had 'all the emotional uplift of *Mein Kampf*', while Tom Buckley of *The New York Times* called it 'ugly and incoherent'. It is now included in *The New York Times* 'Best 1,000 films of all time'.

But *Mad Max* was just Miller's overture. His symphony was *Mad Max 2* (1981), known in the US as *The Road Warrior* because of the limited release of

Filming *Mad Max*.

Steve Bisley as The Goose in *Mad Max*.

the first movie. Many American moviegoers had no idea the film was a sequel until they saw shots from *Mad Max* cut into the prologue. If *Mad Max* was a bleak story about a good man's descent into barbarism, *The Road Warrior* reverses the process. This is a tale of rebirth and redemption that clearly leans on George Stevens' 1953 western *Shane*, in which a lone and haunted stranger saves a group of decent people from a violent threat that is not his concern. Max's relationship with 8-year-old Emil Minty's Feral Kid therefore mirrors that of Shane and Joey Starrett. An opening voiceover sets the scene in the manner of Russell Hoban's post-apocalyptic novel *Riddley Walker* (1980), in which history has become myth. Since the last movie, time has passed and civilisation has collapsed. This is the voice of an old man (the Feral Kid) from a primitive, post-apocalyptic culture at the end of his life looking back. The newsreel footage of civil unrest and war begin to merge with the previous movie, and the Road Warrior is placed in context: 'a man haunted by the demons of his past, a man who wandered out into the wasteland. And it was here, in this blighted place, that he learned to live again.'

Still in the supercharged Ford Falcon from the first movie – now with an Australian Cattle Dog – Max is a scavenger fighting other scavengers on the road for resources, mostly fuel to keep moving aimlessly. In a nod to the previous movie, Max's cop leather has an arm cut away where he was run over by Bubba

Zanetti, and he now has a squeaky metal knee brace having also been kneecapped. His signature weapon also remains the sawn-off shotgun. Like *Mad Max*, the film opens with a stunning chase scene in which Max duels with a pack of marauders led by Wez, a post-punk biker with a short red mohawk on a battered black KZ 1000 (tricked out to look like a Suzuki Katana – a new model the production crew loved but couldn't get in Australia), played with explosive aggression by Vernon Wells.

The plot of *The Road Warrior* is even more simple and high concept than *Mad Max*. With information from Bruce Spense's colourful but craven Gyro Captain, Max finds a group of peaceful settlers in the outback living in an oil refinery with a huge tanker full of gasoline. They are besieged by a rag-tag group of marauders made up of different gangs on bikes, dune buggies, and custom cars led by the Lord Humungus (Swedish Olympic-class weightlifter Kjell Nilsson), who wears a hockey mask a year before Jason picked up his in *Friday the 13th Part III*. The settlers, led by the idealistic Pappagallo (Mike Preston), want to use the gas to escape to the Sunshine Coast. Max wants the gas too, and cuts various deals to earn some, his character gradually changing from disinterested mercenary to hero and saviour.

Though still an independent Kennedy Miller Entertainment production, the success of *Mad Max* had given Miller a much bigger budget of $4.5 million AUD. This is all up there on the screen with sweeping crane and helicopter shots, eighty-odd custom vehicles and over 200 stunts, Miller again shooting in widescreen. At the time, this was the most expensive Australian film ever made, and both Gibson and Miller have cited this as their favourite Mad Max movie. Recently, on a panel at MegaCon Orlando in 2025, Gibson told Victor Dandridge: 'I think the second instalment was the best. It was just pure. It was

Mel Gibson in *The Road Warrior* AKA *Mad Max 2* (1981).

just a chase. From an audience point of view, I thought it was the cleanest. It had some excellent thrills. No special effects, they were just throwing stuff out of a truck.' Co-writers George Miller, Terry Hayes and Brian Hannant managed to strip the first film down to its essence as well as amplifying everything in it, distilling it into an exhilarating visual spectacle with an epic climactic chase that lasts almost fifteen minutes, a moving siege as the marauders pursue and attack a Mack truck driven by Max. The story is told through action and character, with tight minimalistic dialogue, as if language is already de-evolving. Gibson, for example, only has sixteen lines, two of which are, 'I'm just here for the gasoline.'

Max shuns human connection, rejecting the cheery overtures of the Gyro Captain, Pappagallo's earnest entreaties to join them, and even Virginia Hey's unnamed Warrior Woman, who in a lesser screenplay would have been failing the Bechdel Test as a love interest. His only relationship is with his dog, which he clearly prefers to people. His return to humanity is subtle and ambiguous, mostly made up of unspoken protective gestures towards the kid, and in a half-smile exchanged with the Gyro Captain in the third act. Miller was reading Joseph Campbell's *The Hero with a Thousand Faces* (1949) and thinking about mythic archetypal heroes, telling *The New York Times* in 1982: 'This is a mythological tale, and Max takes a journey and learns some things about himself during it ... I think this kind of story is told over again in many cultures.'

Miller was also inspired by L.Q. Jones' post-apocalyptic black comedy *A Boy and His Dog* (1975), based on the novella by Harlan Ellison, which has a similarly neo-medieval desert setting. To this familiar *mise en scène*, Miller's film brings a sense of barbarian chic through the inspired costume designs of Norma Moriceau, an Australian designer based in London who had worked with Malcolm McLaren and Vivienne Westwood. Like McLaren and Westwood, Moriceau took a lot of inspiration from the

Vernon Wells as Wez in *The Road Warrior.*

S&M scene, raiding leather bondage boutiques, as well as sporting goods stores for the hockey and American football armour. As with punk fashion, Moriceau understood the tribalism and semiotic guerilla warfare of youth culture, and exaggerated it in the gang costumes. This gives the movie a unique and much imitated sense of style, as well as telling its own story, again without words. Western motifs also remain in play, the settlers wearing practical, light-coloured clothing, while the outlaws wear black, as does Max, signalling his broken state at the start of the movie.

Voted 'Greatest Action Movie of All Time' in a 2015 *Rolling Stone* poll, contemporary reviews were equally gushing. Gary Arnold in *The Washington Post* compared Miller to Sam Peckinpah, Sergio Leone, and Kurosawa. 'Never has a film's vision of the post-nuclear-holocaust world seemed quite as desolate and as brutal,' wrote Vincent Canby in *The New York Times*, 'or as action-packed and sometimes as funny.' Charles Michener in *Newsweek* praised Gibson and predicted 'an international male star', and everyone agreed that this was one of those sequels that transcended the original.

Like the punks that inspired its distinctive visual style, it's difficult to overstate the influence of *The Road Warrior* on popular culture. As Gibson told *The New York Times* in 2010, 'Look at the music in the 1980s, Billy Idol and Duran Duran. They all took this look, the Mohawks, the black leather and studs. All the bondage stuff.' In motorcycle culture, the matt black streetfighter rode straight out of Miller's universe, as well as much of the designer gear and custom clothing that went with it, rockers becoming post-punk and gothic. And as to the science fiction road movie, the junkyard aesthetic is now *de rigueur*.

The sincerest form of flattery soon followed, with the Mad Max knock-off becoming a new exploitation subgenre. Wasteland fashion calls for a striking outfit, signature weapon, and intimidating vehicle, after which you can embark on cool, episodic adventures. Muscle cars and dune buggies are obviously popular, though motorcycles have their place. This is the case, for example, in the first of the Mad Max copies, Harley Cokliss' *Battletruck* (1982), a UK-New Zealand co-production in which Michael Beck's Hunter rides a futurised Suzuki RM 125. Beck, who had memorably played Swan in *The Warriors*, is the Max figure. He's a loner who can handle himself who ends up helping a peaceful post-nuclear community menaced by a rogue army officer turned warlord in a heavily armoured truck, before leaving enigmatically at the end of the movie.

Another early adapter was the South African *Survival Zone* (1983) written, produced and directed by Percival Rubens. Explained in the obligatory opening narration, neutron bombs have wiped out most living things on earth. Fortuitously, there are small radiation-free areas dotted about known as Survival Zones where a few people, flora and fauna remain. The main storyline concerns a family on a farm besieged by a motorcycle gang of mutant cannibals who

Trash (Mark Gregory) takes Hammer (Vic Morrow) for a ride in *1990: The Bronx Warriors* (1982).

have a similar look to the Toecutter's crew, on Z 1000s in black leathers and full-faces. The leader (Ian Steadman) looks a bit daft though, with 'Big Man' studded across the back of his jacket and a doll's head inexplicably stuck to his lid. After a promising opening chain and bike duel between Big Man and a challenger, and an attack on a convent, the film drifts off into a boring reverie structured around the film's key premise that 'Where there's life, there's hope', as Gary Lockwood and his family look on the bright side in an apocalypse that doesn't look all that bad, at least until Big Man shows up. A poor script and some terrible acting detract from what could have been quite an interesting B-movie.

As with zombies and sharksploitation, though, all the truly great Maxploitation movies came from Italy, banged out by the dozen in the first year or so after *The Road Warrior*. The first, and one of the best, is Enzo G. Castellari's *1990: The Bronx Warriors* (1982), which manages to steal in roughly equal measure from *Mad Max*, John Carpenter's *Escape from New York*, and Walter Hill's *The Warriors*. Castellari is a veteran Italian film-maker who cut his teeth on westerns in the Sixties, and whose previous movie, *The Last Shark* (1981), had swum close enough to *Jaws* to be sued by Universal and withdrawn from theatres in America. As critic Kim Newman remarked wryly in his review of *Bronx Warriors* in *The Monthly Film Bulletin*, 'Castellari nimbly steals back all the stylistic elements that Carpenter and Hill poached from Leone's Westerns in the first place.'

Like the original *Mad Max*, *Bronx Warriors* is dystopian and pre-apocalyptic. The film's set-up is explained with an intertitle: '1990. The Bronx is officially declared "No Man's Land". The authorities give up all attempts to restore law and order. From then on, the area is ruled by the Riders.' The Riders are ruled by Trash (17-year-old Mark Gregory in his debut role), a bodybuilder and avid motorcyclist with Jim Morrison good looks on a Moto Guzzi California with a glowing Halloween skull stuck on the steering head. The skulls and Guzzis mark out the central characters from the extras, who were recruited from the New York biker scene and are mostly on big Japanese cruisers and custom Harleys. The Hells Angels are credited for stunt work and appear in crowd scenes wearing their own colours. Like *The Warriors*, the Bronx is carved up between rival gangs whose looks are colourful and surreal, like the roller-skating Zombies led by George Eastman's Golem, the tap-dancing Iron Men led by real-life ballerina Carla Brait, and the Tigers led by Ogre, blaxploitation legend Fred Williamson essentially recreating Isaac Hayes' Duke of New York. There are also Jackals, Scavengers, and Sharks, all existing under an uneasy truce with rivals Trash and Ogre at the top of the heap controlling opposite sides of the borough.

James Clayton and Beryl Cunningham in *Exterminators of the Year 3000* (1983).

Into this uneasy mix comes Ann (Castellari's daughter Stefania Girolami), heir to the morally bankrupt Manhattan Corporation. Rescued from the Zombies by Trash, the pair quickly form a relationship.

The company sends in the psychotic mercenary Hammer (Vic Morrow) to retrieve Ann. He kills some Riders and plants evidence implicating the Tigers to play the gangs off against each other. The Riders want to go to war but Trash smells a rat. With a small group, he fights his way across enemy turf to parley with Ogre ...

It was good enough for a sequel. Set a few years after *Bronx Warriors*, *Escape from the Bronx* (1983) was also directed by Castellari with Mark Gregory reprising his role from the first film. In a plot that anticipates the later *Robocop* franchise, the Bronx is being cleared by an evil conglomerate with political ties to create a 'city of the future'. Although residents are being promised relocation to better housing, the reality is that a sinister private militia is killing anyone who refuses to leave, including Trash's parents. Trash is now a lone guerilla on a Kawasaki Z 250 who teams up with a crusading journalist and an underground resistance to fight villainous Henry Silva's flamethrower-wielding 'Disinfestors' and expose the truth.

Castellari also knocked out *The New Barbarians* in 1983, AKA *Warriors of the Wasteland*. Set after a nuclear war in 2019, Giancarlo Prete is the Max figure, Scorpion, who drives around in a futuristic Pontiac Firebird. Scorpion ends up protecting survivors along with the Amazonian Alma (model and beauty queen Anna Kanakis), and Fred Williamson's Nadir, who seems to have wandered in from a Conan movie. George Eastman is the warlord who leads the Templars, a death cult that ride around in what appear to be armoured golf carts supported by riders on dirt bikes. As these things only travel at about 5mph, Castellari shoots all the action in slow motion, which is much less effective than the speed and style of the *Bronx* movies, which had significantly higher budgets.

Water rather than gas is the key resource in Giuliano Carmineo Italian-Spanish co-production *Exterminators of the Year 3000* (1983), which has better car and bike chases as loner Alien (Calvin Klein model Robert Iannucci) joins a kid with a robotic arm, a former astronaut, and a cheeky female carjacker to locate a legendary source of fresh water that lies across a wasteland controlled by Fernando Bilbao's warlord Crazy Bull and his motorcycle raiders. Jamaican actress Beryl Cunningham is very cool as Crazy Bull's lieutenant, Shadow, and Bilbao's dialogue is hilarious: 'Onward my merry mother-grabbers!' and 'Hit their flank you lousy squad of aberrations!' His riders have a nice range of European scramblers including KTMs, SWMs, Montesas, and Bultacos.

Sergio Martino's *2019, After the Fall of New York* (1983) has bike riders Parsifal (Michael Sopkiw), Bronx (Vincent Scalondro), and Ratchet (Romano Puppo) on a mission from the president to find the last fertile woman twenty years after a nuclear war has rendered all human beings sterile. The hero's name suggests chivalric romance, but the story's actually more like *Sleeping Beauty*, with the quest object Melissa (Alessandra Tani) kept in suspended animation. Parsifal succeeds after a series of episodic encounters with various wasteland factions, including the Harlem Hunters, the Needle People, the Rat Eater King (Hal Yamanouchi), and George Eastman's Big Ape, who Brandon Tenold described in his *Cult Movie Review* as looking as if 'Bigfoot had decided to dress like a pirate'.

David Worth's US-Italian *Warrior of the Lost World* AKA *Mad Rider* (1983) has a hero on a 'supersonic speedcycle' equipped with a really annoying talking computer called Einstein that looks to be a BMW R80 covered in aluminium cladding. Set 'generations after the radiation wars', what's left of humanity is ruled by a fascist dictator called Prosser (Donald Pleasence slumming it a bit), backed up by a brutal militia known as the Omega, who ride Moto Guzzi V 7s. There is a resistance movement called the Outsiders allied to a small group of mystics called the Enlightened Elders, and in the middle a barbaric wasteland, 'a forbidden zone populated by roving tribes of desperate Marginals'.

The (unnamed) Rider (*The Exterminator*'s Robert Ginty) is more Luke Skywalker than Mad Max, chosen by the Elders to aid the resistance, which includes Persis Khambatta, whose film career had taken a bit of a dive since *Star Trek: The Motion Picture*. Fred Williamson also turns up, though whose side

French lobby card for *2019, After the Fall of New York* (1983) – Alessandra Tani and Michael Sopkiw.

he's on is unclear, along with Geretta Geretta, another American regular on the Italian exploitation circuit. *Warrior of the Lost World* was a big hit on *Mystery Science Theatre 3000*.

One of the best entries in the spaghetti apocalypse is Joe D'Amato's *Endgame* (1983). Made four years before Schwarzenegger's *The Running Man*, *Endgame* features a similarly gladiatorial gameshow broadcast to the masses in a dystopian post-nuclear America. The military government, meanwhile, use the game as a bread and circuses distraction, under cover of which the Security Services are purging telepathic mutants. 'Hunter' Shannon (*Zombie Flesheaters*' Al Cliver) agrees to help mutant Lilith (erotic actress Laura Gemser) lead a group across the radioactive wasteland to a telepathic community after she saves his life from fellow Hunter Kurt Karnak (George Eastman). In a nod to *The Seven Samurai*, Shannon assembles a team of mercenaries including familiar spaghetti western bandit Nello Pazzafini and *Warrior of the Lost World*'s Mario Pedone as bikers, on a Honda XLR 125 and a Goldwing both covered in fur. Pursued by Karnak and the Security Services, the group battle blind warrior monks, 'regressive mutants', and a biker army led by a blue mutant fish man. D'Amato always said this was his favourite film.

D'Amato and Eastman also threw *2020 Texas Gladiators* together in 1983, again starring Cliver (Pierluigi Conti). In this one a group of 'Rangers' maintain a kind of frontier justice after the collapse of civilisation following a series of wars and natural disasters. The group fractures after Catch Dog

(Daniel Stephen) tries to rape a woman they've just saved, and ends up leading a biker gang for Nazi warlord Black One (Dr Butcher MD himself, Donald O'Brien). Catch Dog rides a well-loved black Guzzi which I swear I've seen in several of these movies. The film is fundamentally a futuristic spaghetti western, but then so was *The Road Warrior*. Worth it for a mad climax involving dirt bikes, Nazi stormtroopers, and Native Americans on horseback.

Best known for his notorious *Cannibal Holocaust*, Ruggero Deodato's *The Atlantis Interceptors* (1983) lifts elements from Kevin Connor's 1978 British movie *Warlords of Atlantis* and combines them with the iconography of *The Road Warrior*. In a convoluted plot, radiation from a derelict Russian submarine triggers the rise of Atlantis near the island of San Pedro off the coast of Florida. Discovering their world overrun with human beings, the reactivated Atlanteans wipe out the population of San Pedro, their sadistic and merciless 'Interceptors' a gang of punky bikers with a lot of leather, studs, mohawks and make-up on spikey, armoured Japanese superbikes led by a warlord wearing a crystal skull helmet. It's up to a trio of Vietnam vets led by *Peyton Place*'s Christopher Connelly and a couple of shipwrecked academics to sort this mess out, although where 12,000-year-old reanimated Atlantean warriors came by all those Suzuki GS 1100s at such short notice remains a mystery.

Tonino Ricci's *Rush* (1983) is another Italian post-atomic movie with an evil warlord and a taciturn, enigmatic hero played by Bruno Minniti, but aside from the setting the influence here is obviously *Rambo*. There aren't any bikes in it, either. Minniti returned in the 1984 sequel *Rage*, which is much more *Road Warrior* inspired, with an epic climactic chase involving a train pursued by dirt bikes and dusty muscle cars. Minniti's mercenary Rage (formally known as Rush) is hired

Spanish lobby card for *Endgame* (1983), sold as a Bronx Warriors sequel: *Bronx Final Battle*.

by a group of survivors to lead a team across the 'Forbidden Land' to an abandoned research facility to retrieve a stash of uranium to provide power for their settlement. While dealing with mutants and scavengers, the group are also pursued by a gang of two- and four-wheeled marauders led by Rage's old enemy Slash (Stelio Candelli), who's also after the uranium. In the end, they find an 'even greater treasure' of old books of science, history, and philosophy, but end up just taking the Bible.

Romolo Guerrieri's *The Final Executioner* (1984) has some conceptual links to *Endgame*, being another 'Most Dangerous Game' story in which human beings are hunted. Post-nuclear society is divided between those rich enough to have avoided radioactive fallout and the contaminated, who are consigned to wasteland preserves policed by wardens on Guzzi Californias to be hunted for sport by the elite, one of whom, Erasmus (Harrison Muller), rides a black Honda CB 900 F and carries a samurai sword. Scientist Alan Tanner (William Mang) has discovered that contamination is no longer a problem and that the hunts exist only to get rid of political opponents and social undesirables. For his trouble, he's sent to the wasteland with his wife, who is raped and murdered in front of him by Erasmus' group of rich kids and sadists. Alan survives, and with the help of ex-cop Sam (Woody Strode on top form), gains the fighting skills to turn the tables on the hunters. Alan becomes 'the final executioner', ruthlessly killing the parasitic rich in a satisfying climax that anticipates James DeMonaco's *The Purge: Anarchy* and Craig Zobel's controversial political satire *The Hunt*.

Infamous exploitation director Bruno Mattei worked in many genres – western, sword and sandal, zombie, women's prison, sharksploitation, Nazisploitation, nunsploitation, and cannibal. His contribution to the Mad Max era is therefore memorable. *Rats: Night of Terror* (1984) isn't just another eco-horror about animals attacking; Mattei also makes the setting post-apocalyptic and the protagonists a biker gang. Set 225 AB ('After the Bomb') and shot on the set of Sergio Leone's *Once Upon a Time in America*, a group of wandering two-wheeled survivors decide to stay the night in an abandoned bar where they find fresh food and a hydroponic lab, but also a lot of recently dead and obviously eaten bodies – and rats. A lot of rats. You might say they bring this on themselves, and once the rats have chewed up their tyres they're trapped. With extreme gore, a brilliant twist ending, and Geretta Geretta, this is one of the good ones, although Mattei follows slasher rules so the characters are so dumb it's remarkable they lived this long, especially in an apocalypse. Leader Kurt (Ottaviano Dell'Acqua) is on that familiar black Moto Guzzi, and there's gear and laser guns from *Texas Gladiators* and *The Final Executioner*.

The Atlantis Interceptors (1983).

Horror and *giallo* legend Lucio Fulci put in a strong entry with *Warriors of the Year 2072* (1984), AKA *New Gladiators* and *Fighting Centurions*, starring *Dallas*' Jared Martin and Fred Williamson, supported by genre regulars Hal Yamanouchi, Donald O'Brien, and Al Cliver. Leaning on *Rollerball*, *Bladerunner* and *Endgame*, not to

Cindy Leadbetter, Gianni Franco, and Geretta Geretta in *Rats: Night of Terror* (1984).

mention anticipating *The Running Man*, Fulci depicts a consumer society obsessed with violence in which the TV show *Kill Bike* (which is exactly what it sounds like) tops the ratings. A rival network counters with a new show based on the gladiatorial games of Ancient Rome in which criminals are sentenced to fight to the death on motorcycles. *Kill Bike*'s star Drake (Martin) is framed for murder and stuck in the game which, when it finally starts, is impressive, with a 'Battle of the Damned' conducted on armoured Jawas.

The genre began to die a natural death after George Miller's disappointing *Mad Max Beyond Thunderdome* (1985). This was not a sequel Miller and Gibson had initially wanted to make and was a Mad Max story grafted onto another Miller screenplay about children in the wasteland inspired by *Lord of the Flies* and *Peter Pan*. Pacing therefore suffered, with an interminable second act before the obligatory junkyard chase finale. Though the film turned a modest profit, it was the end of the franchise until Miller revived it with *Mad Max: Fury Road*.

Coming late to the party in Italy was Giuseppe Vari's *Urban Warriors* (1987) and Deran Sarafian's *Interzone* (1989). *Urban Warriors* is visually closer to Miller's world than the early Eighties films but still suffers from a hackneyed script and underwhelming performances. It is a good symbol for the whole genre, though, as after scientists emerge from a bunker following a nuclear war the surface has become

'Warriors of the Future.' French lobby card for *Wheels of Fire* (1985).

Max-world literally overnight, as if everyone raided biker, goth and S&M stores and just got out on the road with distressed muscle cars and matt black dirt bikes, which I'm sure is exactly what would happen. Made by Joe D'Amato's Filmirage company and written by notorious B-movie hack Claudio Fragasso, *Interzone* is rougher and cheaper but more fun. *Re-Animator*'s Bruce Abbott is the leather-clad drifter Swan, up against the female warlord Mantis, played with verve by former bodybuilder Teagan Clive, and her raiders on dirt bikes. The plot is ridiculous, and involves hidden treasure and telepathic monks, but Abbott is a great Max figure, adding humour and making the character a likeable rogue, the way Bruce Campbell might have played it if that proposed *Mad Max* TV series had ever been made in the Nineties.

Roger Corman, of course, got in on the act as well, working with prolific Filipino exploitation filmmaker Cirio H. Santiago. Santiago produced, co-wrote, and directed the early *Road Warrior* rip-off *Stryker* for New World in 1983. The world now a post-nuclear desert, the principal commodity is water, though bullets, gasoline, and nifty leather clothes are apparently plentiful. The Max figure, cowboy Stryker, played by jobbing TV actor Steve Sandor, is a loner in a black Mustang who saves trike-riding Amazon Delha (Andria Savio) from the mobile barbarian hordes of warlord Kardis (Mike Lane), a Captain Hook figure who has history with Stryker, who cut off his hand. Delha comes from the Colony, a peaceful outpost built around an underground spring, and wants to form an allegiance with Stryker's estranged brother, Trun, (Ken Metcalfe), a more benevolent military leader, to protect the Colony from Kardis. Her Amazon sister Laurenz (Julie Gray) views this as a betrayal and her warrior women on trikes are also after Delha. Following the pulp sci-fi tradition, while the men all wear leather armour, the women are in diaphanous tops and leather hotpants. Kardis has Scorpion tanks, and the movie ends with a protracted gun battle, so unlike *The Road Warrior*, the climax is static. The trouble with Santiago's style, however, is pacing. The movie is virtually all action, with little or no reflective scenes to break it up, a breathless pace that allows for no real suspense, character development or even basic story details.

Also out of the Philippines, colourful director Willy Milan's *W is War* (1983) copied the original *Mad Max* in having hero cop W2 (Anthony Alonzo) take down a biker crime lord's brother in a pre-apocalyptic society. W2 is about to be married, but rather than follow the standard formula of killing the hero's fiancée, Den Montero's Nosfero instead castrates W2, who builds a supercar and embarks on an orgy of eunuch revenge. Milan went full *Road Warrior* the following year with *Mad Warrior*, also starring Alonzo, now called Rex.

Santiago followed *Stryker* with *Wheels of Fire* in 1985, by which time Corman had left New World and set up Concorde Pictures, catching the boom in home video. Also known as *Vindicator* and *Desert Warrior*, *Wheels of Fire* was again shot in the Philippines, using many of the same locations and vehicles from *Stryker*, but this time with more dirt bikes. The story, such as it is, concerns lone road warrior Trace

(Gary Watkins) trying to rescue his sister Arlie (*Playboy* model Lynda Wiesmeier) from evil warlord Scourge (veteran Filipino actor Joe Mari Avellana) and his horde of football-armoured marauders. In the background, an apparently benevolent but in actuality imperialist group known as the Ownership are consolidating their powerbase, while a doomed pacifist group called the True Believers are trying to build a rocket to just go somewhere else, which doesn't seem like a bad idea. Again, like *Stryker*, the pace is way off, moving faster than Trace's rocket-powered Camaro.

Staying in the same universe, Santiago followed up with *Equalizer 2000* (1987), based on a story by Joe Avellana and again mostly shot in the same Filipino quarry as *Stryker* and *Wheels of Fire*. Australian martial artist Richard Norton makes for a stronger lead than Gary Watkins, giving us an idea of what a post-apocalyptic Chuck Norris movie might have looked like. Norton would later play the Prime Imperator in *Fury Road*.

Away from Corman and Santiago, Columbia's US-Canadian co-production *Spacehunter: Adventures in the Forbidden Zone* (1983) was an attempt to put a *Star Wars* plot in a Mad Max environment, with mutant raiders and fortified vehicles, including a couple of bikes with roll cages that seem to anticipate the horrors of the BMW C1. This was a big budget movie starring TV heart-throb Peter Strauss and brat-packer Molly Ringwald, but it was rushed out in 3D to hit theatres a week before *Return of the Jedi* and barely broke even. At the other end of the scale, low-budget impresario Charles Band banged out *Metalstorm: The Destruction of Jared-Syn* (1983), also in 3D, with 'sky-bikes' and *The Road Warrior*'s Mike Preston as the evil warlord of the title.

Predicting the BMW C1? *Spacehunter: Adventures in the Forbidden Zone* (1983).

putting it closer to *The Searchers* and *The Road* than *The Road Warrior*. Star Kodi Smit-McPhee played the Boy in *The Road*.

Finally, George Miller made another Mad Max movie himself. With a budget estimated at between $155 and $185 million, Australian-US co-production *Mad Max: Fury Road* (2015) probably cost more than all the impersonators combined, discounting *Waterworld*, which had a similar price tag.

It was a long time coming. Miller doesn't always tell exactly the same story, but the gist is that he started thinking about another possible sequel at the end of the Eighties that would be a continuous chase, but studio changes, scheduling conflicts, the Gulf War, and Mel Gibson's fall from grace meant that principal photography didn't begin until 2012. Miller wrote the script with British comics artist Brendan McCarthy and the Australian actor and screenwriter Nico Lathouris, who incidentally played Grease Rat in the original *Mad Max*. Tom Hardy took over from Gibson, supported by Charlize Theron as Imperator Furiosa and Nicholas Hoult as Nux. In his final role, Hugh Keays-Byrne returned to the franchise as the disfigured warlord Immortan Joe. Hardy and Theron hated each other on set, and Miller uses the tension, what he called Hardy's 'damage', to strike sparks as the antagonists gradually become allies. The film was shot in the Dorob National Park in Namibia. About 150 vehicles were built for the production, including forty-seven motorcycles, designed by McCarthy, Australian motocross legend Stephen Gall, stunt co-ordinator Guy Norris, and production designer Colin Gibson. Only fifteen vehicles survived. Australian cinematographer John Seale (*Gorillas in the Mist*) came out of retirement just to shoot the movie, and digital cameras were strapped to the heads of actors and used as crash cams in

Milla Jovovich in *Resident Evil: Extinction* (2007).

Doomsday (2008) – the Scottish *Road Warrior.*

action sequences. Although the first Mad Max movie to contain CGI, over 80 per cent of the effects were still practical. On the ground, Guy Norris was in charge of over 150 stunt performers, including Olympic athletes and Cirque du Soleil performers, leading Robert Rodriguez to ask Miller after a screening, 'How the hell did you film that?'

There is genius, too, in simplicity. As Miller told Christina Radish in *Collider*: 'I wanted to have one extended chase, in which you discover the backstories of the characters on the way.' Like *The Road Warrior*, Miller wanted very little dialogue. In a two-hour movie, Max has fifty-two lines, including the opening narration at which he is at his most poetic and voluble.

Depth is added through character development and meticulous world building. Immortan Joe's most trusted lieutenant, Imperator Furiosa, helps his Five Wives to escape in a War Rig, a huge, multi-sectioned and armoured truck, heading across the wasteland to the home she was taken from as a child. Max, captured by Joe's War Boys and repurposed as a 'blood bag' to transfuse the cancer-ridden Nux, is taken along for the ride when the War Boys are dispatched to recapture the women, and ends up on the truck. This unlikely trio is forced to work together to evade Immortan's Joe's mobile army and save the women.

As in *The Road Warrior*, Max is traumatised and withdrawn, haunted by memories of people he failed to save. The 'Fury Road' is his path back to sanity and also redemption, a spiritual rebirth also sought by warrior woman Furiosa. Furiosa's desire to return home and to save the wives is the dramatic engine that drives the story, making her ultimately more of a relatable protagonist than Max. This gives the movie a strong and refreshing feminist dimension.

Maggie Q in *Priest* (2011).

The Buzzards in the wasteland drive spikey cars in a nod to *The Cars That Ate Paris*, while the Rock Riders perform insane stunts while attacking the truck on junkyard bitzer Yamaha YZ 450s and Gas Gas TXT 250s. Furiosa's matriarchal tribe, the Vulvalini, all ride bikes, giving Max a Yamaha YZF-R1 sand dragster with an extended swingarm, barkbusters, sissy bar, knobby tires, and a mammoth rear sprocket. Furiosa rides a BMW R80 chop with sand skis on the front forks. Then there's a mad Honda Gold Wing and a Royal Enfield sidecar outfit covered in animal hide. Everything is built from scraps, and covered in carpet, random repurposed metal objects, and bones. The Gold Wing looks as if there's a bit of lawn mower in there.

Fury Road was, of course, a massive critical success. The first of the Mad Max films to be nominated at the Oscars, it took away six. Mel Gibson loved it, and critics were similarly enthralled. While most justifiably raved about the pace and action, Lindsay Bahr of the Associated Press described the film as 'radically visionary', which is not the language usually associated with this genre. Even academics have taken *Fury Road* to their hearts, particularly in Women's Studies, praising Furiosa's dramatic dominance and the range of other atypical female roles, such as the elderly and self-sufficient Vulvalini. Miller has also been praised for his positive, non-stigmatising portrayals of physical disability and mental illness. Whether it turned a profit, however, remains open to conjecture. Though the highest-grossing Mad Max film, taking $380 million at the global box office, its high production costs and advertising budget resulted in a deficit of between $20 and $40 million, which would make it the first Mad Max movie to actually lose money – none of which detracts from the simple fact that *Mad Max: Fury Road* is one of the greatest films ever made. Sometimes, you just can't put a price on Art.

On a somewhat more modest budget, Ana Lily Amirpour's *The Bad Batch* (2016) takes on many of the tropes of the desert apocalypse movie, although the only bike is Jason Momoa's Honda CN 250 Helix. A surreal dystopian political satire, the 'Bad Batch' are undesirables stripped of their citizenship and expelled to a desert in Texas where no laws apply. British actress, model and singer Suki Waterhouse plays Arlen, who is quickly captured by cannibals and spends the majority of the movie with a prosthetic leg and missing an arm.

Waterhouse returned to the desert as an android in James Franco and Bruce Thierry Cheung's *Future World* (2018), which might be described as a cross between *The Road Warrior* and *Cherry 2000* and has the distinction of being one of those films on Rotten Tomatoes that has a 0 per cent approval rating. In a 'new Dark Age' where resources are so depleted that no one even has names, Prince (Jeffrey Wahlberg, nephew of Mark) leaves the safety of Oasis on a quest to find a mythical medicine for his dying mother, Queen (Lucy Liu). In the wasteland, Prince falls foul of Franco's Warlord, the leader of a gang of motorcycle crazies, and his android lover and enforcer Ash (Waterhouse). Sticking to the Tin Man science fiction archetype, Ash develops a conscience and helps Prince, asking questions like 'What are souls?' Along the way, they encounter an outpost called Love Town, where enslaved women are sold by the Love Lord (Snoop Dog), and Paradise, a kind of post-apocalyptic crack house run by the Drug Lord Milla Jovovich, who steals the movie, all the while pursued by the demented horn-wearing Warlord, an obvious satanic archetype.

At a guess, Franco has something like John Bunyan's seventeenth-century Christian allegory *The Pilgrim's Progress* in mind, which has a similar approach to symbolic naming. Or he might be going for some sort of fairytale motif. Instead, it comes off as at best generic, the names more like place markers in the early draft of the script, and at worst pretentious. The story is similarly

Mary Death (Christian Pitre) in *Bounty Killer* (2013).

predictable and familiar and even the title's recycled, *Futureworld* (1976) being the sequel to the original *Westworld* (1973). As these films concerned androids rebelling against their masters, perhaps this is intentional, but again it just seems like lazy writing. (Costumes from *Waterworld* are also reprocessed.) At one point, the Drug Lord asks Prince, 'So, are you doing this whole tourist thing of the wasteland, or is there something else you're after?' This is a good question, which I doubt Franco could answer.

George Miller's returned to the wasteland with *Furiosa: A Mad Max Saga* in 2024, another Australian-American co-production. Miller had wanted to shoot *Furiosa* back to back with *Fury Road*, making the first film's joint protagonist the focus, but protracted wage disputes with Warner Bros. held it up for nine years.

Max only gets a cameo in *Furiosa* (played by Jacob Tomuri, one of Hardy's stunt doubles). The Max figure in *Furiosa* – aside from Furiosa herself – is Praetorian Jack, played by Tom Burke, who particularly distinguishes himself in a memorable high-octane set piece in which flying bikers lay siege to Immortan Joe's War Rig.

While, in common with *The Road Warrior* and *Mad Max Beyond Thunderdome*, the theme of *Fury Road* was redemption, *Furiosa* returns to the original *Mad Max* in being a revenge tragedy. Kidnapped as a child from the Green Place of Many Mothers by Chris Hemsworth's Dementus and his Biker Horde, young Furiosa watches her mother being tortured to death by the charismatic warlord rather than give up the location of the feminist farming collective. In the fifth and final chapter of the film, the adult Furiosa goes after Dementus just as Max pursued the Toecutter. *Furiosa* is also a coming-of-age

Tom Hardy picks up the mantle in *Mad Max: Fury Road* (2015).

Dementus (Chris Hemsworth) and his Biker Horde in *Furiosa: A Mad Max Saga* (2024).

story that starts twenty years or so before *Fury Road* and follows the protagonist from childhood into early adulthood. A brief denouement then sets up *Fury Road*.

Furiosa's backstory was pretty implicit in *Fury Road*. She tells Max she was taken from her home by raiders as a child, and has obviously risen through Immortan Joe's ranks, losing an arm along the way. Her character arrives fully formed at the start of *Fury Road*, beautifully interpreted by Theron, raising the question: *Do we really need a 148-minute biography?* Prequels can be tricky to pull off. There's ultimately no suspense as survival is guaranteed and major outcomes are already known.

Miller clearly loves the character, to the extent that *Fury Road* was already as much about Furiosa as it was Max. Furiosa was not the first strong female character in Miller's Mad Max universe either. There was Virginia Hey's Warrior Woman in *The Road Warrior*, and the ruthless matriarch Aunty Entity (Tina Turner) in *Thunderdome*. In a genre that is overwhelmingly macho, Miller then used *Fury Road* to offer audiences both a male and female action hero, giving Furiosa more emotional depth as an exile yearning for home and the saviour of a group of enslaved women. In *Furiosa*, Miller finally gives us a female protagonist, with Tom Burke's Max surrogate only appearing in a couple of chapters, gender roles reversed so he becomes the doomed love interest.

In a five-chapter saga, running 28 minutes longer than *Fury Road*, with almost an hour on *The Road Warrior*, *Furiosa* never entirely captures either the pacey, post-punk intensity of *The Road Warrior* or the Classical unity of *Fury Road*. It is, however, *epic*. The ideas are not new, just bigger. Dementus' Biker Horde epitomises this. Whereas the Toecutter led a motorcycle gang in low double figures and the Humungus had consolidated a bunch of small gangs into a respectable raiding party, Dementus has a mobile army. As the camera sweeps back and up, we see there are *thousands* of them streaking across the red sand, like some huge Bedouin cavalry charge in *Lawrence of Arabia*. And in Miller's trademark

Anya Taylor-Joy as Furiosa.

visual style, every bike and every outfit is unique. There's even a Norton Commando, which must be a tip of the hat to *Stone.* Dementus rides a chariot hooked up to three motorcycles. I have no idea how that works, but it looks fantastic, adding to the sword and sandal feel alongside Immortan Joe's penchant for Imperial Roman ranks.

As Dementus, Chris Hemsworth steals every scene he's in as the playful despot; intelligent and charming, but also sadistic and increasingly deranged. The Toecutter would have liked him. For some reason, he's sporting a fake nose, which makes him less gorgeous and Thor-like while also recalling Alec Guinness' Fagin from David Lean's *Oliver Twist.* As the great Hugh Keays-Byrne passed away in 2020, Lachy Hulme puts in a good turn as Immortan Joe. The most notable casting change, however, is Furiosa herself. Alyla Browne plays the character as a child, Anya Taylor-Joy (*Last Night in Soho*) taking over as the young adult Furiosa. Miller told the *New York Times* in 2020 that he'd rejected the option of de-aging technology for Theron (who was 40 in *Fury Road*) because of the 'uncanny valley' effect, though machine learning CG was used to blend Browne and Taylor-Joy's features to replicate the same person aging. Following Mel Gibson, Tom Hardy, and Charlize Theron into the wasteland, Taylor-Joy does well in adopting the persona of the post-apocalyptic badass: cool hair, outfits and vehicles, signature weapon, limited dialogue and emotional range, and episodic adventures. How well you think she fills this role will ultimately decide your view of the success or failure of the movie.

Even after all these years, *The Road Warrior* remains the genre yardstick. Although it shared a common protagonist, Miller made the premise new again by moving beyond the traditional biker movie format of the original into audacious mythmaking. The conceptual leap from *Mad Max* was quite brilliant. In *Fury Road*, Miller had again harnessed the demon that created *The Road Warrior*, though it took him thirty years to find it again. In *Furiosa*, Miller's challenge was to once again build on the previous movie while taking it in a new and different direction. Unfortunately, like the lacklustre *Mad Max Beyond Thunderdome*, the story never really lives up to its first act, enlivened as it is by the antics of Dementus and his chariot, and *Furiosa* was not a box office success. As a result, Miller's planned follow-up, *Mad Max: The Wasteland*, seems unlikely to go ahead, leaving us only with the Asylum mockbuster *Road Wars: Max Fury* (2024), starring Vernon Wells, returning the desert apocalypse movie to the land of the low budget.

'And the Road Warrior? That was the last we ever saw of him.'

CHAPTER 9 HERITAGE CLASSICS

IN CINEMA, ALL genres have their heyday. We associate the Gothic, for instance, with the Universal monster movies of the Thirties just as slasher films were a product of the Eighties. The era of the Hollywood musical, meanwhile, was from about 1930 to 1950, while the Golden Age of the western ran from the Forties to the Sixties. This is not to say the genres disappear entirely, but they never command the same kind of audience and critical interaction again.

The biker movie, which was always going to be niche, was no different. Historically, it can be mapped from *The Wild One* in 1953, which pulled the trigger, to *The Road Warrior* in 1981, noting, of course, the outlaw biker film cycle, which ran from *The Wild Angels* in 1966 to *The Dirt Gang* in 1972, as a genre within a genre. Biker movies did not stop, and neither did westerns, musicals, or period Gothic. Instead they became diasporic, marginalised, *occasional*, and never original again. In a trend nowadays common across increasingly soulless and corporate Hollywood products, everything is a legacy picture: a remake, a sequel, a revival. As magnificent as *Fury Road* is, for example, it is just an epic reimagining of *The Road Warrior*. We are in the post-modern paradigm. Nothing is new. Everything's been done. All that is left is homage and pastiche. Like the Harley-Davidson Heritage series, the product may be modern but the design looks back to a different era.

For example, mostly in the Eighties, there was a brief, fascinating flurry of movies that revisited the juvenile delinquent films of the Fifties that had gathered around *The Wild One*: stylish period pieces with leather boys on classic bikes.

Set in 1959, *The Loveless* (1981) was inspired by Kenneth Anger's *Scorpio Rising*, *The Wild One*, the film noir *Detour*, Douglas Sirk's Southern Gothic melodrama *Written on the Wind*, and Sergio Leone's *Once Upon a Time in The West*. Co-written and co-directed by Kathryn Bigelow and Monty Montgomery, *The Loveless* is a moody, character-driven period piece that grew out of the overlapping New York arthouse and underground film scenes that punches well above its weight given that it was the first feature film Bigelow and Montgomery worked on, and the first lead role for star Willem Dafoe, then an avant-garde theatre actor. Montgomery had done some music production work and was able to fund the project, which cost around $80,000, while Bigelow was just out of the Columbia University graduate film programme.

Dafoe plays Vance, the de facto leader of a small group of greasers forced to hang around a truck stop in Georgia to fix a bike en route to Daytona along the old US 17 superhighway. Like the Black Rebels in *The Wild One*, their presence acts as a catalyst, igniting the simmering and complex tensions of the local community, leading to a violent and tragic climax.

'We're going nowhere… fast.' Poster for video release of *The Loveless* (1981).

The world building of *The Loveless* is impeccable, using authentic props borrowed from the Museum of Modern Art. The bikers wear vintage Schott Perfectos and ride stock and bagger Harley FLE panheads. The soundtrack, meanwhile, is a mixture of period rock 'n' roll and Fifties-style instrumentals by 'Lounge Wizard' John Lurie and rockabilly singer Robert Gordon, who also appears in the movie as the edgy biker Davis. His nymphomaniac girlfriend Sportster Debbie is played by Tina L'Hotsky, an icon of the New York club scene. In another inspired piece of casting, the widowed waitress Augusta, who performs an impromptu exotic dance that oozes sexual frustration, was played by real-life stripper Elizabeth Gans.

The influence of *Scorpio Rising* is apparent in the undercurrent of homoeroticism and sexual ambiguity, personified by the androgenous and effeminate biker Ricky (Danny Rosen), who it is implied might have been castrated in a crash. There is also Anger's sense of extreme Americana and folk art in props and setting – with locations frozen in time after Interstate 95 was built and all the bars and truck stops were abandoned – and the replication of the 'Boys & Bolts' section of *Scorpio Rising* as a Harley transmission is repaired. Like Johnny in *The Wild One*, Vance provides a limited reflective voiceover, framing the inevitable disaster. Echoing the words of *Detour*'s antihero Al Roberts (Tom Neal), who had warned, 'Fate or some mysterious force can put the finger on you or me for no reason at all,' Vance similarly concludes, 'Every one of us: dollar chips in one big floatin' crap game.'

The film-makers were able to more explicitly explore the sexual tensions that were always simmering in *The Wild One*, while also looking at the politics of race, class, and gender in the South. Dialogue is smart, tight, and hip, while you can feel the heat of the setting physically and emotionally. Characters are languid, bored, longing; waiting for something to happen, always on the edge. If Tennessee Williams had written *The Wild One* it might have looked like this.

Though a very different-looking film, Francis Ford Coppola's *Rumble Fish* (1983) is similarly brooding and existential. Based on the 1975 Young Adult novel by S.E. Hinton, *Rumble Fish* is a companion piece to *The Outsiders* (1983), another gang-related Brat Pack coming-of-age story also written by Hinton and directed by Coppola that shares many of the same actors. While *The Outsiders* is a cross between *Rebel Without a Cause* and *West Side Story* that recreates the vivid hues of Technicolour, *Rumble Fish* feels more like film noir, shot in stark, Expressionistic high-contrast black and white. Both set in Tulsa, *The Outsiders* takes place in 1965, whereas *Rumble Fish* is more contemporary. Wannabe teenage gangbanger Rusty James (Matt Dillon) aspires to be like his older brother, known only as Motorcycle Boy (Mickey Rourke), a local legend who ruled the street gangs before disappearing suddenly. When Motorcycle Boy returns on his Kawasaki GPZ 550 as a much more reflective young man, Rusty James does everything he can to live up to the reputation his brother is now trying hard to live down. Dennis Hopper plays their drunken father. The film's title refers to Siamese Fighting Fish in a local pet shop, a symbol of the gangs, and the only thing shown in colour. While *The Outsiders* is a complex melodrama, *Rumble Fish* is more of an avant-garde mood piece – a sad, strange and beautiful film with a simpler, more allegorical story held together by stunning visuals and a hypnotic performance by Rourke.

Cast after director Walter Hill saw *The Loveless*, Willem Dafoe was back in the saddle for the neo-noir fantasy *Streets of Fire* (1984), on a matt black Harley FLH, wearing waders and a leather shirt

Mickey Rourke in *Rumble Fish* (1983).

Kaneda (voiced by Mitsuo Iwata) in *Akira* (1988).

and wielding a sledgehammer. That would have been a film in itself, but his job here is to play the villain to Michael Paré's hero, Tom Cody, returned home to save his first love from Defoe's Raven and the Bombers MC, which was mostly made up of real LA clubs the Crusaders and the Heathens, all of whom have a *Wild One* look about them on coal black bobbers. The film is subtitled 'A rock 'n' roll fable' and is set in a hyper-real alternative version of Chicago captioned 'Another time, another place'. The setting is a stylised blend of early Fifties design, DA haircuts, and Ford Mercuries – with a distinct post-war feel in which Cody and his tomboy sidekick McCoy (Amy Madigan) are both ex-military – and an incongruously modern Eighties music scene. Diane Lane, fresh from *The Outsiders* and *Rumble Fish*, plays Ellen Aim, rock star and local girl made good who's kidnapped by Raven. Cody is hired by Ellen's manager (Rick Moranis) to get her back, but he ends up doing it for love not money, leading to the inevitable showdown with Raven and the Bombers.

After the success of *48 Hrs*, Hill could make what he liked, and *Streets of Fire* was a passion project intended to utilise all the features he believed made the 'perfect film' when he was a teenager, including 'rumbles, rock stars, motorcycles, jokes in tough situations, leather jackets and questions of honour'. Cody was intended to launch a franchise, but although the film looks great, the script is hackneyed and silly, and the musical format doesn't work, clashing with the action plot and the Fifties aesthetic.

Streets of Fire was, however, very popular in Japan, its retro-futurism inspiring several manga and anime titles, including Katsuhiro Otomo's stunning *Akira* (1988). Based on his manga of the same name, Otomo's film is a cyberpunk epic with an elaborate plot about post-nuclear mutant telepaths that centres on a group of *bōsōzoku* – disaffected teenagers on futuristic sports bikes – who blunder into a sinister military conspiracy like the rockers in *The Damned*. The opening scene in which the heroes joust with a rival gang dressed as clowns on Harleys across Neo-Tokyo remains one of the most memorable and influential moments in the history of modern animation. Protagonist Kaneda's sliding sideways stop – probably inspired by Japanese motorcycle racer and 'father of drifting' Kunimitsu Takahashi – is one of the most imitated motorcycle moves in subsequent action movies.

Bōsōzoku is a youth subculture that mirrored the growth of the American outlaw biker scene after the war with returning veterans struggling to settle back into ordinary life. As in the States, there were accompanying exploitation movies, though these are still hard to find outside Japan, for example the 'Alley Cat Rock' series about a gang of tough biker girls and Teru Ishii's *Detonation!* trilogy in the Seventies, and Sogo Ishii's punky, manga-inspired *Crazy Thunder Road* and *Burst City* in the Eighties. *Bōsōzoku* culture was also explored in Mitsuo Yanagimachi's 16mm black-and-white documentary *God Speed You! Black Emperor* (1976), which shows the life of a teenage member of the Tokyo Black Emperors MC.

Transgressive cult director John Waters took on the teen rebel movie with the musical comedy *Cry Baby* (1990), closing a loose trilogy that had begun with his playful satire of Douglas Sirk, *Polyester*, followed by his much-loved period musical *Hairspray*. Set in 1954, local singing sensation Wade 'Cry

Baby' Walker (Johnny Depp, keen to escape his *21 Jump Street* image) is 'the happiest juvenile delinquent in Baltimore' having been presented with a K-Series Harley by his grandparents, Iggy Pop and Susan Tyrrell. With a similar though quirkier *West Side Story* dynamic to Coppola's S.E. Hinton films, teens are divided into the working-class rockabilly Drapes led by Cry Baby and the middle-class Squares led by the preppy Baldwin (Stephen Mailer). Baldwin's girl Alison (*Melrose Place*'s Amy Locane) falls for Cry Baby, who ends up in Juvenile Hall guarded by Willem Dafoe, making *Cry Baby* a cross between *Romeo and Juliet* and *Jailhouse Rock*. This may sound like *Grease*, but trust me, *Cry Baby* is way stranger. *Grease* never included lines like 'Let Jesus Christ be your gang-leader!'

Coming late to the pack and at the same time anticipating the Grindhouse revival, John Milius' *Motorcycle Gang* (1994) took its title from the 1957 AIP film of the same name, though little else other than the period setting. This was part of a series of TV movies made for Showtime under the banner of *Rebel Highway*, a revival of AIP drive-in classics produced by Samuel Z. Arkoff's son Lou and John Carpenter's long-time collaborator Debra Hill. Ten films were made using AIP titles that sometimes did and sometimes didn't remake the original, including *Roadracers* directed by Robert Rodriguez, Ralph Bakshi's *The Cool and the Crazy*, and Mary Lambert's *Dragstrip Girl*.

Sometime in the Fifties, 442nd Infantry veteran Cal Morris (*Simon & Simon*'s Gerald McRaney) and his dysfunctional family are driving from Texas to California where he has a new job. He and his wife Jean (Milius' wife Elan Oberon) have drifted apart and she's been having an affair, and their daughter Leann (a 22-year-old Carla Gugino) is flirty and rebellious. Cal has become increasingly withdrawn with age as a result of war experiences he won't talk about. He's cautious and defensive and sees everything around him as a potential threat, especially a group of bikers led by Jake (Gary Busey's son Jake) that Leann interprets as typical teenagers in light of *The Wild One* and *Rebel Without a Cause*. Unfortunately, the gang are smuggling heroin across the border from Mexico and the Kerouac-quoting Jake is currently on a rape and murder spree. He takes a shine to Leann and gaslights her into riding away with him on his beaten up Harley (an aged FXSTS Softail Springer). Cal soon discovers that the police on either side of the border won't help, and has to use his specialised military training to track the gang down and save Leann.

Johnny Depp in *Cry Baby* (1990).

In the UK in the Eighties, the spirit of the motorcycle-oriented kitchen sink drama was still kicking, with issues of social class and national identity reflecting the cast iron grip of Margaret Thatcher after the Falklands War in

1982 and her landslide victory in the 1983 General Election. Scotland, which had overwhelmingly rejected the Conservative government at the ballot box, was hit particularly hard, with high unemployment and the running down of traditional industry, leaving little but tourism to sustain the broken economy. Michael Hoffman's pioneering Scottish film *Restless Natives* (1985) is thus an astute piece of cultural response, as two skint mates from an Edinburgh council estate played by Vincent Friell and Joe Mullaney become modern-day highwaymen, holding up coachloads of American and Japanese tourists in the highlands on a Suzuki GP 125. The pair become folk heroes and, ironically, a tourist attraction themselves. 'You're bigger than the Loch Ness monster,' one copper tells them.

Joe Mullaney, Vincent Friell and Teri Lally in a promo shot for *Restless Natives* (1985).

Written by Scottish author Ninian Dunnett, *Restless Natives* was the winner of the 1984 Lloyds Bank National Screenwriting Competition, and was subsequently picked up by Thorne EMI, probably because of the emergence of the Scottish film as a distinct medium through the work of director Bill Forsyth (*Gregory's Girl*, *Local Hero*). The film was memorably scored by the Scottish rock band Big Country, and beneath the bittersweet coming-of-age drama and picturesque shots of waterfalls, mountains, and glens, there's a distinct sense of growing Scottish Nationalism.

Shot on location in the Bog of Allen, Peter Ormrod's Irish movie *Eat the Peach* (1986) is also about two broke working-class chancers with big ideas. Bike riding brothers-in-law Vinnie (the perpetually morose-looking Stephen Brennan) and Arthur (Eamon Morrissey) are made redundant when the Japanese factory they work at closes, leaving few legal ways to make money. Inspired after seeing *Roustabout* on video, they decide to build a wall of death in Vinnie's back garden, using scrap wood and an equally scrap Honda CG 125.

Vinnie is convinced that people will pay to see the attraction, dreaming of sponsorship and a touring show. The project becomes an obsession that costs him his home and almost his family, funded by working for local gangsters smuggling petrol and whiskey across the border into Northern Ireland. The lads succeed in building and mastering the wall of death, but this isn't a rags to riches story. It's more about hopeless dreamers. The film's title, which is never explained, is taken from T.S. Eliot's 'The Love Song of J. Alfred Prufrock', a poem about regret and thwarted desires that was in those days a standard text on the Irish Leaving Certificate Examination. Based on a true story, Connie Kiernan

Stephen Brennan and Eamon Morissey in *Eat the Peach* (1986).

and his brother-in-law Michael Donoghue really did build a wall of death in a back garden in County Longford, inspired by *Roustabout* and legendary Dublin stunt rider Tommy Messham. Despite some interest from local TV, they never achieved sponsorship and the wall was eventually destroyed by a storm.

Though a little clunky and underwritten at times, Screenwriter-director Frank Deasy's *The Courier* (1988) is the other Irish biker picture from this era. Set in Dublin, Padraig O'Loinsigh plays Mark, a recovering addict who's getting his life back together, pursuing his school crush Colette (Cait O'Riordan), restoring his late father's Commando, and working as a motorcycle courier. After a spill causes a package to open, he begins to realise the company he works for is a drug-running front for local gangsters Val and Christy (played by future stars Gabriel Byrne and Patrick Bergin). Worst, they've killed Colette's junkie brother for talking to police Detective McGuigan – a gritty performance by the great Ian Bannen. Caught between the brutal gangsters and the unscrupulous copper, Mark tries to bring the operation down. This is where it gets a bit daft. As Colette says, 'You think you're Clint Eastwood!'

This film should not confused with Zackary Adler's US-UK co-production *The Courier* (2019), an action thriller starring Ukrainian-French Bond girl Olga Kurylenko riding a blacked-out BMW S1000 R. In this movie, an unnamed female motorcycle courier and former special ops soldier inadvertently delivers a package intended to kill a murder witness in protective custody in a locked-down London tower block. She saves the man, and, realising his guards have been compromised, uses her Ninja skills to protect him

Olga Kurylenko in *The Courier* (2019).

in a protracted battle against hired guns in an underground car park. Gary Oldman in an eyepatch plays the villain, and he literally phones it in, his character being based in New York. Unfortunately, Oldman's performance was so bad the critical response dragged the film down with him. Anton Bidel in *Sight & Sound* got it about right when he compared the film to *Die Hard*, *The Transporter*, and *Con Air*. It's not deep, but at least *The Courier* reverses the biggest action movie cliché by making the hero a capable woman. Purists will note, however, that although Kurylenko looks stunning in her leathers, in real life all London couriers have to wear a hi-vis vest showing their company name or logo.

Getting back to the Eighties, London motorcycle courier Cyril (*Quadrophenia*'s Phillip Davis) does wear his vest in Mike Leigh's 1988 social satire *High Hopes*. With the tagline 'A comedy about optimism in the face of pessimism', *High Hopes* is a snapshot of Thatcher's Britain in which some people were making a lot of money while others were being left behind. A family saga of sorts, the film forensically deconstructs Cyril and his family over a short period leading up to his mother's seventieth birthday. Bearded, bespeckled, and on a dirty Honda Super Dream, dope-smoking Cyril is a working-class Marxist who manages to be cynical and idealistic at the same time. He wants everyone to have enough to eat, somewhere to live, a job, and realising this is impossible is paralysed by indecision. His long-time partner Shirley (Ruth Sheen) likes to grow things and is desperate for a baby but Cyril is equivocating. His widowed mum (*Eastenders*' Edna Doré) is the last council tenant in a gentrified street in Islington, and Cyril's *nouveau riche* sister and her slimy, entrepreneurial husband have their avaricious eyes on the place.

For all the bleak depictions of poverty, unhappiness, and old age, *High Hopes* still manages to be uplifting, largely because of the core relationship between Cyril and Shirley, and the latter's relentless optimism, kindness, and humour. Cyril and Shirley are authentic representations of a particular type of low-income, left-wing, alternative culture that prevailed back then: harder edged than hippies, post-punk, and politically defiant.

We didn't get another motorcycle movie in Britain for twenty years. Jon Ivay's *Freebird* (2008) started life as a play which probably accounts for its dramatic structure, which has beautiful character design and dialogue worthy of Joyce or Beckett – literary but authentically working class and very funny – but lacks much action, despite having built up a climactic gang fight throughout the narrative that is never actually shown on screen.

Freebird follows three old friends and motorcycle couriers who leave London for a weekend in Wales. Fred (Gary Stretch) is running an errand for an old gangster, buying a load of home-grown designer weed from a mysterious hippie (played by prog rock legend Arthur Brown) who lives off the grid somewhere in the Black Mountains. Hard nut and petty criminal Tyg (Geoff Bell) has never been outside London, and drug-addled Grouch (Phil Daniels shifting from young mod to aging rocker) is having one last blast before settling down with a respectable middle-class girlfriend. It's a poignant trip for Fred, whose ex-partner and young daughter live in the area. Unbeknown to the lads, they have blundered into the middle of a gang war between the Wessex Men from London and the Welsh Iron Horse motorcycle clubs. Doing what they always do, which is get out of their heads, each man experiences his own epiphany. Lynyrd Skynyrd's anthemic 'Free Bird' is the controlling metaphor for the libertarian leanings of the biker lifestyle as well as its limitations.

Like *High Hopes*, *Freebird* is an affectionate, realistic and non-sensational depiction of motorcyclists and drug use. Although the *Motorcycle News* objected at the time to the implication that we're all permanently wasted, this wasn't the point. *Freebird* is at heart a character study, held together by the obvious chemistry between Stretch, Bell and Daniels, playing middle-aged stoners at a crossroads. Drugs and their effects are therefore part of character and subculture, and depicted honestly,

How much can three men take? Geoff Bell, Phil Daniels, and Gary Stretch in *Freebird* (2008).

humorously, and non-judgementally in the manner of *Trainspotting* and *Withnail and I*. And unlike the majority of biker film-makers, lifelong motorcycle enthusiast Ivay knows his subject. The attention to detail is remarkable, right down to the choice of lead characters' bikes. Fred's a racing fan on a Suzuki Bandit, Tyg just got a bike to be a courier so has that old standby, the Kawasaki GT 550, and motorised hippy Grouch has an older Guzzi California.

With the exception of Jennie Kermode of *Eye For Film*, who got it, and a *Sun* reviewer who expansively saw the film as 'The best biker movie since *Easy Rider*' (which it isn't), critics hammered *Freebird* and it did not do well, the BBC's Jamie Russell comparing it unfavourably to Hollywood biker comedy *Wild Hogs*. This is an example of the French phenomenologist Maurice Merleau-Ponty's belief that the perception of others always originates from a point of difference between the 'lived through' and the 'displayed'. When a biker finally makes an authentic biker movie, nobody understands it other than bikers, the irony being that if Ivay had packed his film with stereotypes and clichés – like *Wild Hogs* – it might have reached a wider audience. For those of us that do know, however, it's the best British biker movie since *Quadrophenia*.

Speaking of stereotypes and clichés, it is the figure of the outlaw biker that has most stubbornly persisted in the movies. In the early Seventies, like a corpse that wouldn't stop twitching, the sudden demise of the outlaw biker film cycle did not save us from a couple of stragglers. In David L. Hewitt's *The Tormentors* (1971), a vigilante insurance salesman working with a detective infiltrates a Neo-Nazi group called the Fourth Reich, who rob banks on motorcycles, after they murder his girl. Their evil plan is to assassinate the 'Messiah', a hippie Jesus, then artificially avenge him so his youthful acolytes will follow them instead. When they shoot him at the base of a huge cross, I can't help feeling they missed something. Hewitt had previously directed *Hells Chosen Few*. When he ran out of money, producer Kimberly Hyatt was brought in to throw something together using whatever was already in the can. Nazi leader Bruce Kimball's German accent comes and goes.

Rene Martinez Jr.'s *Road of Death* (1973) manages to feel even cheaper and inexpertly put together. Frank (Jack Birch) is a former outlaw biker who's got his life together playing guitar for club band the Joe Banana Thing. He and Joe and their girlfriends share an apartment that looks like a hardcore movie set, especially as Linda is played by *Deep Throat*'s Carol Connors. When the swinging couples are attacked by the Muthas MC at a picnic and Linda is kidnapped, Jack rips off his shirt like Bruce Lee and teaches the bikers humility. 'It's a story that had to be told sooner or later. We're telling it now,' intones the trailer, unaware that 'now' is far too late for anyone to care. Connors and Birch are the parents of Thora Birch, who is a much better actor.

Finally, John Lawrence's even sleazier *Cycle Psycho* (also 1973), goes for a *Strangers on a Train* plot as lawyer Tom Drake (Richard Ridelander) does a deal with rich psycho Harry (*Bladerunner*'s Joe Turkel) to murder his unfaithful wife and provide an alibi. Instead, Harry starts blackmailing Tom to provide more victims, and he ends up hiring a motorcycle gang led by Stephen Oliver to procure them, though they ultimately turn the tables. Stafford Repp – Chief O'Hara from *Batman* – turns up in cameo. Saints preserve us!

Though Blaxploitation was one of the emergent exploitation genres that had killed off the biker movie, there was still occasionally crossover. Matt Cimber's *The Black Six* (1974) from Jerry Gross' Cinemation Industries was the movie *Black Angels* should have been. A peaceful group of African American Vietnam vets drifting around the country on big Triumphs return to one of their home towns in the South after he learns of the mysterious death of his brother. We know he was beaten to death by racist bikers with a Viking fetish because of a pre-credit scene in which he was shown dating a local white girl, the sister of one of his killers. Bubba Daniels (the San Francisco 49ers' Gene Washington) and his crew investigate the death no one wants to talk about until they finally track down the girl and the gang, leading to a violent but frustratingly inconclusive confrontation. The Black Six were all played by NFL football stars, their teams included in the credits, Washington taking the lead having had previous acting experience. All things considered, they acquit themselves pretty well, and this is a solid drama about avenging a murder that gets around a clichéd storyline by genuinely engaging with racism, although the pace drops off noticeably during the second act when Bubba is talking to potential witnesses.

While *The Black Six* stuck very close to western archetypes, William Witney's *Darktown Strutters* (1975) from New World sits somewhere between social satire, science fiction and screwball comedy. The Strutters are a gang of glamorous black women on custom trikes led by the statuesque Syreena, played by dancer and actor Trina Parks (Thumper from *Diamonds Are Forever*).

Syreena's mother has disappeared, and the search leads her to politically ambitious fast food king Commander Louisville Cross (Norman Bartold sending up Colonel Sanders), the KKK on motorcycles, and a cloning machine. The police are presented as incompetent, imbecilic, and easily outwitted, the black community confident and empowered: 'Don't let them scare you anymore,' Syreena tells her grandfather (*Amos 'n' Andy*'s Alvin Childress), 'Those days are gone.'

Darktown Strutters is mad, bold, and colourful, with the 'Motorcycle Queens' decked out in feathers, sequined jumpsuits, winged crash helmets, and gold platform boots. There are custard pie fights, speeded up chase scenes, and random musical numbers, including a nice turn from the soul group The Dramatics.

Mickey Rourke and Don Johnson in *Harley Davidson and the Marlboro Man* (1991).

Shot in 1974 but not released until 1976, *Northville Cemetery Massacre* is a good movie that was just made too late. The political preoccupations of the co-writers and directors William Dear and Thomas L. Dyke all come from the Sixties. Torn between making a horror or a biker movie, they intended the film to be a challenge to what they saw as creeping authoritarianism in the US and the death of individual freedom, and to call out prejudice and stereotyping. The Spirits MC were mostly cast from the Scorpions out of Detroit, where the film was shot, and although not the greatest actors they have an authentic look. The music was by Michael Nesmith of The Monkees.

Sadistic policeman Puttnam (J. Craig Collicut) forms a vigilante group funded by a right-wing businessman to hunt down bikers, covering his tracks as a rapist by pinning the blame on the peaceful Spirits. Had it appeared a few years earlier, *Northville Cemetery Massacre* would have been a strong entry in the outlaw biker film cycle, with some serious thought behind it while maintaining its exploitation roots. By 1976, it was probably more relevant as an early slasher movie.

The last of the old school outlaws were finally well and truly reduced to parody in the form of the Black Widows MC in the popular Clint Eastwood action comedies *Every Which Way but Loose* (1978) and *Any Which Way You Can* (1980). The bikers – who look as if they really ought to start acting their age – are positively tortured by Eastwood and his pet orang-utan Clyde, who they are notionally pursuing, their outdatedness reinforced by a comedic doo-wop theme song. When one tries to evoke the image of the deadly spider to inspire terror, the answer is, 'Most people I know just step on 'em and squish 'em.' The long-suffering president Cholla (John Quade) is another Eric Von Zipper, even down to the catchphrase: 'Why me, Lord? Why me?'

Less parodic than wistfully affectionate, CBS' 1981 TV movie *Return of the Rebels* depicts the Brando generation more realistically, as respectable middle-aged citizens who haven't ridden a bike in years. The story feels like an *A-Team* plot. Widowed Mary Beth Allen (*I Dream of Jeannie*'s Barbara Eden) is struggling to support herself and her teenage daughter running a campsite on the Colorado River. The site has been adopted by a large group of party animals with monster trucks and jet skis led by the creepy K.C. Barnes (Patrick Swayze in a very early role), and are driving away all Mary Beth's regular customers. The police won't help, her bills are mounting, and K.C. is getting more predatory. In desperation, she reaches out to members of the motorcycle club she belonged to in the Fifties, the Eagle Rock Rebels, proposing a reunion but actually hoping they will scare off K.C. Led by divorced mechanic Sonny (Don Murray) and financed by now successful businessmen Jay (Christopher Connelly) and Big Al (*Soap*'s Robert Mandan), who are all a little sweet on Mary Beth, they manage to put some vintage Harleys together, dig out their leathers (which amazingly still fit), and head for the river. *M*A*S*H*'s Jamie Farr provides comic relief. The pace is gentle, and there's never really any doubt how things are going to turn out, recalling the great T-shirt slogan 'Never underestimate an old man with a motorcycle'.

Another light-hearted bikers-to-the-rescue movie is *Running Cool* (1993), co-written and co-directed by husband-and-wife team Beverley and Ferd Sebastion. Bone (*Lost*'s Andrew Divoff) and Bear (professional TV biker Bubba Baker) leave the Sturgis Motorcycle Rally to come to the aid of their buddy Ironbutt (James Gammon), whose home in the Carolina Wetlands is being threatened by evil property developers. Bone's an old soldier with a tragic past, but despite travelling light he seems to have an inexhaustible supply of sleeveless Harley T-shirts, which he shares with love interest Michele (Dedee Pfeiffer, younger sister of Michelle), who transforms from shrinking violet to sexy biker chick overnight. The story of a group of misfit friends raising money to save someone's home is as old as Ironbutt's Indian Chief, but it's diverting enough for a low-budget Nineties action comedy. Baker does the jokes, and though there's a lot of fist fights, no one ever gets really hurt. What's most interesting is

Wild Hogs (2007): William H. Macy, Tim Allen, Martin Lawrence, and John Travolta.

the way that the bikers are portrayed as honourable, likeable, and heroic, whereas local businessmen and law enforcement are corrupt, a reversal of the usual stereotype.

There's a similar reversal of roles in Thomas J. Wright's 1992 TV movie *Chrome Soldiers* starring Gary Busey and Yaphet Kotto, although the tone is much more sombre. The Chrome Soldiers are a group of veterans on Heritage Specials because, as Busey's Colonel Jim Gordon explains, 'The bike thing was a form of therapy after we came back from 'Nam.' In a similar set-up to *The Black Six* and *Chrome and Hot Leather*, when Gordon's older brother is killed in a mysterious accident, the club, who have not seen each other in years, ride down for his funeral. The indecent haste with which local law enforcement tries to run them out of town suggests foul play, and as the old friends dig deeper they discover a sinister conspiracy involving pillars of the local community. Again, the bike riders are the good guys while policemen and bankers are evil and crooked, although the frequent references to Operation Desert Storm and the patriotic portrayal of military service make this more a film about soldiers than bikers.

Busey and Kotto had previously worked together in Richard C. Sarafian's *Eye of the Tiger* (1986), a low-budget action-adventure in which Busey plays another Vietnam vet and (wrongly convicted) ex-con who takes on a drug-dealing biker gang led by William Smith, who have taken over his home town and murdered his wife while a bent sheriff looks the other way. Smith seems to be channelling Vernon

Cher and Sam Elliott in *Mask* (1985).

Wells in this one, sporting a Mohican haircut, riding a matt black dirt bike, and rarely speaking. Epitomising the madness of the Eighties action movie, *Eye of the Tiger* is not great art but it's a lot more fun than the rather plodding *Chrome Soldiers*. Busey's Buck Matthews becomes increasingly brutal as the film progresses, decapitating a biker with wire strung across a road, suffocating another in cocaine, and inventing the dynamite enema.

Simon Wincer's futuristic neo-western *Harley Davidson and The Marlboro Man* (1991) is another movie with the premise of hero bikers trying to save a friend's property from shady developers. Micky Rourke plays Harley Davidson to Don Johnson's Marlboro Man. Rourke rides a raked and rigid 1989 Harley FXR dubbed the Black Death, while Johnson's on a worn-out KZ 1000 that he eventually shoots. When they discover the bank is about to foreclose on their beloved Rock 'n' Roll Bar & Grille in Burbank, they come up with a plan to rob the bank and pay them off with their own money, a plan that goes horribly wrong when they instead rip off a consignment of the designer drug Crystal Dream that the bank's CEO is dealing.

Set in 1996, *Harley Davidson and The Marlboro Man* seems to anticipate later near-future sci-fi action movies like *Strange Days* and *Johnny Mnemonic*, but it bombed at the box office, blown out of the water by *Terminator 2: Judgement Day*, which had its own Harley-Davidson action going on. Like these movies, it was a major studio product (MGM) with a decent budget ($23 million). The film deliberately draws on *Butch Cassidy and the Sundance Kid*, with parallels such as Johnson being a crack shot while Rourke can't hit a barn door with a shovel, the lost love, a botched robbery, relentless pursuers (cyberpunk hitmen in bulletproof leather trench coats), and a jump off something high into water. Unfortunately, the plot is a mess, with a lacklustre resolution after a downbeat change of gear in which the mission moves from saving friends to avenging them. In 2016, on Alec Baldwin's *Here's the Thing* podcast, Rourke said of the movie: 'I remember doing this film and hating myself every day.'

Daniel Raskov's *Masters of Menace* (1990) is a screwball road movie built around a series of sketches and one-liners. Though not exactly a *Saturday Night Live* movie, it is also enlivened by cameos from Jim Belushi, John Candy, and Dan Aykroyd. David Rasche plays Buddy, the freewheelin' pres of the Road Masters MC who believes in his Constitutional 'right to raise hell'. When a judge puts the entire club under court supervision for three years, Buddy's old lady Kitty (*The Dukes of Hazzard*'s Catherine Bach) thinks this might be a good time to buy a house and settle down. The club's arch nemesis, meanwhile, Republican State Prosecutor Riley Hoover (Ray Baker), figures they won't last five minutes on probation and that he can finally lock them up. But when club member Gypsy (Jim Belushi) 'explodes himself' attempting the land speed record, what can his brothers do but take his corpse to his family in Vegas, partying all the way just like he would have wanted? When the club's young lawyer objects, biker Lazy Larry (John Hazelwood) looks at him over his shades and asks, 'Did you never see *The Wild One*?'

Though outlaw biker comedies are pretty thin on the ground, *Return of the Rebels*, *Running Cool* and *Masters of Menace* all preface Disney's biker movie *Wild Hogs* (2007), which is the one everybody remembers. Despite a budget of $60 million, the presence of such talent as John Travolta, Tim Allen, Martin Lawrence, William H. Macy, Marisa Tomei, Ray Liotta, and Peter Fonda, *Wild Hogs* is a horrible film. Though it looks great, there's just something mean spirited about it. Written by TV writer Brad Copeland (*Arrested Development*) and directed by motorcycle enthusiast Walt Becker, *Wild Hogs* deals with the worst of the Harley-riding clichés: the midlife crisis.

Middle-aged, middle-class friends Woody (Travolta), Doug (Allen) – both on Fatboys – Bobby (Lawrence, on a gorgeous FXSTS Springer Softail), and Dudley (Macy, Sportster) call themselves the Wild Hogs. Facing another boring weekend ride, Woody convinces the group to go on a run to the west coast. This sets up a series of slapstick adventures centred around a run-in with the 'real deal', the Del Fuegos MC ('From the fire' in Spanish) led by Jack Blade (Liotta), who says what we're all thinking: 'The joke is suburban assholes who buy leather outfits who think they're bikers.' This rant is the heart of the film, raising the issue of *authenticity*.

It's an interesting subcultural point, but Copeland and Becker make it very one-sided. The Wild Hogs are the heroes, despite having very little to recommend them. They're all classist, sexist, and hysterically homophobic. They look down on the Del Fuegos, mess with their bikes, and destroy their home; they view their wives as harridans and their families as an inconvenience, and their horror of a gay motorcycle cop is a running gag throughout the movie. Dudley is a menace on a motorcycle, constantly crashing because he isn't paying attention, then jumping back on unharmed like a character in a cartoon. In short, I'm with the Del Fuegos, although they're all lazy stereotypes too. The moral of the story seems to be that the Wild Hogs become the 'real' bikers by standing up to the Del Fuegos, while the Del Fuegos become 'posers' by turning into bullies. Peter Fonda delivers the benediction, so it must be true. But that doesn't work either. There are all sorts of motorcyclists. And whether you're a weekend warrior or a hardcore streetfighter, as *Freebird* teaches us, the point of bikes is to have *fun*. *Wild Hogs* turns it into a competition and then lets the rich urban bikers win.

Speaking of authenticity, after years of negative stereotyping and beset by a RICO trial (Racketeer Influenced and Corrupt Organizations), the Hells Angels finally decided to make a 'real motorcycle movie' to 'tell their own story their own way'. The result was the feature-length documentary *Hells Angels Forever* (1983), a failed exercise in public relations but a fascinating insight into the club in the days when many of the original members were still active. New York Chapter pres Sandy Alexander (who appeared in *Bronx Warriors*) had been collecting footage since the Seventies,

Lance Henriksen contemplates his life choices in *Savage Dawn* (1985).

but the film came together when The Grateful Dead's Jerry Garcia fronted much of the budget and documentary film-maker Richard Chase came on board to knock it into shape.

Narrated by character actor Morgan Paull (Holden in *Bladerunner*), *Hells Angels Forever* opens with a long (177-word) title card that amounts to a defensive libertarian manifesto decrying media misinformation and police harassment, and celebrating the outlaw life of brotherhood and freedom. There is then a brief prologue covering the post-war origins of the club, Hollister, and *The Wild One*, before the credits roll over a huge run comprising literally hundreds of riders on impressive custom chops. Chase uses original and news archive footage, and interviews with members, mamas and old ladies, supporters, lawyers, police, and a handful of detractors. The film covers the roughly ten-year period between Barger's imprisonment in the early Seventies and the campaign for his release, and the failed RICO trials, which act as a framing narrative. The Angel lifestyle is depicted through episodes that include runs, concerts and parties, families and relationships, core values, accusations of racism, and violence. There's even a wedding and a funeral. There are several musical numbers from Angel events, most notably by Jerry Garcia, Bo Diddley, and Willie Nelson. Some talking heads are natural philosophers and raconteurs, others are downright terrifying. Like many documentaries, to be fair, there's a definite bias; legal action is always presented as harassment, Barger is a 'political prisoner', and acts of violence are always 'self-defence'.

But it all ultimately fails to convince. Instead of coming across as misunderstood folk heroes, the Angels repeatedly betray their true selves every time they speak. They can't help it. Every anecdote ends with violence, and they are repeatedly shown armed; fervent denials of racism are littered with racial slurs, and attitudes to women are sexist and misogynistic. What comes over most is a sense of the true outlaw: not some romanticised version, but people who genuinely believe the law does not apply to them and that 'freedom' simply means not doing anything they don't want to. Even Jerry Garcia, the film's producer, can't stay on message. When asked if he's afraid of them, he replies, 'Yeah. They're scary, man ... They're really good in all the violent spaces.'

A much more sympathetic take on outlaw culture can be found in Peter Bogdanovich's *Mask* (1985), based on the life of Roy Lee 'Rocky' Dennis (1961–78), who suffered from *Craniodiaphyseal dysplasia*, an extremely rare and horribly disfiguring bone disorder. Rocky grew up around the LA biker scene, to which his mother, Florence 'Rusty' Tullis, belonged.

The Turks MC are Rocky's extended family, nurturing and protective, and a community in which he is unconditionally accepted. *Mask* is heartbreaking and uplifting in roughly equal measure, as the highly intelligent and doomed dreamer Rocky (Eric Stoltz) negotiates daily prejudice based on his appearance with almost relentless positivity, and experiences first love with a blind girl, Diana (played by Laura Dern). 'Why don't you take off your mask?' is a frequent insult as well as a symbol for the defences and affectations people use to disguise their true selves. He dreams of riding a Harley across Europe, as family friend Gar (Sam Elliott) had done when he was young.

Screenwriter Anna Hamilton Phelan (*Girl, Interrupted*) strips Rocky's story down to its essence, conflating and fictionalising real-life events to fit them into his final year, with a focus on character. The real Rusty Tullis was surprised at how central she had become to the story, in a deeply moving performance by Cher. *Mask* is about Rocky *and* the rebellious, determined, vulnerable, and deeply flawed Rusty. Elliott, meanwhile, is excellent in support as Rocky's father figure and the only man Rusty ever truly loved. Bogdanovich was looking for 'Gary Cooper on a motorcycle', which is exactly what he got.

James Bryan's *Hell Riders* (1984) returns to the small-town takeover stereotype. Its only claim to fame is the presence of *Batman* star Adam West as the doctor who opposes the bikers and *Gilligan's Island*'s Tina Louise as the woman he saves. Reputedly shot at a western-themed strip mall, Louise

Brian Bosworth in *Stone Cold* (1991).

and West only worked for a day, their parts filmed mostly in close-up then intercut into scenes utilising body doubles. Exploitation queen Renee Harmon co-wrote and acted in the film, while most of the cast were her film students. Also released in 1984, writer-director Frank Roach's *Nomad Riders* is equally clunky. In a predictable revenge plot that foreshadows Steve Austin's much better *Recoil*, Tony Laschi plays a tough cop who's out for revenge against the bikers that murdered his family and the gangsters that gave the order, accompanied by a jaunty Eighties synth-pop soundtrack by Rob Walsh.

The cast of *Savage Dawn* (1985) alone should have made it brilliant: Lance Henriksen, George Kennedy, Richard Lynch, William Forsythe, and Karen Black. Instead, it's a disaster from start to finish. Former Green Beret Stryker (Henriksen) rides into the desert mining town of Aqua Dulce on a Suzuki GS 1000 to visit his old army buddy Tick Rand (Kennedy). The paraplegic Rand and his teenage kids are trying to reopen a gold mine to bring hope to the dying town, which has unfortunately just been adopted by cliché-ridden biker gang the Savages, led by Forsythe's Guzzi-riding Pigiron. Stryker is sick of battle and looking for absolution, but we all know that eventually the Savages will push him over the edge.

Belgian-born director Simon Nuchtern was a low-budget indie grifter who among other things re-edited and dubbed foreign films for the grindhouse market, most notably the notorious Argentinian film *Snuff* (1976). Co-writer Bill Milling mostly did softcore, while writing partner Max Bloom was a cameraman. None of this team seem to have any idea how to structure a movie. There's a catfight between Karen Black and Claudia Udy that goes on forever, corrupt preacher Lynch is seduced and blackmailed for no adequately explored reason, and Black ultimately manages to run herself over with a tank. Henriksen has described this as the worst film he ever made.

The Last Riders (1991) is another dog's breakfast starring Erik Estrada – Ponch from the TV crime series *CHiPs* – and a rather frail-looking William Smith. Estrada plays Johnny, an original member of the Slaves MC who gives up his colours in a familiar plot device in which an outlaw goes off on his own to start a new life and it all goes horribly wrong. Syria-born director Joseph Merhi made a series of straight-to-video action movies for his PM Entertainment Group in the Eighties and Nineties but *The Last Riders* is not one of his best. The film starts promisingly with bikini-wearing former female wrestler Mimi Lesseos beating up two Slaves but it's all downhill from here as the film shifts gear to become an interminable love story in which snooty single mother Anna (Kathrin Middleton) succumbs to Johnny's charms after initially hating him, only to be murdered by the Slaves who mistakenly believe he's ratted them out. Johnny then goes after the club and the bent cop who set him up, only most of this happens in montage, absurdly accelerating what should have been the main storyline.

Estrada would later appear in cameo in Dax Shepard's ghastly 2017 film version of *CHiPs*, a $25 million box office bomb for Warner Bros. in which Michael Peña plays Ponch as a sex addict who has to stop and masturbate in public toilets every time he sees a cute girl – a running gag that makes the gay jokes in *Wild Hogs* seem almost tasteful. For a much better motorcycle cop drama, try Fred M. Wilcox's *Code Two* starring Ralph Meeker (MGM, 1953).

The police are better represented in two underrated and very different undercover cop movies. Even by contemporary action movie standards, the climax of Craig R. Baxley's *Stone Cold* (1991) is insane, as outlaw bikers attack the Mississippi State Capital building to spring a brother on a murder rap and assassinate the District Attorney and the Supreme Court, shouting 'First the Courthouse, then the White House!' The title suggests a remake of *Stone*, but aside from the basic premise there's no similarity. In a role originally offered to Arnold Schwarzenegger, the colourful Seattle Seahawks' linebacker Brian Bosworth plays a motorcycle-riding Alabama cop on suspension for insubordination who is tasked by the FBI with infiltrating the outlaw club the Brotherhood, drug traffickers and arms

Charlie Sheen and Michael Madsen in *Beyond the Law* (1993).

dealers with links to the Mafia. He gets close the club president Chains (Lance Henriksen), much to the chagrin of his suspicious sergeant-at-arms Ice (William Forsythe), the actors reunited from *Savage Dawn.* Henriksen is clearly enjoying playing the villain, delivering lines like: 'At moments like this I think of my father's last words: "Don't son, that gun is loaded!"'

Though the bikers default back to the barbarian model, *Stone Cold* is still a diamond in the rough. Bosworth's a bit wooden, but no more than Dolph Lundgren or Schwarzenegger when they were starting out. The film also had a respectable budget of $25 million and was released by Columbia. It's well-paced, it delivers on the action, and there's a nice undercurrent of gallows humour. Alas, *Stone Cold* was a commercial flop, with poor reviews focusing on Bosworth's performance, probably influenced by his bad NFL rep rather than the actual movie.

Though sharing its core premise with *Stone Cold, Highlander* screenwriter Larry Ferguson's directorial debut *Beyond the Law* (1993) is a much more serious drama. Based on the true story of 'Undercover Angel' Dan Black, a narcotics agent who spent two and a half years in deep cover with outlaw bikers in northern California, *Beyond the Law* explores the common theme of the undercover cop's divided loyalties and loss of identity. Black acted as an advisor and appeared as an extra in the movie. Charlie Sheen plays Dan Saxon, an undercover policeman of Native American heritage suffering from the unresolved trauma of an abusive childhood that has made him empathetic but also wary of authority and tormented by nightmares. Ferguson is interested in the battle for Dan's soul, which he allegorises through an old Indian fable about a man who loses his shadow and must face Death to retrieve it, and, oddly, Classical and Renaissance literature. The film opens with a quotation from the *Aeneid* and the mechanic who teaches Dan to become a biker is called Virgil (Leon Rippy), mirroring Dante's guide through the *Inferno.* Death is represented by the president of the Jackals MC, Blood, a powerful performance from Michael Madsen just before his breakout role in *Reservoir Dogs*.

Dealing drugs and arms and raising hell, the Jackals are similar to *Stone Cold*'s Brotherhood in being presented as a criminal organisation, though they're depicted much more realistically. Madsen is excellent as the intelligent, violent, yet almost noble leader, though Sheen never really looks the part. Overall this is a good crime thriller as well as a biker movie, although it feels overloaded with symbolism. Though made in 1990, distribution problems kept the film on the shelf for almost three years, until it was eventually released quietly on late-night cable. With an $18 million budget and some solid actors, had it been shown in cinemas to capitalise on *Point Break* or *Reservoir Dogs* it might have done quite well.

Michael Madsen and Quentin Tarantino were also instrumental in bringing Larry Bishop's *Hell Ride* (2008) to the screen. This was not a Grindhouse copy so much as a genuine attempt to recreate a true AIP-style biker movie, casting veteran genre actors Dennis Hopper, David Carradine and Bishop himself, who also wrote and directed, alongside more contemporary actors Madsen, Eric Balfour (*24*), and British footballing legend Vinnie Jones. Quentin Tarantino was a fan of Bishop's exploitation films, and the two men met through mutual friend and actor Laura Cayouette. Tarantino gave Bishop a part in *Kill Bill: Volume 2*, where he befriended Madsen. The legend, as repeatedly told by Bishop, is that after Tarantino invited him to his house to watch *The Savage Seven* together, he told him it was his 'destiny' to make the best biker movie ever, which Tarantino would produce. Bishop wrote the script and the film was released by Dimension under the banner 'Quentin Tarantino Presents'. Bishop wrote the role of the tuxedo-wearing Gent specifically for Madsen.

There is more style than substance to *Hell Ride*, but it looks and sounds great, Daniele Luppi's moody neo-western soundtrack seamlessly blending with original music from *The Wild Angels*, *Devil's Angels*, *Hell's Belles*, *The Savage Seven*, and *The Hard Ride*. There's a similar attention to detail with the bikes. Motorcycle consultant Justin Kell built these around the characters, so the Gent's ride is an *Easy Rider*-style chopper, while Bishop's pres Pistolero rides a bobbed Seventies shovelhead that looks as if it's gone around the world, and Hopper's Eddie Zero rides an immaculate post-war Indian Chief sidecar outfit. Balfour's Comanche was inspired by Eddie's Indian as a kid, but he rides a ratty unrestored one, a real Forties bobber like something out of the Hollister photographs.

The influence of Tarantino is obvious, particularly *Kill Bill*, in the non-linear narrative and drip-fed secrets from the past. There's also the stylised and often very funny dialogue. Visually, however, Bishop is much more inspired by the films of Sergio Leone, with a lot of lens flair, intense close-ups, and enigmatic desert scenes. Viewing the genre as one of primitive violence and sexuality, he's also taken the brutality and eroticism to places that the Sixties biker movies couldn't go, probably too far in the latter case, Pistolero winning the 2008 Women Film Critics' Circle Award for 'Most Offensive Male Character'.

Hell Ride's premise is relatively straightforward, but Bishop convolutes it with flashbacks, hallucinations, and MacGuffins. At heart, it's about Pistolero, the president of the Victors MC,

Michael Madsen, Larry Bishop, and Eric Balfour in *Hell Ride* (2008).

keeping a promise he made to a long-dead woman he loved, and finally avenging her. This has been precipitated by the return of the Victor's arch-rivals the Six-Six-Sixers MC, who had disbanded after the disappearance of their president Deuce (Carradine) in 1976. Now Deuce's right-hand man Billy Wings (Jones) is back, killing Victors who are loyal to Pistolero and recruiting those who aren't.

Bishop's previous outing as a writer/actor/director had been the 1996 ensemble crime comedy *Mad Dog Time*, which had a fantastic cast but was described by *Entertainment Weekly* as 'jaw-droppingly incoherent', and a similar criticism could be levelled at *Hell Ride*. For Bishop, *Hell Ride* is fundamentally a character study. He and Tarantino were fascinated by the almost schizophrenic moral ambiguity Adam Roarke had brought to *The Savage Seven*. He has also said, 'I like the psychopathology of the John Wayne character in *The Searchers*,' and that he wanted Pistolero to 'go further than a normal mind would go regarding vengeance'.

Hell Ride was not a critical or commercial success, and has now been largely forgotten. Like *The Last Riders*, the pace is terrible; you spend much of the movie waiting for it to start and then it's over. Sometimes Bishop tries to copy Tarantino too much and you find yourself wishing he'd trust his own instincts more, and had Tarantino actually made the movie it would be better. But this is a very high bar, and maybe not the right one, even if the selling point is Tarantino's name over the title. The true yardsticks are Bishop's AIP biker movies, and measured by these *Hell Ride* is glorious. And, as he told Brian Gallagher of *MovieWeb*: 'The thing with the motorcycle movie, it's psychopathic in a sense that it's not interested in what anybody thinks about it ... It's almost like a motorcycle gang in real life. It's not looking for your approval. It's just a take it or leave it.'

Staying in the grindhouse, if *Hell Ride* is Tarantino-inspired, Joseph Guzman's *Nude Nuns with Big Guns* (2010) takes its lead from Robert Rodriguez right down to stealing the theme music from *Planet Terror*. Released the same year as Rodriguez's *Machete* but made for a tenth of the budget, *Nude Nuns with Big Guns* is a film that stays true to its title, indicating that, like Rodriguez, Guzman is working through a lot of religious issues. Like Guzman's previous film *Run! Bitch Run!*, this is a retro rape and retribution story looking back to the nunsploitation films of the early Seventies, although stylistically it's much more like an Italian western.

Asun Ortega plays Sister Sarah, a young nun who learns after her final vows that the Church is a drug cartel working with outlaw motorcycle club Los Muertos (literally 'The Dead'), who act as enforcers and distributors. Given to Los Muertos by her priest, she is drugged and put to work in one of their brothels. After overdosing, God tells her to become an instrument of His vengeance, and the Los Muertos doctor that saves her gifts her a brace of silver-plated Colt .45s.

David Castro steals the show as Chavo, the Sportster-riding president of Los Muertos, whose bottom rocker reads 'Dondequiera', which is Spanish for 'Wherever'. Chavo recalls the bandit king El Indio (played by the great Gian Maria Volonté) in Leone's *For a Few Dollars More* – charismatic, charming, and completely psychotic, in a way that makes him almost likeable. He also gets all the best lines: 'There's a vigilante on the streets going around killing all the bad guys. And in case you forgot, we are the bad guys!'

Based on a short film of the same name, *Nude Nuns with Big Guns* is not for the easily offended, even by exploitation movie standards, moving beyond the objectification of women that made *Hell Ride* overly and needlessly sleazy into repeated scenes of sexual violence. In the same camp as Meir Zarchi's notorious *I Spit on Your Grave* and Abel Ferrara's *Ms .45*, there are equally strong arguments for denouncing Guzman's film as a rape fantasy dressed up as a film about female empowerment or applauding it as an ultimately feminist or even LGBTQIA+ movie, as gay lovers Sarah and Sister Angelina (Aycil Yeltan, the star of the original short film) triumph over the corrupt patriarchy of the

Asun Ortega in *Nude Nuns with Big Guns* (2010).

Church and Los Muertos. You pays your money and you takes your choice, but don't expect a film with a title like this to be subtle.

Drug dealing outlaw bikers were also the antagonists in Terry Miles' *Recoil* (2011), a straight-to-video action vehicle for retired professional wrestler 'Stone Cold' Steve Austin. Machete himself Danny Trejo plays the president of the Circle MC, Drayke Salgado, who have taken over the town of Hope in Washington State, which he runs like his feudal fiefdom, the sheriff having 'compromised' with him to keep the town safe. Austin's the vigilante ex-cop in the black '68 Plymouth GTX who rolls into town looking for a rapist who turns out to be Drayke's brother. Could there be a connection between the Circle and the 'biker turf war' that killed his family years before?

Recoil was shot in British Columbia and it has a cold, grey, wet look that makes it noirish and atmospheric, while the violence lacks the sensation normally associated with this genre, making this one of Austin's better movies. There are parallels to be drawn here with the Punisher, the Marvel anti-hero waging a one-man war on crime after the murder of his family. Dolph Lundgren portrayed the

Dolph Lundgren in *The Punisher* (1989).

character in the 1989 Australian-US movie of the same name, riding a wonderfully battered 1974 shovelhead Super Glide.

The outlaw biker had moved to television in 2008 with FX's award-winning and critically acclaimed *Sons of Anarchy* created by Kurt Sutter. The series would run through seven seasons to 2014, and was followed by the five-season spin-off *Mayans M.C.* (2018–23), also created by Sutter. Essentially *The Sopranos* on motorbikes, the genius of *Sons of Anarchy* was that it was loosely based on *Hamlet*. The throne of Denmark thus becomes the motorcycle club – a complex criminal organisation funded by gun running – and instead of being visited by his father's ghost, hero Jax Teller (Charlie Hunnam) finds a manuscript written by his dead dad laying out his original philosophy for the club. As the series progresses, Jax begins to realise that his father may have been offed by his mother (Katey Sagal) and her now husband and club president Clay (Ron Perlman), mirroring Shakespeare's Gertrude and Claudius, but is torn by indecision and divided loyalties. *Mayans M.C.* was less Shakespearean, but continued to explore *Sons of Anarchy*'s themes of brotherhood, loyalty, betrayal, and redemption. Former Hells Angel David Labrava was technical adviser, and Sonny Barger had a cameo. Sutter's epic delivers a levels of drama and authenticity that puts almost all biker movies to shame.

Another Shakespearean biker project unsurprisingly followed. Michael Almereyda's *Cymbeline* (2014) reunited the director with Ethan Hawke, who had also starred in Almereyda's contemporary version of *Hamlet*. Like the previous film, *Cymbeline* uses the original text of the play but in a modern setting, making

Ron Perlman in a promo shot for *Sons of Anarchy* (2008–2014).

Ed Harris' King Cymbeline the president of the Britons MC and the Romans the Police Department. That David Rooney of *The Hollywood Reporter* could describe this as 'a mashup of *Sons of Anarchy* with *Game of Thrones*' can only suggest that he has never seen either. This is a poor Shakespeare adaptation and a worse biker movie, doubly so given that *Sons of Anarchy* had shown how well these elements could work together. The Britons just wear leather jackets; there was no attempt to design colours, and biker iconography is never integrated successfully. Motorcycles are represented mostly by engine noises and characters entering carrying crash helmets, aside from a brief shot of Cymbeline on a Heritage Softail Classic, a couple of Yamaha XJ 900s, and Imogen and Posthumus riding off on a Kawasaki ZRX. In order to fool unsuspecting moviegoers, *Cymbeline* was craftily retitled *Anarchy: Ride or Die*.

Not to be confused with Alan Taylor's 2008 TV movie *1%* – a forgotten *Sons of Anarchy* cash-in starring Donal Logue and Kim Dickens – Stephen McCallum's Australian film *1%* AKA *Outlaws* (2017) also has links to a TV show, but not *Sons of Anarchy*. *Bikie Wars: Brothers in Arms* was a six-part mini-series directed by Peter Andrikidis for Network Ten in Australia in 2012. Based on the 1989 book *Brothers in Arms* by Lindsay Simpson and Sandra Harvey, *Bikie Wars* dramatises the events leading up to the Milperra Massacre in 1984, a shoot-out in the Sydney suburb Milperra between members of the Comancheros MC and a breakaway group who had formed the first Australian chapter of the Banditos in which seven people were killed. Scriptwriters Greg Haddrick, Roger Simpson, and Jo Martino focused on the fatal relationship between William 'Jock' Ross (played by Matt Nable), founder and president of the Comancheros, and Anthony 'Snoddy' Spencer (Callan Mulvey), the president of the rival club. Ross had been a father figure to Spencer, who came from a broken home and desperately needed to *belong*. The souring of this friendship made for an intense tragedy about loyalty, betrayal, and guilt. Nable and Mulvey were brilliant, backed up by Susie Porter as Jock's wife Vanessa and Maeve Dermody as Snoddy's girlfriend Lee, both strong, resourceful women exerting a lot of power behind the thrones.

Matt Nable also wrote the screenplay for *1%*, which is also about a divided motorcycle club and the rivalry between two former friends. McCallum had won the prestigious Screenwest West Coast Visions award, which provided most of the funding. Nable plays the original president of the Copperheads MC, Knuck, while Ryan Corr is Paddo, the VP who has been running things for the three years Knuck's been in prison. Only now Knuck's coming out and reasserting his authority, unimpressed by Paddo's attempts to modernise the club. In a darkly comic scene, Knuck orders all the club hoodies designed by Paddo's girlfriend Katrina (*Fury Road*'s Abbey Lee) burned because, 'We're a one per cent club not a fucking netball team!'

Nable's script doesn't always come together, but there's some excellent character work. Paddo is fiercely protective of his self-destructive younger brother (Josh McConville), broken by childhood trauma. Knuck's old lady Hayley (a standout performance by Simone Kessell) is sick of playing second fiddle to Katrina, the Lady MacBeth figure, and is celebrating the return of her man, unaware that prison has fundamentally changed him. Nable plays Knuck like an even scarier version of Jock Ross, now tormented by inner demons he's not smart enough to handle. Enterprising distributers in Germany retitled the film *Brothers of Anarchy*.

And the moral of the story? In the biker movie, it always comes back to outlaws in the end. It may be 1 per cent against the 99 on the road, but on celluloid it will always be the other way round.

CHAPTER 10 FULL CIRCLE

THE BIKER MOVIE finally travels full circle with Jeff Nichols' *The Bikeriders* (2023), which returns to the style, ethos and influence of *The Wild One*, released seventy years earlier. Not since *The Loveless* has the golden age of the post-war American biker been so perfectly realised on screen. Beautifully shot in 35mm anamorphic by cinematographer Adam Stone, *The Bikeriders* brings authenticity, emotional depth and drama to a subculture rarely given such dignity in film.

The Bikeriders is mythic, elegiac, and ultimately tragic, but also charming, romantic and funny. Set episodically in Chicago between 1965 and 1973, *The Bikeriders* documents the rise and fall of the first

Benny (Austin Butler) waits to be arrested in *The Bikeriders* (2023).

Tom Hardy as Johnny in *The Bikeriders*.

generation of the Vandals, a motorcycle club loosely based on the Outlaws, the second largest MC in the world after the Hells Angels. The film takes its name and inspiration from the 1968 photobook by Danny Lyon, a pioneer of New Journalism, who, like Hunter S. Thompson and the Angels, rode with the club, taking pictures and conducting interviews. Writer-director Jeff Nichols uses Lyon's interviews as a framing device, weaving anecdotal accounts together as then student Lyon (played by Mike Faist) talks to various members of the club, most notably Kathy (British actress Jodie Comer), the wife of the free-spirited Benny (Austin Butler, reminding us of his smouldering and Oscar-nominated turn as Elvis in Baz Luhrman's 2022 biopic). It is Kathy's relationship with Benny that holds the narrative together, giving the choppy, non-linear plot its throughline, alongside the story of Benny's best friend Johnny (a brooding Tom Hardy), the founder and president of the original chapter. In their different ways, Kathy and Johnny both love Benny, and both want different things from him. Benny is therefore torn between the more conventional family life Kathy offers (she wants him to give up riding), and his loyalty to Johnny, who is grooming Benny as his successor. Nichols has described the film as 'a combination of two things – Danny Lyon's book and *Goodfellas*'.

With perfect cheekbones, great hair and a devil may care reckless streak, Benny is James Dean to the taciturn working-class nobility of Tom Hardy's Brando. And *The Bikeriders* is a film that pays its dues, namechecking both *The Wild One* and *Easy Rider*. Hardy's Johnny is inspired to found a riding club while watching *The Wild One* on TV, and Lyon's book reproduces the real Johnny Davis' scrapbook, containing *TV Guide* clippings from the film's premier on CBS. This gives us the essentially hyper-real nature of the biker tradition, the truth being that most of us came to the life by trying to emulate romantic depictions in the movies. On one hand, Johnny is a pioneer, like the Second World War veterans who founded the original US motorcycle clubs, but on the other he is already replicating a purely celluloid construction, a copy of a reality that never existed in the first place. The first half of the film is therefore a raucous celebration of the early days of the club and its ethos, as working-class

Austin Butler and Jodie Comer as Benny and Kathy in *The Bikeriders*.

misfits come together to form a family. As Johnny's second-in-command Brucie (Damon Herriman) tells Lyon, 'We don't belong nowhere else, so we belong together.'

It is in these early scenes that *The Bikeriders* shows its affinity with the low-budget biker movie, with a lot of hard riding and hard drinking, and the odd inter-club brawl, followed by more drinking, usually with the guys they've just been fighting. The anecdotal nature of Lyon's original book gives Nichols crisp dramatic vignettes such as the story of Benny running out of gas after a high-speed chase with the cops, only to coast to a halt and light a cigarette, waiting for his pursuers to catch up and arrest him. And in the context of the film narrative, this shows the freedom of spirit that seems to draw Johnny so much to Benny. Although Kathy explains, 'Johnny always loved Benny,' and confronts him directly at one point declaring, 'You can't have him, the club can't have him, he's mine,' Nichols is not suggesting anything as conventional as a physical love triangle. Johnny, for his growing sense of power, wants to be Benny. As Nichols told the *Guardian*: 'He covets him. He'd like to absorb him. I knew it wouldn't be overtly homosexual: that would over-simplify it. But there's something there.' And if he can't be Benny, he wants Benny to be him, taking over command of the club, a role Benny doesn't want, especially as things become darker – first in the 1969 section when events change Johnny from a benign patriarch to, effectively, a warlord, and finally in the film's violent climax in 1973.

Towards the end of his reign, in a scene in which Hardy does what he does best, elevating the dialogue of an ordinary, inarticulate working man to the poetic and profound, Johnny tells Kathy, 'Sometimes you put your whole life into a thing and it's still gonna do what it's gonna do.' Like *Sons of Anarchy*, *The Bikeriders* is very much about the corruption of a dream; with the idealised original family increasingly infiltrated by a new breed of ruthless, unboundaried street kids, and drug-addled, unstable Vietnam vets. (Kathy differentiates between the Fifties greaser 'beer drinkers' and the long-haired 'dope smokers'.) In the second half of the film, these disparate and antagonistic forces move towards their inevitable collision. As Nichols told Steven Richards in an interview for Harley-Davidson, this was the essence of Lyon's book that he was trying to catch: 'It isn't easy to explain, but to me it's the beauty and the romance of motorcycle clubs in contrast with the toxic, negative aspects of the culture – there's a tension there that is hard to capture.'

Structurally, *The Bikeriders* is incredibly elegant. For Nichols, what stood out in Lyon's book were the interviews with Kathy, a street smart, thoughtful, and often very funny working-class Chicago girl. He thus builds his film around these, having Kathy tell what would otherwise be a very male story, often setting up turning points in the club's history before Nichols dramatises them in tight flashbacks. There's a kind of visual and narrative *bricolage* to this technique that nonetheless results in a coherent and forward-moving plot, which at once also feels like a documentary, conveying a gritty authenticity. Jodie Comer (*Killing Eve*), is mesmerising as Kathy, holding her own against Hardy, whose acting style is very different. Their scenes together are electric, with Comer guarded, edgy, defiant and fast-talking while Hardy takes a silent age lighting a cigarette or pulling on a beer before mumbling a two- or three-word reply. Between them, Austin Butler's Benny is both Apollonian and Dionysian, the beautiful boy as destroyer, failing to reconcile the order and chaos within. There's also a nice turn from *The Walking Dead*'s Norman Reedus, a lifelong biker who here plays Funny Sonny, a Californian refugee who ends up paid by a movie theatre to promote *Easy Rider*.

Norman Reedus as Funny Sonny in *The Bikeriders*.

And the motorcycles match the quality of the cast. Stunt co-ordinator Jeff Milburn convinced the production team to use original bikes, not artfully disguised modern Harleys, telling *American Rider*: 'In the end, we went with real, old motorcycles and didn't cheat. It was a pain in the ass to keep that many older bikes running at the same time, but in the long run, it was well worth it.' Johnny, for example, rides a bobbed 1956 Hydra-Glyde, and the screen is awash with vintage Duo-Glides, Electra-Glides, and Sportsters, with Reedus on a chopped knucklehead with hand-change gears and suicide clutch. Dirt racing scenes also showcase some lovely British bikes. There are some gorgeous road shots of solo riders and packs, the period atmosphere supported by a banging contemporary soundtrack. In a particularly memorable scene, when Kathy first gets onto Benny's bike and they are joined by the rest of the club, roaring down a deserted expressway like medieval cavalry, 'Out in The Streets' by The Shangri-Las swells around them as Kathy falls for Benny.

Like one of those old westerns about the ranges being fenced in, *The Bikeriders* offers a stylised portrait of a lost world, playing on all the myths of freedom associated with motorcycling, and the way that such freedom is inevitably compromised. Though I misspent my youth in motorcycle clubs in the Eighties not the Sixties, I cannot deny a certain dewy-eyed nostalgia came over me in the cinema when I watched *The Bikeriders*, remembering what it felt like to belong to something like that, to be part of a community, to be so sure of your own identity. And I'm still doing it today, although more sedately, with an older and wiser crew. For all the mad, bad, and sometimes downright stupid biker movies I've watched over the years, *The Bikeriders* is the first to actually catch that feeling.

BIBLIOGRAPHY

Albright, Brian. *Wild Beyond Belief: Interviews with Exploitation Film-makers of the 1960s and 1970s.* London: McFarland & Company, Inc., 2008.

Barger, Ralph 'Sonny', with Keith and Kent Zimmerman. *Hell's Angel.* London: Fourth Estate, 2001.

Bernstein, Abbie. *The Art of Mad Max Fury Road.* London: Titan, 2015.

Brando, Marlon, with Robert Lindsey. *Brando: Songs My Mother Taught Me.* New York: Random House Inc, 1994.

Cohen, Stanley. *Folk Devils and Moral Panics: The Creation of the Mods and Rockers.* Oxford: Martin Robertson, 1980.

Corman, Roger, with Jim Jerome. *How I Made A Hundred Movies In Hollywood and Never Lost a Dime.* New York: DaCapo Press, 1998.

Farren, Mick. *The Black Leather Jacket.* London: Plexus, 1985.

Gagne, Paul R. *The Zombies That Ate Pittsburgh: The Films of George A. Romero.* New York: Dodd, Mead & Company, 1987.

Halliwell, Leslie. *Halliwell's Film Guide* (7th ed). London: Paladin, 1989.

Harris, Maz. *Bikers: Birth of a Modern Day Outlaw.* London: Faber and Faber, 1985.

Lyon, Danny. *The Bikeriders.* New York: Aperture, 2014.

Mathews, Tom Dewe. *Censored: The Story of Film Censorship in Britain.* London: Chatto & Windus, 1994.

Meadows, Peter. *To Be Someone.* London: Countdown, 2011.

Osgerby, Bill. *Biker: Truth and Myth.* Guilford, Ct: The Lyons Press, 2005.

Rooney, Frank. 'Cyclists Raid'. In Arthur Veno (ed). *Bikers.* London: Robinson, 2007.

Seate, Mike. *Two Wheels on Two Reels: A History of Biker Movies.* New Hampshire: Whitehorse Press, 2000.

Simpson, Lindsay, and Harvey, Sandra. *Brothers in Arms.* Crows Nest, New South Wales: Allen & Unwin, 1989.

Spoto, Donald. *Stanley Kramer, Film Maker.* New York: G.P. Putnam, 1978.

Stanfield, Peter. *Hoodlum Movies: Seriality and the Outlaw Biker Film Cycle, 1966–1972.* New Brunswick: Rutgers University Press, 2018.

Thompson, Hunter S. *Hell's Angels.* London: Penguin, 1967.

Weldon, Michael. *The Psychotronic Encyclopedia of Film.* New York: Ballantine Books, 1989.

Walker, Mick. *Café Racers of the 1960s.* Marlborough: The Crowood Press, 1994.

Wooley, John, and Price, Michael H. *The Big Book of Biker Flicks.* Tulsa: Hawk Publishing, 2005.

PICTURE CREDITS

All images provided under editorial licence by MovieStillsDB and picryl.

CHAPTER 1

Sherlock Jr (1924) – © Buster Keaton Productions.
The Wild One (1953) – © Stanley Kramer Productions.
Hell's Angels (1930) – © The Caddo Company.
Motorcycle Gang (1957) – © Golden State Productions.
Dragstrip Riot (1958) – © Transworld Productions.
Pajama Party (1964) – © Alta Vista Productions.
Scorpio Rising (1963) – © Puck Film Productions.

CHAPTER 2

The Black Rider (1954) – © Balblair Productions.
Some People (1962) – © Vic Film Productions.
The Damned (1963) – © Hammer Films.
The Leather Boys (1964) – © Raymond Stross Productions, Shout Factory!
Up the Junction (1968) – © BHE Films, Crasto.
Girl on a Motorcycle (1968) – © Arès Productions, Mid-Atlantic Film (Holdings), British Lion Film Corporation.

CHAPTER 3

Quadrophenia (1979) – © The Who Films, Polytel.
Brighton Rock (2010) – © StudioCanal, BBC Film, UK Film Council.
The Pebble and the Boy (2021) – © NOW Films.
The Fence (2022) – © Red Anchor Films, Zebrafish Media.

CHAPTER 4

The Great Escape (1963) – © The Mirisch Company, Alpha Productions.
Roustabout (1964) – © Wallis-Hazen.
Motorpsycho! (1965) – © Eve Productions, Harlequin Pictures.

The Wild Angels (1966) – © American International Pictures.
Hells Angels on Wheels (1967) – © Fanfare Films.
The Born Losers (1967) – © American International Pictures, F.P. Productions.
The Glory Stompers (1967) – © American International Pictures, Norman T. Herman Productions.
She-Devils on Wheels (1968) – © Mayflower Pictures.
The Mini-Skirt Mob (1968) – © American International Pictures.
Hell's Belles (1969) – © American International Pictures.
Satan's Sadists (1969) – © Independent-International Pictures.
Run, Angel, Run! (1969) – © Fanfare Films.
The Losers (1970) – © Fanfare Films.
Angel Unchained (1970) – © American International Pictures.
C.C. and Company (1970) – © Namanco Productions, Rogallan Productions.
Outlaw Riders (1971) – © Hawthorne Productions.
Angels Hard as They Come (1971) – © New World Pictures.
Chrome and Hot Leather (1971) – © American International Pictures.
Angels' Wild Women (1971) – © Independent-International Pictures.
The Dirt Gang (1972) – © American International Pictures.

CHAPTER 5

Easy Rider (1969) – © Pando Company Inc., Raybert Productions.
Electra Glide in Blue (1973) – © Guercio-Hitzig.
Roadside Prophets (1992) – © New Line Cinema, Swinson-Starkey Productions.

CHAPTER 6

No Limit (1935) – © Associated Talking Pictures.
Once a Jolly Swagman (1949) – © Wessex Film Productions.
Little Fauss and Big Halsey (1970) © Alfran Productions, Furie Productions, Paramount Pictures.
On Any Sunday (1971) – © Solar Productions.
Sidecar Racers (1975) – © Universal Pictures.
Silver Dream Racer (1980) – © The Rank Organisation.
Rollerball (1975) – © Algonquin, United Artists.
Rollerball (2002) – © Atlas Entertainment, Canada Film Capital, Helkon Media.
Evel Knievel (1971) – © The Fanfare Corporation.
The World's Fastest Indian (2005) – © OLC/Rights Entertainment, Tanlay, New Zealand Film Production Fund.
Spetters (1980) – © VSE Film.
Fast Charlie... The Moonbeam Rider (1979) – © Universal Pictures.
Harley and the Davidsons (2016) – © RAW.
Knightriders (1981) – © Laurel Productions.
Biker Boyz (2003) – © DreamWorks Pictures, 3 Arts Entertainment.
Torque (2004) – © Warner Bros., Village Roadshow Pictures, Original Film.
Burn Out (2017) – © 2425 Films, Wy Productions, Gaumont.
One Fast Move (2024) – © Gulfstream Pictures, Luber Roklin Entertainment.

CHAPTER 7

Tales from the Crypt (1972) – © Amicus Productions.
The Convent (2000) – © Alpine Pictures.
The Walking Dead (2010–2022) – © AMC, Circle Management + Production, Valhalla Motion Pictures.
Bigfoot (1971) – © Ellman Film Enterprises, Gemini-American Productions.
Werewolves on Wheels (1971) – © South Street Films.
Psychomania (1973) – © Benmar Productions.
Race with the Devil (1975) – © Saber Productions, Twentieth Century Fox.
What Have They Done To Your Daughters? (1974) – © Primex Italiana.
Nightmare Beach (1989) – © El Pico S.A., Laguna Films, Overseas FilmGroup.
The Lost Boys (1987) – © Warner Bros.
I Bought a Vampire Motorcycle (1990) – © Dirk Productions Ltd.
Ghost Rider (2007) – © Columbia Pictures, Crystal Sky Pictures, Relativity Media.
Ghost Rider: Spirit of Vengeance (2011) – © Columbia Pictures, Hyde Park Entertainment, Imagenation Abu Dhabi FZ.
The Texas Chainsaw Massacre: The Beginning (2006) – © New Line Cinema, Platinum Dunes, Next Entertainment, Vortex/Henkel/Hooper, Texas Chainsaw Productions.
Dear God No! (2011) – © Big World Pictures (II).

CHAPTER 8

Stone (1974) – © Hedon Productions.
Mad Max (1979) – © Kennedy Miller Productions, Mad Max Films, Soundfirm.
The Road Warrior (1981) – © Kennedy Miller Productions.
1990: The Bronx Warriors (1982) – © Deaf Internacional Film s.r.l.
Exterminators of the Year 3000 (1983) – © 2T Produzione Film, Globe Film.
2019, After the Fall of New York (1983) – © Nuova Dania Cinematografica, Medusa Distribuzione, Les Films du Griffon.
Endgame (1983) – © Filmirage.
The Atlantis Interceptors (1983) – © Regency Productions, Regal Films.
Rats: Night of Terror (1984) – © Beatrice Film.
Wheels of Fire (1985) – © Rodeo Productions.
Spacehunter: Adventures in the Forbidden Zone (1983) – © Columbia Pictures, Delphi I Productions, Zone Productions.
Waterworld (1995) – © Universal Pictures, Gordon Company, Davis Entertainment.
Resident Evil: Extinction (2007) – © Constantin Film, Capcom Company, Estudios Churubusco Azteca S.A.
Doomsday (2008) – © Rogue Pictures, Intrepid Pictures, Crystal Sky Pictures.
Priest (2011) – © Screen Gems, Michael De Luca Productions, Stars Road Entertainment.
Bounty Killer (2013) – © Just Chorizo Productions, Kickstart Productions.
Mad Max: Fury Road (2015) – © Warner Bros., Village Roadshow Pictures, Kennedy Miller Mitchell.
Furiosa: A Mad Max Saga (2024) – © Warner Bros., Domain Entertainment (II), Kennedy Miller Mitchell.

CHAPTER 9

The Loveless (1981) – © Pioneer Films.
Rumble Fish (1983) – © Zoetrope Studios, Hotweather Films.
Akira (1988) – © Akira Committee Company Ltd., Akira Studio, TMS Entertainment.
Cry Baby (1990) – © Universal Pictures, Imagine Entertainment.
Restless Natives (1985) – © EMI Films, The Oxford Film Company, Thorn EMI Screen Entertainment.
Eat the Peach (1986) – © The Irish Film Board, Channel Four Films, Strongbow.
The Courier (2019) – © Lionsgate, Grindstone Entertainment Group, Capstone Entertainment Group.
Freebird (2008) – © Freebird Films.
Harley Davidson and The Marlboro Man (1991) – © MGM, Krisjair, Laredo.
Wild Hogs (2007) – © Touchstone Pictures, Tollin/Robbins Productions, Wild Hogs Productions.
Mask (1985) – © Universal Pictures.
Savage Dawn (1985) – © Mag Enterprises.
Stone Cold (1991) – © Stone Group Pictures, Vision International.
Beyond the Law (1993) – © Polar Entertainment Corporation, Live Entertainment, Capitol Films.
Hell Ride (2008) – © Dimension Films.
Nude Nuns with Big Guns (2010) – © Freak Show Entertainment.
The Punisher (1989) – © New World Pictures, New World International.
Sons of Anarchy (2008–2014) – © SutterInk, Linson Entertainment, Fox 21.

CHAPTER 10

The Bikeriders (2023) – © Focus Features, Regency Enterprises, New Regency Productions.

INDEX

1% (*Outlaws*, 2017) 173
1990: The Bronx Warriors *129*, 130–131, *133*, 163
2019, After the Fall of New York 131, *132*
2020 Texas Gladiators 132–134
59 Club 29–30
77 Sunset Strip 18, 66

Ace Café 27, *28*
Adamson, Al 58, 63, 69, 72–73, 118, 120
Adventures of Priscilla, Queen of the Desert, The 71–72
Agostini, Giacomo 82
AJS 83
Akira 151
All Hell Breaks Loose 120–121
Altamont Free Concert 56, 60, 66, 70
American International Pictures (AIP) 15, 17, 19, 47–49, 51–52, 55–56, 59–60, 64–65, 67, 69, 71–75, 125, 152, 167, 169
American Motorcycle Association (AMA) 11, 84, 87, 95, 102
Amityville Horror, The 51
Angel Unchained 65–66
Angels Die Hard 63
Angels from Hell 45, 50, 56, 63, 66, 109
Angels Hard as They Come 69–71
Angels' Wild Women 72–73, 113
Anger, Kenneth 20–22, 58, 60, 77, 148–149
Ann-Margret 66, *67*
Any Which Way You Can 160
Aprilia 100, *101*
Ariel 19
Arkoff, Samuel Z. 15, 17, 48, 75, 97, 152
Atlantis Interceptors, The 133, *134*
Bad Batch, The 142–143
Band, Charles 116, 137
Barbeau, Adrienne *105*, 106
Barger, Ralph 'Sonny' 48–50, 60, 64, 75, 78, 164, 172
Batman 50, 158, 164
Battletruck 129
Baxter, Les 55–56
Beach Blanket Bingo 20
Beach Boys, The 44
Beach Party 19, 50, 75, 106
Beard, Elspeth 95
Beatles, The 29, 47–48
Being Evel 93
Bennett's War 101–102
Beyond the Law 167
Bigelow, Kathryn 22, 148–149, 115
Bigfoot (1970) 71, 106, *107*, 109, 115
Bigfoot 109, 119–121, 131
Biker Boyz 67, 99–100
Biker Zombies from Detroit 115
Bikeriders, The (1968) 21, 175, 177
Bikeriders, The (2023) 174–178
Bikie Wars: Brothers in Arms 173
Bikini Beach 20, 59
Bishop, Larry 53, 65, 71, 167–169
Bisley, Steve 124–125, *126*
Black Angels 66–67, 158
Black Rider, The 23–24
Black Six, The 158, 161
Blackboard Jungle 10, 15
Bladerunner 134, 158, 164
Blaxploitation 66–67, 71, 130, 158, 161
Blob, The 106, 116

Blood Freak 109, 115
Blow-Up 24
BMW 71, 95, 131, 137, 138, 142, 154, *155*
Bogarde, Dirk 84, *85*
Bogdanovich, Peter *47*, 48, 164
Bonet, Lisa 99
Bonner, William 55, 67, 69, 73
Book of Eli, The 138-139
Boon 116
Born Losers, The 50–53, 56, 67
Bōsōzoku 151
Bounty Killer 139, *143*
Boy and His Dog, A 128
Brando, Marlon 10, *12*, 13–15, 19–21, 44, 66, 160, 175
Brighton Rock 37, *39*
British Board of Film Classification 10
Brooks, Ray 24–25
Brough Superior 23
Brown Bunny, The 100–101
BSA 19, 23, *25*, 30, 35, 84, 86–87, 116
Bultaco 131
Burn Out 102
Bury Me an Angel 69
Busey, Gary 70, 152, 161–162
Butch Cassidy and the Sundance Kid 79, 87, 162
Butcher Brothers 118–119
Byrds, The 48, 77

C.C. and Company 66, *67*, 98
Campbell, Bruce 113, 136
Campbell, Joseph 128
Carradine, David 80, 92, 96, *97*, 167, 169
Carrol, Regina 58, 72, *73*
Cars That Ate Paris, The 123, 142
Cassavetes, John 48, 50
Castellari, Enzo G. 130–131
Centauro 102
Chaplin, Charlie 10, 83
Cherry 2000, 138, 143
Children of Light, The 26
CHiPs 166
Chopper Chicks in Zombie Town 113–114
Chrome and Hot Leather 71, 161
Chrome Soldiers 161–162
Cliver, Al 132, 134
Clockwork Orange, A 26
Code Two 166
Cohen, Stanley 34
Comer, Jodie 175, *176*, 177
Convent, The *105*, 106
Coppola, Francis Ford 78, 150, 152
Corman, Roger 17, 20, 44–45, *47*, 48–49, 52, 56, 58–59, 63, 69, 75, 92, 96, 118, 136–137
Courier, The (1988) 154
Courier, The (2019) 154, *155*, 156
Cramps, The 54
Crown International 51, 54, 59, 71
Cry Baby 151–152,
Curb, Mike 53, 58, 60
Cycle Psycho 45, 158
Cycle Savages, The 58, 60
Cymbeline 172–173

D'Amato, Joe 132, 136
Damned, The 26–27, 151
Daniels, Phil 34–35, *36*, 37, 156, *157*
Darktown Strutters 158
Davie Allan and the Arrows 48, 58
Dawn of the Dead (1978) 97, 106, 122
Dean, James 10, 15, 20, 51, 175
Dear God No! 119, *120*
Death Race 2000 (1975) 92, 99
Deathsport 92
Deep Throat 158
Delon, Alain 31, *32*
Demme, Jonathan 69–70
Dern, Bruce 48, 60, 63, 138
Dern, Laura 63, 164
Detour 149–149
Devil on Wheels, The 10
Devil's Angels 48–49, 53, 168
Dirt Gang, The 73, *74*, 148
Doctor Who 25
Donner, Clive 24–25
Doomsday 138, *141*
Dr Strangelove 27, 75

Dr. Goldfoot and the Bikini Machine 20
Dragstrip Girl 17–19, 152
Dragstrip Riot 17–18, *19*
Duke of Edinburgh Awards Scheme 24–26
Dunn, Nell 30
Dylan, Bob 77

Eastman, George 130–132
Easy Rider A.D. 81
Easy Rider 15, 49–50, 52, 56, 60, 63–65, 72, 75–79, 81, 87, 157, 168, 175, 177
Easy Rider: The Ride Back 80–81
Easy Wheels 113–114
Eat the Peach 153, *154*
Ekins, Bud 43, 66, 71
Electra Glide in Blue 79, *80*
Empire of Ash 138
Endgame 132, *133*, 134
Endless Summer, The 87
Equalizer 2000, 137
Escape from the Bronx 131
Essex, David 90
Evel Knievel (1971) 92, *94*
Evel Knievel (2004) 93
Every Which Way but Loose 160
Evil Dead, The 113, 115–116
Excelsior-J.A.P. *85*
Exterminators of the Year 3000 *130*, 131,
Eye of the Tiger 161–162

Faithfull, Marianne 31, *32*
Fanfare Films 49, 56, 59, 63–64, 72, 92, 109
Fast and the Furious, The 99–100
Faster 103
Faster, Pussycat! Kill! Kill! 44, 54
Fence, The *41*, 42
Final Executioner, The 134
Fishburne, Laurence 99
Fist of the North Star 138
Fonda, Peter *47*, 48, 75–78, 80–81, 110, 117, 163
Ford v Ferrari 82
Ford, John 75, 79
Formby, George 24, 83–84
Frankenstein Created Bikers *120*, 121
Freebird 156–157, 163
Freeman, Gillian 28
Friday the 13th Part III 127
Furie, Sidney J. 27–28, 87
Future World (2018) 143–144
Futureworld (1976) 144

Gallo, Vincent 100–101
Garwood, John 18, 50, 52
Gas Gas 142
Geretta, Geretta 132, 134, *135*
Ghost in the Invisible Bikini, The 20
Ghost Rider 116–117, 121
Ghost Rider: Spirit of Vengeance 117, *118*
Giallo 112–113, 134
Gibson, Mel *124*, 125, *127*, 128–129, 140, 142, 147
Gimme Shelter 60
Girl on a Motorcycle 31, *32*, 33
Glory Stompers, The 51, *52*, 58, 63, 69
God Speed You! Black Emperor 151
Goodfellas 175
Gothic 44, 109, 110, 116, 125, 129, 148
Great Escape, The 43, *44*
Griffith, Charles B. 47–48
Guevara, Che 95

Hagen, Ross 54–55, 59, 73
Haggerty, Dan 69, 71, 76, 78
Hailwood, Mike 83
Hamlet 172
Hammer Films 26, 27, 106, 110, 114
Harbutt, Sandy 122–123, 125
Hard Ride, The 67, 69, 168
Hardy, Tom 140, *144*, 147, *175*, 176, 177
Harley and the Davidsons 97, *98*
Harley Davidson and the Marlboro Man *159*, 162
Harley-Davidson 10, 14, 18, 20–21, 31, 33, 43, 48, 50, 53, 58, 64, 66, 69, 74, 79, 87, 90, 93, 95, 97, 100, 104, 106, 114–115, 117, 121, 123, 130, 139, 148–152, 160, 162–164, 177–178
Hatcher, Harley 58, 67
Hell Comes to Frog Town 138
Hell Ride 53, 167–169
Hell Riders 164, 166
Hell's Angels (1930) *13*, 45
Hell's Angels (1966) 10, 21

Hell's Angels '69 64–65
Hell's Belles 50, 56, *57*, 168
Hell's Bloody Devils 50, 63, 72
Hellcats, The 54, 59, 69, 106
Hells Angels Forever 60, 163-164
Hells Angels Motorcycle Club 13, 22, 24, 44–45, 47–48, *49*, 56, 60, 64, 75, 78, 109, 116, 122, 130, 163, 164, 175
Hells Angels on Wheels 18, 49–50, 52, 56, 64
Hells Chosen Few 54–55, 69, 158
Hemmings, David 24, *25*
Henriksen, Lance 93, *163*, 166–167
High Hopes 156
High Noon 51, 124
Hills Have Eyes, The 110, 121
Hinton, S.E. 150, 152
Hollister 10–11, 34, 164, 168
Honda 42–45, 55, 91, 95, 98–100, *106*, 112, 115–116, 132, 134, 138, 142, 153, 156
Hopper, Dennis 10, 51–52, 75–76, *77*, 78, 80–81, 138, *139*, 150, 167–168
Horror 15, 17, 50, 51, 54, 71, 104–121, 123, 134, 160
Hot Angel, The 19, 40
Hot Rod Girl 17
Hot Wax Zombies on Wheels 115
Hotchkiss, Avis and Effie 95
House of a 1000 Corpses 119
House of Un-American Activities Committee 26
How to Stuff a Wild Bikini 20
Huston, Tony 54, 59, 69

I Bought a Vampire Motorcycle 115–116
I Spit on Your Grave 169
I Was a Teenage Werewolf 17
Independent-International Pictures 58–59, 63, 69, 72–73, 118, 120
Indian 94, *95*, 97, 160, 168
Interzone 135–136
Invasion of the Saucer Men 17
Isle of Man TT 23, 82–83, 103
It's a Revolution Mother 60
Ivy, Bill 31, 82

Jailhouse Rock 17, 152
Jam, The 34, 37, 39
Jawa 135
Jeavons, Steph 95
Johnny Mnemonic 162
Juvenile delinquency 10, 15, 17, 19, 20, 26–27, 47, 115, 148, 152

Kasem, Casey 52, 58–60
Kawasaki 66, 102, 122–123, 125, 127, 130–131, 150, 157, 162, 173
Keaton, Buster 10, *11*
Keays-Byrne, Hugh 123–124, 138, 140, 147
Kendall, Suzy 30, *31*
Kidd, Eddie 93–94
Kill Bill 168
King Kong 18, 86, 106
Knievel, Evel 92–93, *94*, 98, 116–117
Knightriders 97–99
Kovács, László 49, 76
Kramer, Stanley 13–14, 48
KTM 131
Kuhn, Thomas 71
Kurosawa, Akira 52, 69, 129

Ladd, Diane 48, 63
Lambretta 30, 35, 37, 39
Last Riders, The 166, 169
Laughlin, Tom 51
Lawrence of Arabia 24, 145
Lawrence, T.E. 23
Le Mans 82, 138
Leather Boys, The 27–28, *29*, 72, 87
Leigh, Mike 42, 156
Lembeck, Harvey 19–20, *21*
Leone, Sergio 129, 130, 134, 148, 168–169
Lewis, Herschell Gordon 53–54
LGBTQIA+, 28, 71, 169
Little Fauss and Big Halsey *86*, 87
Little Shop of Horrors, The 47
Loach, Ken 30
Loners, The 72
Losers, The 18, 50, *62*, 64–65
Losey, Joseph 26–27
Lost Boys, The *114*, 115
Loveless, The 148–150, 174
LSD 47–48, 53, 58, 60, 75, 77, 122

Luke, Derek 99, *100*
Lynch Report 45
Lyon, Danny 21, 175–177

*M*A*S*H* 110, 160
Mabel at the Wheel 10
Mad Dog Time 169
Mad Max Beyond Thunderdome 135, 138, 144–145, 147
Mad Max 73, 88, 99, 117, 122–123, *124*, 125–127, 129–131, 136–138, 140, 144, 147
Mad Max: Fury Road 123, 135, 137–142, *144*, 145, 147–148
Mad Max: The Wasteland 147
Mad Warrior 136
Madsen, Michael 167–168
Magnificent Seven, The 66, 138
Man Who Knew Too Much, The 24
Manson, Charles 60, 73
Marvin, Lee 10, 14, *16*
Mask *162*, 164
Masters of Menace 162–163
Maxploitation 129–138
Mayans M.C. 172
McBain, Diane 55, 59
McQueen, Steve 43, *44*, 88, 96, 106, 138
Meadows, Peter 37
Meadows, Shane 39, 42
Merleau-Ponty, Maurice 157
Metalstorm: The Destruction of Jared-Syn 137
Meyer, Russ 44–45, 54
Miller, George 112, 123–125, 127–129, 135, 140–142, 144–145, 147
Mini-Skirt Mob, The 55–56, 59
Mizer, Bob 20
Modern Way, The 40, 42
Mods and Rockers 29–30
Mods 24, 27, 29–30, 33–35, *36*, 37, *38*, 39–40, 42, 45, 156
Money for Speed 24, 82–83
Monkees, The 76, 160
Montesa 131
Motocross 87, 89, 95, 101–102, 140
MotoGP 23, 31, 82, 84, 87, 90–91, 100, 102–103
Motorcycle Diaries, The 95
Motorcycle Gang (1957) 117–119, 152
Motorcycle Gang (1994) 152
Motorpsycho! 44–45, *46*, 47, 109
Ms .45 169
Munro, Burt 94, *95*
Murdercycle 116
Murphy, Mary 13, *14*,
Muscle Beach Party 20
Mystery Science Theatre 3000, 132

Naked Angels 59–60, 69
Namath, Joe 66, *67*
Necropolis 121
New Barbarians, The 131
New World Pictures 59, 63, 69, 72, 92, 136, 138, 158
Nicholson, Jack 49–50, 63, 75–76, 78, *79*
Night School 112
Nightmare Beach 112, *113*, 115
No Limit 24, 83–84, 87
Nomad Riders 166
Northville Cemetery Massacre 160
Norton 28, 31, 56, 83, 95, 104, 112, 115, 147
Nude Nuns with Big Guns 169, *170*
Nunsploitation 134, 169, *170*

Occult 58, 109, *110*, 112, 116
Oliver, Stephen 45, 109, 158
On Any Sunday 87–88
On the Waterfront 15
Once a Jolly Swagman 24, 84, *85*
One Fast Move 102–103
Outlaw Riders *68*, 69, 106

Pace That Thrills, The 84, 86
Pajama Party 20, *21*
Parks, Michael 79, 89, 113
Pebble and the Boy, The 37, 39, *40*
Peckinpah, Sam 63, 125, 129
Peeters, Barbara 69
Phillips, Stu 50, 56, 63
Pink Angels, The 71–72
Poor White Trash 50–51
Post-apocalypse 73, 81, 92, 122–147
Presley, Elvis 10, 15, 18, 19, 20, 43, 44, *45*, 54, 68, 117, 175

Psychomania 109–110, *111*, 115
Psych-Out 52
Punisher, The (1989) 171
Punk 33–34, 42–43, 79, 115, 121–122, 127, 129, 133, 138, 145, 151, 156

Quadrophenia 15, 29, 33–35, *36*, 37, *38*, 39–40, 42, 157

Race for Glory 90–91
Race with the Devil 50, 98, 110, 112
Rage 133–134
Rainey, Wayne 82, 103
Rambo: First Blood Part II 62, 64, 133
Rats: Night of Terror 134, *135*
Read, Phil 82
Rebel Rousers, The 63
Rebel Without a Cause 10, 15, 17, 118, 150, 152
Recoil 166, 171
Redford, Robert *86*, 87
Reed, Oliver 26
Reedus, Norman *106*, 177–178
Resident Evil: Extinction 138, *140*
Restless Natives 153,
Return of the Rebels 160, 163
Revenge tragedy 45, 74, 124, 144
RICO 163–164
Riddley Walker 126
Riding High 93–94
Road of Death 158
Road Warrior, The (*Mad Max 2*) 15, 62, 64, 73, 112, 122, 125–126, *127*, *128*, 129–130, 133, 136, 138, 140–141, 143–145, 147–148
Road Wars: Max Fury 147
Road, The 138–140
Roadside Prophets 79–80, *81*
Roarke, Adam 49–50, 52–53, 56, *57*, 64
Roberts, Kenny 82
Rock Around the Clock 10
Rockers 10, 23–30, 34–35, 37, 45, 129, 151
Rodriguez, Robert 119, 141, 152, 169
Roger Wonders Why 30
Rollerball (1975) 91–92, 97–99, 134
Rollerball (2002) 92, *93*
Romeo and Juliet 11, 29, 152
Romero, George A. 97, 98, 106, 122
Rooney, Frank 11, 13
Rossi, Valentino 82, 103
Rourke, Micky 150, *159*, 162
Roustabout 43, *45*, 153–154
Royal Alloy 39
Royal Enfield 29, 142
Rumble Fish 150–151
Run, Angel, Run! 50, *61*, 63–65
Running Cool 160, 163
Rush (1983) 133–134
Rush (2013) 82
Rush, Richard 49–50, 52

Salute of the Jugger, The 138
Santiago, Cirio H. 136–138
Satan's Sadists 58–59, 63, 119
Satanic Rites of Dracula, The 106
Saturday Night and Sunday Morning 24
Savage Dawn *163*, 166–167
Savage Seven, The 18, 50, 52–53, 56, 168–169
Savages from Hell 51
Scharf, Sabrina 49–50, 76
Schott 14–15, 17, 20, 149
Schwantz, Kevin 82, 103
Schwarzenegger, Arnold 132, 166–167
Scorpio Rising 20–22, 28, 60, 77, 148–149
Scorsese, Martin 22, 78
Scream Free! 58–60, 69
Searchers, The 139–140, 169
Sergeant Bilko (*The Phil Silvers Show*) 10, 20
Seven Samurai, The 52, 132
Sex Pistols, The 34
Shakespeare, William 11, 29, 84, 124, 152, 172–173
Shane 51, 80, 126, 138
Shangri-Las, The 178
Shanty Tramp 50, 59, 69
She Devils on Wheels 53–54, 113
Sheene, Barry 82, 103
Sherlock Jr 10, *11*
She-Wolves of the Wasteland 138
Sidecar Racers 88, *89*
Sidecars 20, 59, 69, 71, 87–89, 95, 142, 168
Sidehackers, The 59
Sidewinder 1 89–90

Silver Dream Racer 90, 93
Sinatra, Nancy 20, 48
Sinner's Blood 59
Sirk, Douglas 148, 151
Slasher movies 58, 110, 112, 118–119, 121, 127, 134, 148, 160
Slate, Jeremy 51, 56, 64
Smith, William 63–64, 66, *71*, 138, 161, 166
Solomon, Joe 49, 56, 59, 64, 69, 109
Some People 24–26, 28
Sons of Anarchy 172–173, 176
Sorority Girl 17
Southern, Terry 75–78
Spacehunter: Adventures in the Forbidden Zone 137
Speedway 24, 82–84, 91, 92, 100
Spetters 95–96
Stanton, Harry Dean 54, 56, 63
Star Trek 56, 131
Starrett, Jack 49–50, 56, 63, 64, 76, 112
Steel Dawn 138
Stone 88, 122–123, 147, 166
Stone Cold *165*, 166–167
Strange Days 162
Streets of Fire 150–151
Stroud, Don 65–66
Stryker 136–137
Survival Zone 129–130
Sutton, Dudley 28, *29*
Suzuki 99, 127, 129, 133, 153, 157, 166
SWM 131

Tales from the Crypt (1972) 104
Tamblyn, Russ 58, *59*
Tank Girl 138
Tarantino, Quentin 119, 167–169
Taste of Honey, A 24
Tate-LaBianca murders 60, 70
Taylor-Joy, Anya 146, 147
Teddy boys 10, 24
Tenold, Brandon 131
Terminator 2: Judgement Day 98, 162
Tessier, Robert 52, 69
Texas Chainsaw Massacre, The 110, 119
Texas Chainsaw Massacre: The Beginning, The *119*, 121
Then Came Bronson 79, 89
Theron, Charlize 140, 145, 147
They Saved Hitler's Brain 17
This is England 39–40, 42
Thompson, Hunter S. 10, 13, 15, 45, 121, 175
To Be Someone 37, 39
Tormentors, The 157–158
Torque 100, *101*
Townsend, Pete 34, 37
Trip, The 52, 75
Triumph 14–15, 17, 24, 28, 43, 56, 58, 65, 72, 74, 80, 86–87, 100, 106, 122
Troma Entertainment 113, 115
TT3D: Closer to the Edge 103
Tushingham, Rita 28

Up the Junction 30–31
Urban Warriors 135–136

Van Buren, Augusta and Adeline 95
Vanishing Point 69
Vespa 35
Veteran Motocross Foundation 102
Vietnam War 45, 47, 55, 58, 60, 64–65, 67, 75, 92, 109, 123, 133, 158, 161, 177
Village of the Damned 24, 27
Vincent, Gene 15
Violent Kind, The 118–119
Viva Knievel! 92–93, 98

W is War 136
Wagner, Clara 95
Walking Dead, The 106, 177
Warrior of the Lost World 131–132
Warriors of the Year 2072, 134–135
Warriors, The 63, 129–130
Waters, John 22, 151
Waterworld 138, *139*, 140, 144
Weller, Paul 39–40
Wells, Vernon 127, *128*, 138, 147
Werewolves on Wheels 45, *108*, 109, 119
West Side Story 10, 29, 58, 150, 152
West, Adam 164, 166
West, Del 'Sonny' 54, 68–69, 106

Western 18, 40, 45, 51, 56, 63–65, 70, 74–75, 82, 86, 116–117, 125–126, 129–130, 132–134, 138–139, 148, 158, 164, 168–169, 178
Westworld (1973) 144
What Have They Done To Your Daughters? 112
Wheels of Fire 136–137
Who, The 34–35, 37
Wild Angels, The 20, 44, *47*, 48, 50, 53, 56, 58, 72, 75–76, 148, 168
Wild Hogs 157, *161*, 163, 166
Wild One, The 10–11, *12*, 13, *14*, 15, *16*, 17–20, 24, 27, 43, 47–48, 50, 58, 84, 87, 122, 148–152, 162, 164, 174–175
Wild Rebels, The 51
Wild Wheels 59
Williamson, Fred 130–132, 134
Women in Cages 59, 69
Women's prison movies 59, 69
Wood, Edward D. 72
World Gone Wild 138
World War I 23, 82, 84, 96, 97
World War II 10, 14, 23–24, 27, 80, 84, 151–152, 175
World's Fastest Indian, The 94, *95*
Wright, James Gordon 51
Wynette, Tammy 63

Yamaha 50–51, 82, 92, 94, 100, 106, 115, 117, 121, 142, 173
Young Ones 139–140

Zombie, Rob 119, 138